FIT FOR THE CALLING

Aligning your faith and fitness to fulfill
your ultimate purpose

KYLE RECCHIA

HOUSTON, TX

Kyle Recchia/Fit for the Calling
Printed in the United States of America

For more information please visit: kylerecchia.com/book

Fit for the Calling/ Kyle Recchia -- 1st ed.

ISBN 979-8-9942739-3-7 Print Edition

CONTENTS

To Tiff, who never stopped believing I would heal
and loved me through every season—
you are my anchor in every storm.
And to our four boys:
may you always know you are beloved
and use your strength to serve
the people you love most.

"Therefore I urge you, brothers and sisters, by the mercies of God, to present your bodies as a living and holy sacrifice, acceptable to God, which is your spiritual service of worship. And do not be conformed to this world, but be transformed by the renewing of your mind..."

— Romans 12:1–2

A LETTER TO YOU

Dear Reader,

I never planned to write a book about faith and fitness. But if I'm honest, it's been writing itself in my heart for years.

It's not just that I've worked in the health and fitness world for well over a decade. Or that I've seen thousands of people transform physically through strength training, healthier habits, or better nutrition. It's that I've watched something deeper unfold—within others and in myself. A kind of spiritual clarity that comes not just from belief, but from embodiment. When your body gets healthy, your heart opens. Your thoughts change. Your service expands to your family, your community, and God. And most of all—you become available.

That word—available—is what this entire book is about. Being available for God. Available for your spouse. Your kids. Your community. Your purpose. Your calling.

But we can't give what we don't have. And many of us are trying to serve God and others with an exhausted mind, a sluggish body, and a distracted spirit.

I want to help you change that.

To be clear, I'm not a doctor. I'm not a pastor. I'm a guy who's spent most of his life chasing two things: God's calling and whole-person health. And after years of struggling, learning, failing, and getting back up again—I've come to believe that God's calling and whole-person health are not two separate pursuits, but one.

When we honor God with our whole selves—body, mind, and spirit—we step into our most powerful role: vessels for His glory.

Before we begin, I need to tell you something important: This book almost didn't get written.

Not because I ran out of time or ideas, but because for a long stretch of my life, I was too sick, too exhausted, and too lost to write anything worth reading. I was the CEO of a fitness company and could barely get out of bed. A health advocate who couldn't figure out what was wrong with his own body. A man with a calling he couldn't answer because he didn't have the capacity to show up.

If you picked up this book hoping for another expert to tell you what to eat and how to exercise, I should warn you—that's not quite what you're getting. What you're getting is a fellow traveler. Someone who has stumbled through the wilderness, face-planted more times than he can count, and somehow emerged on the other side with a few hard-won truths worth sharing.

This book is for the Christian who knows they should take better care of themselves but can't seem to make it stick. It's for the leader who pours out for everyone else while running on fumes. It's for the person who has tried every diet, every program, every hack—and still feels stuck.

But more than that, this book is for anyone who suspects that their health and their calling might be more connected than they've been taught to believe.

You are right. They are. And that's what we're going to explore together.

More Than a Health Book

I want to be honest with you about what I'm trying to do here because it's bigger than just helping you lose weight or build muscle.

This book is the first in a trilogy. Not because I love writing (I find it terrifying), but because I believe there's a journey that most people never complete—a journey from *identity* to *calling* to *leadership* to *kingdom impact* (which is just the way Christ followers express the quality of making a difference that lasts in all the ways that matter—to your family, your community, and the world beyond you.)

In this book, we start at the beginning: Who are you, really? And how do you become the healthiest version of yourself—body, mind, and spirit—so you can live out the calling God has for you?

In the second book, *Called to Lead*, we'll tackle something most Christians don't realize: You're already a leader. Someone is watching your example right now. The question is whether you're leading well—and in a world full of division and confusion, what does strong leadership look like?

In the third book, we'll explore the amazing purpose of it all: the Kingdom of God, here and now. Not just a future hope, but a present reality we're invited to participate in. Every healthy habit, every act of leadership, every moment of service—it's all training for something more.

But here's the thing: none of that matters if you can't get out of bed. None of it works if you're too exhausted to be present for your family, too foggy to hear God's voice, too depleted to serve anyone but yourself.

This book might be the most important of the three—because everything else depends on what we build here.

How to Use This Book

I didn't write this book to sit on your shelf looking impressive. I wrote it to change your life. That said, nothing you read here should suggest it is the only way to achieve your calling. It is simply Kyle Recchia's way. But it's what I know worked for me, and I believe it could work for you as well.

That's why every chapter ends with something called "Ready, Willing, Able." It's a simple framework that meets you where you are:

Ready actions are things you can do right now, today, in the next five minutes. No preparation needed. No excuses allowed.

Willing actions are things you can accomplish this week with a little planning and intention.

Able actions are bigger commitments you can tackle over the next month as you build momentum.

Here's what I've learned after years of working with people: Most folks fail at health changes because they try to jump straight to "Able" without building the foundation. They go from zero to hero overnight—and crash within weeks.

Start with Ready. Build to Willing. Grow into Able. This is how lasting change works.

If you read something that grabs your attention and you feel a need to follow up on it with some action, don't think you must wait until you get to that point in the book. I want you to use what is useful for you now and get to the rest of it as you are led. It will be here.

You'll also find Scripture[1] woven throughout—not as decoration, but as foundation. And you'll encounter science that might surprise you, stories that might make you laugh (or cry), and perspectives that might challenge what you thought you knew about health, faith, and the connection between them.

A Word About Science

What you will read in this book reflects current science. Science that isn't based on trends, but on carefully evaluated data. That means that the science presented here isn't likely to change overnight. However, the wonderful thing about science is that it isn't stagnate; it continues to evolve. As advancements are made, consideration must be given to utilize that new knowledge, and new editions of this book will be published as necessary.

Traditional medicine has come a long way, but that doesn't mean there aren't gaps. Medical professionals continue to learn, but no one can be a specialist in all areas. If you have a physician you trust, continue to do so, but I believe it's important to keep your mind open to other possibilities.

As you read this book, please understand that my intention is not to be dogmatic on any level. Please accept my apologies now if you ever feel that way as you read.

A Word About Grace

Before we dive in, I need you to hear this: You are already loved.

Not after you lose the weight. Not when you finally get your act together. Not someday when you deserve it. *Right now*. Exactly as you are. With all your false starts, your broken promises to yourself, your confusion and exhaustion.

The health journey we're about to take isn't about earning God's love; it's about becoming available to receive and share the love you already have.

This distinction matters more than you know. I spent years trying to get healthy out of guilt, shame, and performance anxiety. It never worked—not for long. Real transformation only came when I understood that I was working *from* acceptance, not *for* it.

So, take a deep breath. Release the shame. Let go of the scoreboard.

You're not here to become good enough. You're here to become available.

Let's fill your tank.

Let's build your foundation.

Let's get you fit for your calling.

With hope and gratitude,

Kyle
Houston, Texas

1

HOW I GOT HERE

Childhood: A Seed of Faith and Health

I grew up in Texas with my twin brother and older sister. For most of our early life, it was just us and our mom. She was strong. Resilient. Resourceful. She did whatever it took to raise us, even if that meant delivering pizzas at night with her kids hiding under a blanket in the backseat so her boss wouldn't know. I'm sure she looks back at that season with some level of pain or even shame, but the great thing about kids is their perspective. I remember it being a fun game we'd play, crouched down, giggling in the dark, eating Cheetos (a rare and thrilling gift) while trying not to get caught.

My parents divorced when I was six, but the truth is they were hardly ever together even before that. We lived with my mom in Houston while my dad worked in different cities across Texas, visiting when he could. Eventually Dad moved to Florida with the spoken intention that one day we would follow him there. As I've gotten older, I've come to realize that the dynamics between my parents were far more complex than I could have appreciated back then.

One of my earliest and most treasured memory of my dad was a visit he made to our small apartment in Houston, the two of us curled up together on a La-Z-Boy recliner, watching old Superman movies from the 1970s. Later he brought me a Superman action figure. It may or may not have been new, but what I do remember is that it was missing an arm. I loved it anyway. In fact, I loved it fiercely. Since we didn't have much, new toys were rare. But that one-armed Superman was, to me, the most powerful superhero in the world.

Looking back, I see the parallel now in ways I couldn't have articulated as a child. My dad wasn't around much, but to me he was Superman. Distant, yes. Missing pieces, sure. But special. Powerful. Mine.

From an early age, I was also a dreamer. I used to tell people I wanted to be an astronaut. I'd visit NASA's Space Center and get lost in the wonder of the stars, mesmerized by the thought of exploring something bigger than myself. I wasn't chasing a title—I was chasing awe. I wanted to be part of something beautiful and much greater than me, something that connected the dots between purpose, beauty, and our creator.

As I grew, I began to experience those same feelings of awe toward the human body, nature, and the miracle of being alive. My curiosity widened from space to science, from stars to biology, from wonder to wisdom. And at some point, I realized the same sense of purpose I once attached to space exploration now lived in my passion for helping people live longer, healthier, more meaningful lives.

Mom remarried when I was eight. My stepdad came with his own kids, and then we welcomed my half-brother, Dylan. Besides our new nuclear family, at any given time we might have distant relatives or exchange students living with us as well. It was chaos—kids coming, kids going, some related, some not. We lived with a revolving door of family and almost-family, held together by faith and not much money.

My stepdad changed jobs constantly. Metro buses. church staff positions. Police chaplain. UPS driver. Pest control entrepreneur. His work ethic was incredible, but he couldn't find his place. Nothing stuck.

Mom worked odd jobs, but her real passion was herbs and natural health. She was a believer—spirit-filled and prayerful—and she cared about what went into our bodies just as much as what came out of our mouths. Eventually they decided to open an herb store. Mom partnered with friends who were deep into herbalism and natural health. I didn't know it then, but she was planting seeds that would later grow into my career, my convictions, and this book.

The store wasn't in a good part of town, so, not surprisingly, the foot traffic was nonexistent. Mom would sit behind the counter while we kids found ways to entertain ourselves. There was a small back room that functioned as a makeshift nursery for Dylan, who was just a baby then. We'd hang out there among the inventory, watching our little brother while our mom waited for customers who rarely came. When we got restless, we'd walk across the street to the gas station—the kind of place where you had to check expiration dates carefully because half the products were past their prime. Then we'd wander over to an old park nearby that had a mile-long walking track and just ... walk. Loop after loop, killing time until evening when we could finally go home.

The herb store didn't last long. It never turned a profit. In fact, I think it was one of the things that contributed to my parents' eventual bankruptcy. But those seeds—the chalky sweetness of rice-milk popsicles, the bitter smell of tinctures, the belief that what you put into your body matters—they took root in me even though I didn't know it at the time.

Years later, when I started studying nutrition and wellness, when I began helping others transform their health, I'd think back to that little shop in the rough part of South Houston. My mom was ahead of her time in some ways. She just didn't have the resources, the location, or maybe the business sense to make it work. But she planted something in me that would eventually grow into my career, my convictions, and this book.

Our revolving door chaos also included church and connection. We were active in a spirit-filled church community, deeply involved in worship, youth group, and everything in between. Our lives were soaked in community and faith.

But there was another side to my story.

Every summer, my siblings and I would fly to Florida to spend time with my dad. He was a deeply kind man—funny and affectionate in that loud, expressive, Italian kind of way.

My aunts—his sisters—were the same. Family above everything. There was never a dull moment. Disagreements would break out with passion that could rattle the windows, but somehow always ended in laughter and food. From him—from that part of my family—I learned that family matters more than anything, even when that family comes with complications, are far away, and come with missing pieces.

But his life couldn't have looked more different. He smoked constantly, ate fast food every day, never exercised, and struggled financially. He was the kind of person everyone loved, yet his lifestyle quietly broke the hearts of those closest to him. My siblings and I often found ourselves trying to motivate him to quit smoking, eat better, and move more. He'd nod and smile, but the changes never stuck.

It was hard. We knew he loved us. We knew he had a good heart. But it became clearer each year that his health choices were limiting his availability—not just physically, but relationally and spiritually too. Those summers left an imprint on me: Kindness isn't enough. Intentions don't equal health. And a good heart doesn't always come with a strong body.

I've come to appreciate, though, that my dad wasn't an outlier. In fact, the more I've learned about what we're truly up against in today's environment—ultra-processed food, addictive technology, chronic stress, misinformation—the more grace I've developed for why so many of us struggle. Like Paul wrote, "For I do not understand what I am doing; for I am not practicing what I want to do, but I do the very thing I hate." (Romans 7:15). And Paul didn't even have to live in this toxic, hyper-addictive modern world! I'll dive much deeper into this in the chapters ahead, but if you're reading this book, take heart—you're not broken. You're not weak. You're up against real forces. And with the right knowledge, support, and faith, change is absolutely possible. You can do this. You are not alone.

Discovering Strength and Weakness

As a kid and teenager, I loved sports. I wasn't the best on the field, but I was passionate. Football, baseball, soccer, cross-country—you name it, I played it. I loved the camaraderie, the structure, the intensity. Movement felt good. It made sense. When I wasn't playing organized sports at school, I was outside playing with the other eight or so boys who lived on our street—Carefree Lane. It's almost poetic, really. What a fitting name for the place where we ran barefoot, played pick-up games until the sun went down, and rode bikes like we were invincible. Those memories are woven into me—moments of pure energy, joy, and connection. And in many ways, I think that's what we're all trying to get back to. A life that feels more carefree—not careless or irresponsible, but rooted in freedom, simplicity, movement, and connection. A life where we're not bogged down by chronic stress, fatigue, and confusion, but energized, playful, and open. I believe that kind of life is still available. And I believe reclaiming your health—body, mind, and spirit—is the path back to it.

But like many people, after high school ended, so did my activity level. I went into sales. I sat at a desk. I ate poorly. I moved less. The change happened so slowly that I didn't even notice—until one day a girl I liked made a casual comment about my stomach sticking out in my dress shirt. That moment embarrassed me. Not because she was mean, but because I realized how far I'd drifted from the person I wanted to be.

So, I hired a personal trainer.

The experience was … complicated. I tried to follow the advice I was given: strict diets, long workouts, conflicting recommendations. It all felt unsustainable. I'd make progress, then slide back. I wasn't lazy. I was overwhelmed.

Part of what made it so overwhelming was my own insecurity. I've always been someone who wanted to do things right (in the minds of others), to be respected, to be taken seriously. And early on, I thought the way to earn that was by gaining others' approval. I'd listen to everyone, try every plan, and get lost in the noise trying to please. I thought if I could just gain approval from other people they would believe in me, and then maybe I could too.

If you've ever felt that way, you're not alone.

Let me introduce an important concept: the Dunning-Kruger effect[2]. It's a cognitive bias where people with low expertise overestimate their knowledge; ironically, the more someone learns, the more they realize how little they know. I was taking advice from people who sounded confident but were often just as confused as I was. The fitness and nutrition world is flooded with confident voices and very little clarity.

Over the years, I've come to appreciate how much bad data exists in our industry. Epidemiological research gets twisted into clickbait headlines. Conflicting studies confuse the public. We hear bold claims like "meat is toxic" or "carbs are evil" or "if you don't do 90 minutes of fasted cardio, you're wasting your time."

The deeper I went, the more I realized that most people are just trying to make sense of a noisy, contradictory, broken system. It's no wonder so many of us give up.

This book is my attempt to clear the noise. To go back to simple, sustainable, life-giving truths. To remind us that honoring God with our bodies doesn't require perfection or performance—it requires stewardship, wisdom, and grace.

My focus on perfection and performance at that time caused me to walk away from it all again.

But God wasn't done with me.

I ended up working at a church, mentoring troubled teens. It was a deeply shaping time for me spiritually. I grew as a leader, a servant, and a man of faith. And it was there that my passion for health found new life.

One day, a fellow staff member and friend—now a pastor—joked with me, "Why don't you lift weights? You've got tube arms." It was funny, but it hit a nerve. I didn't have a good answer. He was one of those guys everyone looked up to, including me. He was a man's man—strong in character, clear in conviction, and allergic to BS. You always knew where you stood with him. He didn't speak much, but when he did, people listened. There was something deeply grounding about the way he carried himself. When he invited me to start lifting weights with him during our lunch breaks, I said yes. And I was hooked.

Strength training became a new form of worship for me. It wasn't about vanity. It was about dignity. Ownership. Alignment.

Eventually, I began to realize that my need for approval wasn't just draining—it was distracting me from the deeper calling God had placed on my life. I thought I needed others to believe in me so I could believe in myself, but that was never the path. True confidence—real confidence—comes from alignment with truth, not applause. God wasn't asking me to be liked. He was asking me to be faithful.

From Curiosity to Calling

The deeper I went, the more curious I became. I signed up for premed college classes—partly to impress my then-girlfriend (now my wife), who was studying to be a nurse—and partly because I genuinely wanted to understand how the body worked.

Something began to click.

I got straight A's in anatomy and physiology—not because I was a natural academic (I barely passed high school math), but because I was obsessed with understanding the human body. Learning about it was like discovering secrets of the universe.

I remember pestering my professor with questions like, "How does RNA know to do its job?" He eventually shrugged and said, "I don't know. It just does." That moment stuck with me: The gap between what science could explain and what it couldn't—that's where I would find God.

I became a certified personal trainer. I loved working with clients. But soon I began to dream bigger. What if I could help people not just get fit—but stay that way? What if I could create a platform that combined wellness with purpose?

That's when I launched a business called Beloved World—a hybrid of Thrive Market (an online, health-centered grocery store), Amazon Smile (a defunct program where .5 percent of a member's purchases would be donated to an organization of that member's choice), and church-based wellness outreach. The dream was to make it easy for people to buy healthy products while supporting their local church community.

It was a beautiful idea.

And it failed miserably.

When the Dream Dies

I put everything into Beloved World—money, time, passion, belief. I worked late nights. I networked. I marketed. I pitched. I poured my heart into what I thought would be a breakthrough for the church, for people's health, and for the future.

Nothing I did worked.

To make matters worse, I was newly married and our firstborn son, Liam, was just a few months old. Nine months into the venture, I was close to going through our life savings. I was out of energy, out of clarity, and honestly—out of faith.

I remember praying late one night in September and feeling what I believed was a prompting from God: "Give it until November." I held onto that like a lifeline. It felt like a sign that breakthrough was coming. And then—almost unbelievably—a major church reached out. They were interested in what I was building and invited me to make a presentation about Beloved World to them in November. I could hardly believe it. This was the moment. The door was opening.

I showed up. I made the presentation.

And they told me it wasn't for them.

That night, I sat alone and came undone. I remember yelling at God with raw, unfiltered frustration (and a few choice words that I am not proud of): "Why would You let this happen? I thought I was doing something good—for You!"

For years, I told this story as if it were a total failure. And at the time, it sure felt like one. But looking back, I see it differently. I used to think we made plans and God laughed. But now I see the deeper truth: We define success too narrowly, then blame God when things don't go our way.

I had decided what the win was supposed to look like. I had mapped it all out, prayed over it, worked for it. But I wasn't open to where the journey might lead—or who it would shape me to become.

God hadn't failed me. He was forming me.

That painful season wasn't wasted. It was necessary. Every setback, every "no," every sleepless night and slammed door—it was all part of the pruning process. A realignment. A preparation.

After that dark night of heartbreak, I woke up with nothing left but surrender. I got online, searched for personal trainer jobs, and found one that stood out: The Perfect Workout. It just so happened that they were expanding into Texas, and—as "luck" would have it—this was their very first hiring post in the state.

I went to their hiring seminar with dozens of other applicants. At the end, they did a sort of "speed dating" style interview process—two minutes per person. I remember boldly telling them I didn't want to work weekends or nights, and that this job was just a stepping-stone because I was working on my own business. To this day, I still can't understand why they hired me! I wouldn't have hired myself with that attitude.

Fast forward thirteen years—and I'm now the CEO.

I can't fully explain how it all came together. But I can clearly see God's hand in every piece of it: the failures, the weird childhood memories of herbal tinctures, the contrast between my parents, the moments of shame, the weight room epiphany, the business heartbreak.

Just about a month after I started working at The Perfect Workout, my dad passed away suddenly at the age of fifty-five. After I heard the news, my thoughts went to Superman and those quiet evenings on the La-Z-Boy, pressed against his belly, watching a hero fly across the screen.

That loss was devastating—and yet, it clarified something deep in me. It was as if God closed one chapter with finality, and in doing so, He illuminated the next one. My dad's death became a turning point. It cemented my conviction that health, fitness, and strength training weren't just professional interests. They were part of my calling. His life—and his early passing—became a powerful motivator for the mission I've committed myself to.

The journey hasn't been easy. The last thirteen-plus years at The Perfect Workout have been filled with meaningful growth but also plenty of trials and setbacks. I've made mistakes. I've had to unlearn and relearn more than I ever expected. And I've personally battled through a diagnosis and health challenge that I'll share more about in a later chapter. What I've come to believe is that God doesn't waste anything—not pain, not failure, not even disease. It's all part of the preparation and pruning He uses to deepen our purpose and strengthen our impact.

Even my grandparents, who I haven't yet mentioned but who absolutely shaped me—played a role. My grandfather, a PhD and retired nuclear medicine professor, became a successful business leader in network marketing. He taught me that readers are leaders, and that success is possible with clarity, grit, and faith. That voice is still in my head today. His example, along with my dad's story and my own journey, reminded me that legacy is built in layers—sometimes through triumph, sometimes through pain. Those seeds, too, were part of the preparation. They taught me to think big, stay grounded, and trust in something larger than myself.

The Real Reason I Wrote This

We're living in a cultural moment that's breaking us.

Our minds are overloaded. Our bodies are undernourished. Our spirits are numb. We scroll instead of pray; we consume instead of create; we burn out instead of build up.

We are the most overstimulated, under-recovered, and biologically confused generation in history—and it's killing us. Slowly, silently, but surely. And what's worse is that many Christians have unknowingly separated faith from physicality. We act like the body is an afterthought, or worse, a distraction from what really matters.

But Romans 12:1–2 tells us otherwise. It reminds us that our bodies aren't distractions from our spiritual lives—they're instruments of worship. That true transformation doesn't come from following cultural patterns or chasing wellness trends but from renewing our minds in God's truth. This isn't about conforming to the world's definition of health. It's about offering every part of ourselves to God—body, mind, and spirit—as a living sacrifice.

Your body is part of your worship. Your mind is part of your transformation. Your health is not about abs or aesthetics—it's about availability.

This book is an invitation. Not into shame. Not into hustle. Not into perfection.

But into stewardship.

I want to show you how exercise, nutrition, recovery, and even things like gut health are not just scientific tools—they are spiritual ones. Tools that prepare you to say yes to God when He calls. To show up fully for your family. To lead with integrity. To feel energized, clear-headed, and purpose-driven.

And we'll do it all through a biblical lens—grounded in truth, not trends. With grace, not guilt. With evidence, not emotional hype.

My hope is simple: that by the end of this book, you will see that becoming your healthiest self isn't just good for you.

It's good for the kingdom.

So, let's begin.

Let's become available—for the people, the purpose, and the life God has called us to.

What to Expect from This Book

Before we get too far, I want to be upfront about something important: I'm not a doctor. I'm not a licensed therapist or a functional medicine practitioner. My background is in exercise and nutrition coaching. What I share in this book doesn't come from a medical degree—it comes from years of experience helping real people get healthier, stronger, and more available for the life God is calling them to.

I've read hundreds of books, attended dozens of conferences, and have learned a great deal from mentors and leaders in the field of health and performance. I deeply admire the work of experts like Dr. Michael Ruscio, Dr. Gabrielle Lyon, and Dr. Layne Norton. I don't personally know them, and I'm not claiming their authority—but I've learned a lot from their research, teachings, and courage to challenge popular narratives.

Nothing in this book is "original" in the sense that I invented it. But what I've done—and what I hope to do for you—is take what's most useful, clear, and life-giving, and make it simple and actionable. I'm a translator. A guide. A fellow traveler. My goal isn't to add noise or complexity—it's to offer clarity, confidence, and a walkable path forward.

And I want to be clear about something else: I'm not here to present dogma. This book isn't about promoting one right way to train, eat, or live. I know how tempting it is to want black-and-white answers—especially when it comes to health, faith, or anything that feels high-stakes. But the truth is, life is complex. Bodies are complex. Science is complex. Even Scripture, when taken seriously, invites deep reflection, tension, and nuance.

We're learning more all the time. There are things we know, things we think we know, and things we haven't even begun to understand. Books like *Ingredients: The Strange Chemistry of What We Put In Us and On Us* by George Zaidan, do a great job showing just how messy and unreliable some of the studies—especially around nutrition—can be. That doesn't mean we throw out evidence or wisdom. It just means we hold it all with humility.

Throughout this book, you'll find what I believe to be the most helpful, actionable, and life-giving principles I've found across decades of reading, coaching, studying, and failing forward. I ask that you hold them with openness. Try what resonates. Wrestle with what doesn't. And let God guide you into the version of health that helps you serve Him and others more fully.

This is not your typical health book.

You won't find rigid rules, gimmicks, or shame-based motivation here. You also won't find pages of fluff or theory with no real action. This is a whole-person health guide built on two foundations: biblical inspiration and scientific evidence—designed to help you become fit for the calling God has placed on your life.

Over the coming chapters, we'll explore:

- Why your body matters to God—and what Scripture really says about honoring it,
- The power of strength training (especially slow-motion, high-effort training),
- How to eat in a way that's simple, sustainable, and effective,
- Why recovery, sleep, hydration, and gut health are essential—not optional,
- How your thoughts, habits, and self-talk shape your health and your faith,
- Why metrics like blood work, muscle mass, VO_2 max, and body composition matter,
- And how to cut through the noise and take clear, simple, practical steps toward lasting change.

You'll also find biblical encouragement in every chapter, real science explained clearly, and straightforward action steps to help you build momentum as you go.

This book was written to make you feel hopeful, not heavy. Empowered, not exhausted. Clear, not confused.

My goal is not to impress you—it's to free you. So you can become strong, healthy, and fully available for the life and calling God has for you.

2

A BELOVED WORLD

"and behold, a voice out of the heavens said, 'This is My beloved Son, with whom I am well-pleased.'"
— Matthew 3:17

What if every person on earth truly knew they were loved?

Not hypothetically. Not intellectually. But deep in their bones. What if every person—Christian or agnostic, athlete or addict, CEO or student—knew with absolute certainty that they were fully loved, accepted, and enough—not because of what they've done, but because of who they are in Christ?

What would the world look like if every person walked around with that kind of freedom? That kind of peace? That kind of power?

Would we still numb ourselves with food, alcohol, social media, or perfectionism? Would we still chase approval or achievement like oxygen? Would we still neglect our bodies or mistreat others?

Or would something change—not just within us, but around us?

A Vision of Wholeness

I mentioned that years ago, I started a business called Beloved World. It was more than a name—it was a statement of belief. That's when God declared from heaven, "This is My beloved Son, with whom I am well pleased," He wasn't just speaking about Jesus in isolation—He was speaking through Jesus to all of humanity. In Christ, we are the beloved. As Ephesians 2:8–9 reminds us, "For by grace you have been saved through faith; and this is not of yourselves, it is the gift of God; not as a result of works, so that no one may boast. "This is the scandalous beauty of the gospel: Our identity as God's beloved isn't something we earn—it's something we inherit. And that inheritance changes everything.

Not because we've earned it. Not because we've achieved it. But because we've been adopted into that same identity. We are now and forever loved by God.

But I didn't always believe that.

I grew up with a very different view of God. It was the classic "fire-and-brimstone" model. God was holy and angry. I was sinful and small. The best I could do was behave, try hard, and hope to be tolerated. I had this mental image of God watching from a distance with arms crossed, waiting for me to mess up again.

So, I worked hard. I tried to be good. I tried to earn my way into favor. But underneath all the striving was a current of fear—fear that I wasn't enough.

That fear didn't just show up in my relationship with God. It showed up everywhere. My parents were separated, and like many kids in that situation, I internalized it. I wore a lens that said love had to be earned, not received. I found myself trying to win the approval of my mom, my dad, my grandparents, my teachers—any authority figure in my life. If I performed well, I felt safe. If I failed or disappointed someone, I felt vulnerable.

This is the story for so many believers—and non-believers, too. We wear invisible scoreboards. We hustle for our worth. We think if we just get the grade, the job, the body, the house, the approval—we'll finally feel okay.

It's all about our fears.

Fear can be a powerful motivator. But it's also a cruel master.

The Day Everything Shifted

It wasn't a lightning bolt moment. It was a slow unraveling. A new season. A quiet invitation.

I started reading voices I hadn't grown up with—voices like Pastor Joseph Prince in *Destined to Reign*, Rob Bell, John Crowder, and Richard Rohr. (You can find these authors and others in the Resource section at the back of this book.) These authors weren't denying sin or holiness. They weren't watering down the gospel. They were magnifying the cross. They were saying: Look at what Jesus did. Not just for you—but to you!

He didn't just forgive your sins. He gave you a new name. He didn't just give you another chance. He gave you a new identity.

And that identity? Beloved.

It was like someone ripped the veil off a deeper truth I had always missed: that all my efforts to become "good enough" were keeping me from believing that I already was enough in Christ.

Hillsong United captured this beautifully in their album *A Beautiful Exchange*, based on Colossians. The lyrics, the themes all pointed to a staggering truth: We don't work our way into God's love. We wake up to the love we already have.

What We Believe Shapes What We Do

This shift wasn't just theological. It was practical. Suddenly, I began to see how deeply our identity shapes our actions.

If you believe you are broken, unworthy, and barely tolerated, how will you treat your body? If you believe you are an orphan—spiritually or emotionally—how will you eat, rest, and move? If you believe life is a competition for love and attention, how will you live in community?

This isn't abstract. It's neuroscience. Dr. Caroline Leaf[3], a cognitive neuroscientist and Christian author, has written extensively on how thoughts shape the physical structure of the brain. Identity changes biology. Belief rewires behavior. In *Switch on Your Brain*, she shows how toxic thoughts lead to toxic choices—which lead to chronic stress, sickness, and fatigue.

Likewise, in *Dopamine Nation*, Dr. Anna Lembke[4] reveals how most modern addiction isn't about pleasure, it's about escape. Escape from emptiness. From unworthiness. From pain. From a life that doesn't feel good enough.

What if the deepest need wasn't more discipline, more hacks, or more self-help? What if the answer was identity?

A King Who Forgot He Was a King

Imagine a prince raised in a slum, unaware of his birthright. He hustles, steals, fights for scraps never realizing the throne is his. Then one day, someone shows up with a royal ring and says, "You've been the king all along. Come home."

This is how I see so many people in the church. They're fighting for scraps, addicted, exhausted, ashamed while holding an inheritance they've never been told about, let alone taught to believe in.

One of the most powerful examples of this reality is found in the Old Testament story of Mephibosheth. He was the grandson of King Saul and the son of Jonathan, David's closest friend. After Saul and Jonathan were killed, Mephibosheth was just a child. In the chaos that followed, his nurse picked him up to flee, but she dropped him. The fall left him crippled in both feet. From that moment on, Mephibosheth lived in hiding, in a town called Lo-Debar—literally meaning "no pasture," or "no word." A place of silence, shame, and scarcity.

He believed the king would want him dead. After all, he was part of the former regime. A forgotten heir. A crippled threat. Side note for those of you who don't know—the Bible is full of wild, *Game of Thrones*-level stories. Assassinations, betrayals, palace intrigue, secret lineages, family curses—it's all in there. It's not exactly the watered-down PG book you may have thought it was while growing up. But I digress.

Years later, King David asked a strange question: "Is there anyone still left from the house of Saul to whom I can show kindness for Jonathan's sake?"

When they told him about Mephibosheth, David summoned him—not to destroy him, but to restore him. And when Mephibosheth arrived, trembling before the king, David said, "Don't be afraid … I will surely show you kindness … You will always eat at my table."

David didn't just spare him. He elevated him. He gave him land, provision, and a seat at the royal table for the rest of his life.

This is the gospel.

We were dropped. We were wounded. We were hiding in shame, thinking we were disqualified. And then the King called us by name, invited us in, and seated us at His table—not because of our worthiness, but because of His covenant of love.

This isn't prosperity gospel. This is gospel. The gospel doesn't just promise life after death. It promises transformation now. New life. A renewed mind. A healthy body. A healed soul.

But that starts with believing: *You are the beloved.*

The First Obstacle to Health

Most health books start with habits. This one starts with identity. As Dr. Layne Norton[5]—a respected nutrition scientist and champion powerlifter—often says, true transformation starts with how you see yourself. It's not just about what you do; it's about who you believe you are. Instead of saying, "I need to get healthier," it starts with, "I am someone who prioritizes my health."

Identity shapes behavior. And without that shift, most habits don't stick.

Because nothing will change until you believe you are worth taking care of.

You can't guilt someone into transformation. Not for long. Shame can spark a sprint, but it can't sustain a marathon. What you believe about your body—your value, your worth, your future—will determine how you treat it.

This is why I believe unhealed identity is the first and greatest obstacle to health. Not laziness. Not knowledge. Not even discipline.

I've worked with hundreds of people over the years. I've seen six-figure earners who couldn't get out of bed in the morning, and single moms who deadlifted twice their bodyweight. The difference wasn't willpower. It was identity.

Even in my own life, when I lose sight of my identity, everything else follows. It shows up in how I eat. How I speak to myself. How I rest—or don't. And each time I've returned to the truth of being the beloved, healing has followed.

You Can't Heal What You're Still Ashamed Of

Let's talk about shame.

Shame is the undercurrent of most dis-ease. It's the silent voice that says, "You're too far gone." "You'll never change." "You're not worth the effort."

But shame isn't from God. Romans 8:1 says, "Therefore there is now no condemnation at all for those who are in Christ Jesus." None. Zero. The enemy uses shame to paralyze; God uses grace to mobilize.

Dr. Brené Brown[6], a research professor and leading voice on shame and vulnerability, defines shame as the intensely painful feeling or experience of believing that we are flawed and therefore unworthy of love and belonging. She's spent decades studying how shame affects everything from relationships to leadership to addiction and health. One of her most powerful conclusions? That shame thrives in secrecy, silence, and judgment—and that the antidote is empathy, truth, and connection.

She often draws a sharp contrast between guilt and shame. Guilt says, "I did something bad." Shame says, "I am bad." One points us to change. The other leaves us stuck.

And neuroscience backs this up.[7] Studies show that chronic shame triggers the release of cortisol, our stress hormone, which contributes to inflammation, fatigue, weight gain, auto-immune disease, and even heart disease.[8] When we're locked in shame, our bodies bear the weight—not just emotionally, but physically. The spiritual and physical effects are deeply intertwined.

This is why so many people struggle to make health changes. It's not because they don't know what to do—it's because they're carrying too much shame to believe they're worth the effort. We say we want to change, but shame whispers, "What's the point?"

So, before we ever pick up a dumbbell or meal plan or blood test, we have to pick up the mirror of God's Word and see what's true: You are not your past. You are not your struggle. You are not your diagnosis. *You are the beloved.*

You are not beyond repair. You are not a problem to be fixed. You are a person to be loved—and healed—from the inside out.

The Power of Remembering

Throughout Scripture, God constantly calls His people to remember. Not because they're stupid, but because they're human. We forget. We drift. We default to fear, scarcity, and performance. We believe we must earn God's grace by our actions forgetting that Romans 5:17 tells us we receive the abundance of grace through Jesus Christ. We don't have to earn it.

But when we remember who we are—and whose we are—everything begins to re-align.

Ephesians 1 says we were chosen in Christ before the foundation of the world. Romans 8 says nothing can separate us from God's love. Colossians 3 says our life is now hidden with Christ in God. That's not theory. That's identity. That's the bedrock of health.

There's a powerful story in the Old Testament that illustrates this. In Numbers 21, as the Israelites wandered in the wilderness, they began to complain and rebel—again. In response, venomous snakes entered the camp and began biting the people, and many died. When they cried out in repentance, God instructed Moses to raise up a bronze serpent on a pole. Anyone who looked at it—just looked—would be healed.

It wasn't about effort. It wasn't about worthiness. It was about trust. Look, and live.

This wasn't just a strange moment in history—it was a prophetic image. In John 3, Jesus Himself references that very story: "And just as Moses lifted up the serpent in the wilderness, so must the Son of Man be lifted up, so that everyone who believes will have eternal life in Him."

Joseph Prince and other grace-based teachers have pointed out the profound simplicity here: Healing came not by striving, but by looking. Looking to the source. Looking to the symbol. Looking in faith—to believe.

And don't we need that now?

In a culture of chronic distraction, discouragement, and dis-ease, we need to look again. We need to remember. Because when we remember who Christ is—and who we are in Him—we stop reacting to the world in fear and start responding with faith.

When the foundation is secure, you can build something that lasts.

You can build a body that reflects strength. A mind that reflects clarity. A spirit that reflects peace.

But it starts with remembering—and looking—daily.

What Would Happen If ...

I asked this question at the beginning of this chapter, but it's important. So let me ask you again.

What would happen if you truly believed you were fully loved, fully accepted, and fully empowered by God?

What would your mornings look like? What would you eat? How would you move? How would you talk to yourself? How would you show up for others?

What would the church look like if the body of Christ was full of healthy bodies?

Can you imagine the impact of millions of people living with purpose, energy, confidence, and peace—not chasing perfection, but walking in wholeness?

What if the next great revival didn't just happen in churches—but in kitchens, gyms, homes, and doctors' offices?

What if wholeness was the revival?

This isn't just a spiritual idea—it's grounded in both biblical wisdom and modern psychology. Think of Maslow's hierarchy of needs. At the foundation are physiological needs: sleep, nutrition, movement, safety. When those aren't met, it becomes difficult—if not impossible—to fulfill higher-level needs like purpose, passion, and spiritual growth. We can't pour out from an empty cup. The body matters because the body enables the calling.

Even Scripture aligns with this. In 3 John 1:2, John writes, "Beloved, I pray that in all respects you may prosper and be in good health, just as your soul prospers." The implication is clear: health—physical and spiritual—are meant to work in tandem.

Studies also show that physical health impacts psychological well-being. Regular movement improves mood. Balanced blood sugar regulates emotional stability. Adequate sleep enhances memory, patience, and empathy. These aren't just personal wins—they're relational ones. When you're well, you can lead well. Serve well. Love well.

Imagine what would shift in the world if we stopped treating the body as an afterthought and started stewarding it as a sacred vessel.

What would your family look like if you had the energy to be present? Your business or ministry if you had the clarity to lead? Your neighborhood if your life radiated peace?

This isn't about narcissism or vanity. It's about being ready. Available. Fit for the Calling.

So, I'll ask one more time—what would happen if you truly believed you were the beloved?

What would your life look like if you lived from that truth?

A New Kind of Journey

Before we close this chapter, I want to say something that might bring you a deep breath of relief: It's not your fault.

Yes, we all make choices and have personal responsibility. But many of the things holding you back from health and wholeness aren't because you're lazy or broken. They're the result of a modern world that is fundamentally misaligned with human flourishing. And that's what we'll explore in the next chapter.

Some people assume, "Well, it's just in my genes. My family's always been overweight (or sick or anxious)." But here's what most people don't know: Genetics aren't the full story. In fact, they're only a small part. The bigger player is something called epigenetics—the study of how your environment, lifestyle, thoughts, and habits influence which genes get turned on or off. You might carry the potential for a condition, but it's often your choices, surroundings, and stress levels that determine whether that gene gets expressed.

The hopeful news? Epigenetics shows us that change is possible. You're not locked into your past. You're not stuck in your DNA. You can rewire your health through simple, consistent action.

In the next chapter, we'll talk about the world we live in—a world that's stacked against our health. From the food system, to the dopamine traps in your phone, to the way we've normalized burnout and disconnection, we'll paint the picture of the modern epidemic we're up against.

We'll also start to break down the practical reasons people struggle with their health: Too many calories, not enough sleep, constant stress, pain, lack of time, or simply not knowing where to start. And we'll begin simplifying it all—because my role in this book isn't to overwhelm you with information. It's to clear a path.

This book is not about becoming your best self to earn love. It's about becoming healthy enough to give love—to your family, your neighbors, your calling.

And that starts with this simple truth:

You are the beloved. God is well pleased with you. Not someday. Not after you fix yourself. Now.

Everything else in this book will flow from that foundation. Your nutrition. Your strength. Your mindset. Your recovery.

It's not about striving. It's about alignment. Not hustle. But healing. Not perfection. But presence.

So, as we begin, ask yourself: What would it look like to live from the truth that I am already the beloved?

Your identity.

That's the question. And it changes everything.

3

THE MODERN EPIDEMIC

"My people are destroyed for lack of knowledge"
— Hosea 4:6

If Chapter Two is the Call to Identity (what should be), this is the Wake-Up Call to Reality (what is).

The House Full of Smoke

Imagine waking up every day to the smell of a house slowly filling with smoke. There's no fire—just the faint scent of something smoldering. You crack a window. You light a candle to cover the smell. You open an app that tells you your air quality is fine. You even buy a new air filter. But the smoke never leaves. You grow used to it. Numb to it. You adjust your routines, your breathing, your expectations. Eventually, this quiet fog becomes the background of your life.

That's what it's like to live in the modern world today.

We are the most informed generation in human history. At our fingertips lies a constant stream of health podcasts, biohacks, diet trends, and AI-driven data. We've engineered ways to extend life expectancy, eliminate many infectious diseases, and automate the tasks that once wore down the human body.

And yet—we are the sickest, most anxious, and most confused generation ever recorded.

Life expectancy in the US rose from around forty-seven years in 1900 to nearly seventy-nine by 2019. But while we may be living longer, we're not living better. The average American now spends the last twelve to sixteen years of life in poor health, often battling multiple chronic diseases, pain, or cognitive decline. This gap between lifespan and health span—the years lived in good health—is growing.

Consider the irony: Despite unparalleled access to food, modern medicine, and digital tools for connection and productivity, rates of depression, anxiety, metabolic disease, autoimmune conditions, obesity, and loneliness are all skyrocketing. A study published in *The Lancet* found that mental health disorders now account for more than thirty-two percent of all years lived with disability globally.[9] In the US, the CDC reports that six in ten adults live with at least one chronic disease—and four in ten live with two or more.

How did this happen?

To borrow from scripture, we have "exchanged the truth of God for falsehood" (Romans 1:25). We've been told that comfort, convenience, and consumerism are the pinnacle of the good life. But these promises have left us depleted. This is not an epidemic of germs. It is an epidemic of disconnection—from nature, from stillness, from each other, from our bodies, and ultimately, from our design.

The Wars We're Losing

What we're experiencing isn't random bad luck or inevitable aging. It's the result of three simultaneous battles being waged against human flourishing—battles most people don't even realize they're fighting.

Battle #1: Your Mind

The first battle is neurochemical. Your brain's reward system—designed to help humans survive and thrive—is being systematically hijacked.

Dopamine is your brain's motivation molecule. It's what makes you pursue, anticipate, strive, and feel the thrill of what's possible. In a natural world, dopamine guided our ancestors toward survival: seek shelter, find food, build fire, bond with others. It was about reward and meaningful action.

But now, we live in a world of endless, cheap rewards—none of which require sacrifice, patience, or real effort.

Think about it: A new email lights up your brain like a scratch-off ticket. A scroll of the finger floods your reward system with novelty. Sugar, salt, and fat are delivered to your door within twenty minutes. Pornography delivers false intimacy with the tap of a screen. Video games simulate conquest without risk. Alcohol gives the illusion of calm without addressing what caused the stress.

Most of these aren't inherently evil, but they warp your baseline. Instead of your brain slowly releasing dopamine in response to meaningful effort, you begin expecting instant hits—leaving you—ironically—more anxious, restless, and unmotivated. Ryan Sheridan, NP, says that "We're frying our brains with short-term hits of dopamine that, ironically, leave us feeling demotivated, lethargic, and stressed out in the long run."[10]

The casualty? Your ability to sit with discomfort, to be present, to feel satisfaction from simple pleasures. And that presence is where transformation happens—insight, conviction, gratitude, stillness, prayer and reflection. When your brain is caught in an endless loop of quick highs and fast drops, you lose the signal in the noise.

Take the executive who reaches for his phone 200 times a day, the mom who numbs her anxiety with wine every night, or the teenager who can't focus on homework without constant stimulation. These aren't moral failures—they're predictable responses to an environment designed to exploit ancient wiring.

And let's talk about alcohol specifically, since it's one of the most deceptive partners in this dopamine hijacking. For decades, people believed in the "J-curve" theory: that moderate alcohol consumption might be good for your health, especially your heart. But newer, better-designed studies have debunked that. The curve is flattening—and so is the illusion. The truth is that alcohol is a dose-dependent poison. Even small amounts come with trade-offs.

Neurochemically, alcohol increases GABA, the brain's primary calming neurotransmitter. This is why you feel relaxed at first. But your brain quickly compensates by dialing glutamate (an excitatory neurotransmitter) up—and reducing natural GABA production. This leads to rebound anxiety, sleep disruption, and mood instability—especially after the buzz fades.

At the same time, alcohol boosts dopamine, giving you a spike in reward and pleasure. But the more often you drink, the weaker the reward becomes. Your brain adapts. Over time, the same drink gives you less joy and more dependence. Eventually, you're not drinking to feel good—you're drinking to feel normal.

It also shrinks the prefrontal cortex—where your judgment and purpose reside. It impairs REM sleep and wrecks gut barrier function. And it can turn a night of "unwinding" into a week of hormonal and emotional chaos.

In a world that's already overclocked with stress, distraction, and numbness ... alcohol doesn't give us control—it steals it. And yet it's marketed as medicine.

Battle #2: Your Body

The second battle is biological. While your mind is being chemically hijacked, your body is being systematically poisoned—not by dramatic toxins, but by the slow accumulation of inflammatory triggers.

Your gut—the "second brain"—is under siege. It houses over 100 million neurons, produces around ninety percent of your serotonin, and regulates immunity and inflammation. But processed foods, chronic stress, antibiotics, and environmental toxins have created widespread gut dysfunction. When your gut lining breaks down (leaky gut), particles like undigested food and toxins slip into your bloodstream, triggering systemic inflammation and immune confusion.

This is where autoimmune conditions like Hashimoto's, rheumatoid arthritis, and psoriasis often begin. It's why over 50 million Americans now battle autoimmune diseases—seventy-five percent of them women. It's why anxiety, brain fog, and unexplained fatigue have become normal. While studies are still being done on what is called long COVID, it is likely that could be included in this group as well.[11]

Your hormonal symphony is out of tune. Cortisol—your stress hormone—was designed for short bursts of danger, not the chronic pressure of modern life. When it stays elevated, it breaks down muscle, increases belly fat, disrupts sleep, and suppresses immune function. Eventually, you become cortisol resistant: tired but wired, unable to fall asleep yet unable to get out of bed.

Meanwhile, testosterone levels in men have dropped by more than fifty percent compared to their grandfathers—not from aging, but from sedentary lifestyles, poor sleep, processed food, and endocrine-disrupting chemicals (from plastics, receipts, personal care products, and pesticides). Symptoms aren't just physical—they're psychological: apathy, anxiety, low drive for both motivation and intimacy, loss of muscle and increased fat.

Women face their own hormonal chaos. Estrogen and progesterone fluctuations in perimenopause and menopause can lead to mood instability, sleep disruption, brain fog, hot flashes, and bone density loss. Women with PCOS (Polycystic Ovary Syndrome)—now affecting one in ten—often experience irregular cycles, insulin resistance, and difficulty maintaining a healthy weight, all driven by a hormonal environment completely out of sync.

Thyroid dysfunction is now a major public health issue, especially among women. This tiny gland controls your metabolism, energy, and brain fog. When cortisol stays high, it can blunt thyroid hormone conversion, leading to symptoms like fatigue, weight gain, constipation, and depression.

Your metabolism is confused. Insulin resistance—where your cells stop responding to insulin—now affects eighty-eight percent of American adults. This isn't just about diabetes; it's the engine behind heart disease, fatty liver, and even Alzheimer's. Your body becomes trapped in energy confusion, constantly swinging between highs and crashes.

Think of the mom who can't lose weight despite "eating healthy," the businessman whose afternoon energy crash requires multiple coffees, or the retiree whose joints ache and whose mind feels cloudy. These aren't signs of weakness; they're symptoms of a body trying to function in an environment it was never designed for.

Battle #3: Your Soul

The third battle is spiritual, and it's the most devastating of all. We've lost our sense of rhythm, meaning, and transcendence.

Ancient humans lived by natural rhythms: sunrise and sunset, seasons of work and rest, feast and famine. These patterns weren't just cultural—they were biological and spiritual necessities that kept the human system in balance.

But we've replaced rhythm with chaos. We eat constantly but never feel satisfied. We're stimulated endlessly but never feel fulfilled. We're connected digitally but isolated relationally. We chase comfort but find emptiness.

The result? An epidemic of what researchers call "diseases of despair"—depression, anxiety, addiction, and suicide. Rates are skyrocketing not because life is objectively harder than it was for our ancestors (it's not), but because we've lost connection to meaning, purpose, and the sacred.

Consider the paradox: We have more entertainment options than any generation in history, yet depression rates continue to climb. We have more ways to connect, yet loneliness is at epidemic levels. We have more convenience, yet stress and burnout are normalized.

When you lose the battle for your soul, you lose the war for your health. The spirit, mind, and body aren't separate—they're integrated. Spiritual emptiness manifests as physical illness. Chronic stress becomes chronic disease. Disconnection from purpose becomes disconnection from vitality.

How the Battles Connect

Here's what makes this epidemic so insidious: These three battles reinforce each other in a downward spiral.

The dopamine-damaged brain craves quick fixes, leading to poor food choices, which damage the gut, which sends inflammatory signals to the brain, which increases anxiety and cravings, which lead to more quick fixes.

The chronically stressed body produces cortisol, which disrupts sleep, which impairs decision-making, which leads to more stress and worse choices, which create more inflammation and hormonal chaos.

The spiritually empty soul seeks meaning in consumption, achievement, or stimulation, which provide temporary relief but deeper emptiness, which drive more seeking in all the wrong places.

Most people are caught in this cycle without realizing it. They think they're lazy, broken, or weak-willed. But they're not—they're trapped in a system designed to keep them sick, tired, and dependent.

The New Horsemen of the Apocalypse

The book *Outlive* identifies the "Four Horsemen" of modern chronic disease: heart disease, cancer, type 2 diabetes, and neurodegenerative disease. These conditions kill more people in the Western world than all infectious diseases combined.

But I'd add a fifth horseman that underlies all the others: **autoimmunity**—the body's immune system attacking itself. Over 50 million Americans now live with autoimmune conditions, and the numbers are rising rapidly.

What connects all five horsemen? They're not random genetic lottery tickets—they're the predictable endpoints of the three battles we just described:

Heart disease often begins with chronic inflammation and insulin resistance driven by poor diet, chronic stress, and sedentary living.

Cancer rates correlate with exposure to toxins, chronic inflammation, poor sleep, and compromised immune function.

Type 2 diabetes is fundamentally a disease of insulin resistance caused by overconsumption of processed foods and under-consumption of movement.

Neurodegenerative disease like Alzheimer's (now called "Type 3 diabetes") is linked to insulin resistance, chronic inflammation, poor sleep, and social isolation.

Autoimmunity emerges when chronic stress, gut dysfunction, and toxin exposure confuse the immune system into attacking the body's own tissues.

The common thread? These diseases aren't primarily genetic—they're environmental and lifestyle-driven. They're the body's logical response to an illogical environment.

Gaps in Conventional Medicine

If you walked into a doctor's office today with fatigue, brain fog, weight gain, and anxiety, more often than not you'd likely walk out with prescriptions—maybe several. A sleep aid. An antidepressant. A statin. You might be told it's just "getting older" or "bad genetics."

But what if your symptoms weren't the problem? What if they were the signal?

This is where there is often a gap in conventional medicine: It generally treats symptoms rather than addressing the systems that produce them. It slices the body into disconnected parts and attempts to silence the alarms without asking why they're sounding.

This isn't new. Consider Dr. Ignaz Semmelweis[12], who in the 1840s discovered that physicians washing their hands dramatically reduced maternal deaths during childbirth. His data was overwhelming—death rates dropped from eighteen percent to under two percent in wards where doctors washed their hands. But he was mocked by the medical establishment, ostracized by his peers, and eventually had a nervous breakdown. He was institutionalized and died in an asylum, beaten by guards. It wasn't until decades after his death—after Louis Pasteur's germ theory gained acceptance—that handwashing became standard practice.

Today, the idea that nutrition, environment, stress, movement, and spiritual life deeply affect health is still treated as radical in many medical circles—despite overwhelming evidence. But paradigm shifts often face ridicule before acceptance. This not to say all medical professionals fail to recognize the connections, but sadly many do.

You are not broken. Your biology isn't betraying you. Your body is trying to protect you from a broken world.

Finding the Right Physician

Before I continue with my healing story, I want to pause and offer something practical—because I know many of you are in the middle of your own medical wilderness, and finding the right physician can feel impossible.

I eventually found my way to functional medicine, which transformed my health. But here's what I want you to understand: The path to finding the right doctor isn't always about credentials or specialties. It's about character.

The first doctor who helped me wasn't a functional medicine practitioner. He was a traditionally trained MD in Colorado with no specialized training in gut health or integrative approaches. What made him different wasn't what he knew. It was how he listened.

Not the half-listening where someone's already formulating their response while you're still talking. Real listening. Curious listening. The kind where you feel like your concerns actually matter — even when your labs look "normal."

When I mentioned I suspected I might have SIBO, he didn't roll his eyes or dismiss it as internet hypochondria. He leaned in and said, "Tell me more about that. What makes you think so?"

When I explained I wanted to work with a functional medicine doctor alongside him, he didn't get defensive or territorial. He just said, "That sounds reasonable. Keep me in the loop on what they find."

That response was worth more than any test he could have ordered.

After years of navigating the medical system—both the helpful parts and the frustrating parts—I've learned that good physicians share certain qualities. These have nothing to do with where they went to medical school:

They listen more than they talk. You've been living in your body for decades. A good doctor wants to hear your story, not just scan your chart. They ask open-ended questions. They let you finish sentences. If you feel rushed out the door before you've explained what's wrong, that's a red flag.

They're curious, not defensive. Medicine is evolving fast, and no physician knows everything. The best ones are intellectually humble, willing to say, "I don't know but let me look into that." If a doctor bristles when you bring research or ask questions, they're probably not the right fit.

They look for root causes, not just symptoms. A doctor who reaches for the prescription pad before understanding *why* you're symptomatic isn't serving you well. Medications have their place, but a good physician wants to understand what's driving your symptoms, not just silence them.

They're willing to collaborate. Your health journey may require multiple perspectives—a primary care physician, a specialist, a functional medicine practitioner, a nutritionist, maybe a therapist. The right doctor sees this as a team approach, not a threat to their authority.

They give you time. I know the healthcare system makes this hard. Insurance companies pressure doctors to move fast. But the best physicians push back against this however they can. You can feel the difference between someone who's truly present and someone who's already mentally moved on to the next patient.

Here's a simple litmus test I wish I'd had earlier in my journey. When evaluating a physician, ask yourself:

- Do they make eye contact and seem genuinely interested?
- When I mention something outside their expertise, do they get curious or dismissive?
- Are they open to me working with other practitioners?
- Do they explain their reasoning, or just issue orders?
- Do I feel heard, or do I feel processed?

Finding the right physician might take time. You might need to "interview" several before you find the right fit. That's okay. Your health is too important to settle for someone who doesn't meet you where you are.

And if you're wondering about functional medicine specifically—whether it's worth the investment, how it differs from conventional care—we'll explore that more in Chapter 10 when we talk about building your complete health team.

For now, just remember this: Even the best doctor is still only one member of your health team.

You're the captain. They're the navigator. You need each other—but ultimately, you're the one steering the ship.

The Power of Early Detection

The Ostrich Approach to Health

There's a particular kind of denial that's become socially acceptable—even celebrated—when it comes to our health. It sounds like this:

"I don't want to know."

"If something's wrong, I'd rather not find out."

"My grandfather never went to the doctor and lived to eighty-five."

I get it. I really do. There's something deeply uncomfortable about submitting yourself to tests that might reveal bad news. The colonoscopy you've been avoiding. The skin check you keep rescheduling. The bloodwork that sits in your doctor's patient portal, unopened, because you're afraid of what it might say.

But here's what I've learned, both from my own health journey and from studying the research: when it comes to longevity, early detection is just as important as prevention. Sometimes more so.

Think about it this way: If you had a small, contained fire in your kitchen, would you rather discover it when it's just started smoking, or after it's engulfed the entire first floor? The fire is the same fire. But the timing of discovery changes everything.

The Math of Early Detection

Consider cancer. The five-year survival rate for localized breast cancer (caught early, before it spreads) is ninety-nine percent. Once it's metastasized to distant organs, that number drops to thirty-one percent. Same disease. Radically different outcomes based on when it's found.

Colon cancer tells a similar story. Caught at stage one, the five-year survival rate is over ninety percent. By stage four, it's around fourteen percent.

This isn't meant to terrify you—it's meant to motivate you. Because here's the thing: You have significant control over which scenario you end up in. Not total control, but significant control. And that control is exercised through one simple decision: choosing to look rather than look away.

What Should You Actually Screen For?

The specifics will vary based on your age, sex, family history, and risk factors. But here's a general framework for the screenings that matter most.

Cancer Screenings:

- **Colonoscopy:** Starting at age forty-five (or earlier with family history). Yes, the prep is miserable. Do it anyway. Colon cancer is one of the most preventable cancers precisely because we can find and remove precancerous polyps before they become dangerous.
- **Mammograms:** For women, typically starting at age forty to fifty depending on risk factors and guidelines.
- **Skin checks:** Annual full-body skin exams with a dermatologist, especially if you have fair skin, lots of moles, or a history of sun exposure. Melanoma caught early is highly curable. Caught late, it's one of the deadliest cancers.
- **Prostate screening:** For men, discuss PSA testing with your doctor starting around age fifty (or forty to forty-five with family history or other risk factors).
- **Low-dose CT scan:** For current or former heavy smokers, this screening can catch lung cancer early when it's still treatable.

Cardiovascular Screening:

- **Coronary artery calcium (CAC) score:** This simple, inexpensive CT scan measures calcium buildup in your coronary arteries—a direct indicator of atherosclerosis. It's one of the best predictors of future heart attack risk and can identify problems decades before symptoms appear.

- **Advanced lipid panel:** Standard cholesterol tests tell you part of the story. Advanced panels measure particle size and number, Lp(a), and other markers that give a much clearer picture of cardiovascular risk.
- **Blood pressure monitoring:** Not just at annual checkups—consider a home monitor to track your numbers over time.

Genetic Testing:

- **APOE status:** This gene variant affects your risk for Alzheimer's disease. Knowing your status won't change your genes, but it can dramatically change your motivation to implement the lifestyle factors (sleep, exercise, nutrition, cognitive engagement) that reduce risk.
- **BRCA and other cancer genes:** If you have a family history of breast, ovarian, or certain other cancers, genetic testing can inform screening frequency and preventive strategies.

Metabolic Health:

- **Fasting insulin and glucose:** These markers catch metabolic dysfunction years before diabetes diagnosis.
- **HbA1c:** A measure of average blood sugar over the past two to three months.
- **Comprehensive metabolic panel:** Liver function, kidney function, and other markers that reveal how your systems are functioning.

The Psychology of Knowing

I understand the fear. Truly. When I was in the depths of my health crisis, every test felt like a potential death sentence. I remember waiting for results with my heart pounding, convinced that this would be the one that confirmed my worst fears.

But here's what I discovered: The anxiety of not knowing is often worse than the reality of knowing.

When you don't know, your mind fills the void with worst-case scenarios. You're fighting shadows. But when you know—even if the news isn't what you'd hoped—you can do something. You have a target. You have options. You have agency.

And often, the news isn't catastrophic. It's actionable. It's "your vitamin D is low" or "your blood pressure is creeping up" or "you have a small polyp we can remove right now before it becomes a problem."

That's not scary. That's a gift. That's your body giving you information you can use to change your trajectory.

Stewardship Requires Seeing

Remember our principle: you can't steward what you don't monitor. This applies to your finances, your relationships, your spiritual life—and your physical health.

Avoiding information isn't faith. It's fear dressed up as faith. Real faith says, "I will look at reality honestly, trusting that God will give me the grace to handle whatever I find." The ostrich with its head in the sand isn't safe from predators. It's just unaware of them. And in that unawareness, it loses the opportunity to respond.

You have one body. One life. One shot at catching problems early when they're most treatable. Don't let fear rob you of that opportunity.

Schedule the colonoscopy. Get the bloodwork. See the dermatologist. Open the patient portal.

Look. Because what you find might just save your life.

The Age of Confusion

We also live in the noisiest health era in human history. Every scroll offers a new villain: "Meat causes cancer." "Carbs make you fat." "Fasting cures everything." "Seed oils are poison."

Meanwhile, your neighbor is 50 pounds overweight but runs marathons. Your cousin eats nothing but red meat and swears he's never felt better. Your doctor tells you to eat more whole grains while they sip a Coke.

In this environment, people don't just adopt dietary preferences—they form nutritional religions. Carnivore. Vegan. Keto. Paleo. If you're not careful, you'll spend more time defending your plan than feeling good in your body.

This is why wisdom must trump dogma. Scripture reminds us: "but examine everything; hold firmly to that which is good" (1 Thess. 5:21). That's not just spiritual advice—it's practical health guidance.

What passes the test? Real food. Movement that makes you stronger. Deep sleep. Quiet mornings. Time in the sun. Moments in the Word. It's not sexy, but it works. The most powerful path is rarely the trend—it's the truth.

The Path Forward

Here's the hopeful news hidden in this sobering reality: **You are not defective. You are disconnected.**

Disconnected from rest, from movement, from nature, from meaning, from God. But disconnection isn't permanent. What's been trained can be retrained. What's been lost can be restored.

The same neuroplasticity that allowed your brain to adapt to a toxic environment can help it readapt to a healthy one. The same epigenetics that turned on disease-promoting genes can turn them off. The same body that learned to live in survival mode can learn to thrive again.

You don't need to be perfect. You need to be honest. Honest about where you are. Honest about what's not working. Honest about your need for something different.

Most importantly, you need to know you're not alone. The struggles you face—the cravings, the fatigue, the confusion, the sense that something is "off"—these aren't personal failures. They're normal responses to an abnormal world.

But normal doesn't mean inevitable. And recognizing the problem is the first step toward the solution.

We've drifted far from our design, but the journey home is possible. It requires courage to face the truth, wisdom to discern what's helpful from what's harmful, and faith to believe that healing is still available.

Jesus said in Matthew 11:28-30, "Come to Me, all who are weary and burdened, and I will give you rest." The original Greek word for "burdened" implies being weighed down by something external and ongoing—a perfect description of modern life.

The rest He offers isn't just spiritual—it's holistic. Rest for your overstimulated mind. Rest for your inflamed body. Rest for your exhausted soul. As 3 John 1:2 reminds us, "Beloved, I pray that in all respects you may prosper and be in good health, just as your soul prospers." The implication is clear: Physical and spiritual health are meant to work in tandem.

And that journey toward rest—toward wholeness—begins with understanding that you were never meant to carry these burdens alone.

For me, that understanding came the hard way, through illness that brought me to the edge of myself and back. But sometimes the breakdown becomes the breakthrough. Sometimes getting lost is the only way to find the path home.

That's where we're going next. But first:

A Personal Inventory: Where Are You in the Battle?

Before moving forward, take a few minutes with the questions below. This isn't a test—it's an honest conversation with yourself. No one else needs to see your answers. The goal isn't shame; it's awareness. You can't navigate out of a fog you refuse to acknowledge.

The Battle for Your Mind

- How many times do you reach for your phone before you've been awake for five minutes?
- When was the last time you sat in complete silence—no podcast, no music, no screen—for more than ten minutes? How did it feel?
- Do you use food, alcohol, social media, or entertainment to "take the edge off" more days than not?
- When you try to focus on one task, how long before your mind pulls you toward distraction?
- If you're honest, has your capacity for patience, presence, or deep thought increased or decreased over the past five years?

The Battle for Your Body

- Do you wake up most mornings feeling rested and energized, or do you drag yourself out of bed already behind?
- How often do you experience unexplained symptoms—brain fog, fatigue, digestive issues, joint pain, headaches—that doctors dismiss as "normal" or "just stress"?
- Has your weight, energy, or body composition changed in the last decade despite no major change in your habits?
- Do you rely on caffeine to get through the day and alcohol or food to wind down at night?
- If someone asked you to describe the state of your gut health, hormones, or metabolic function, would you have any idea what to say?

The Battle for Your Soul

- When was the last time you felt genuine awe—not entertained, but truly moved by beauty, wonder, or transcendence?
- Do you have rhythms of rest built into your week, or does every day blur into the next?
- How often do you feel deeply connected to another human being—not just present in the same room, but truly known?
- If you removed work, entertainment, and obligations from your life, what would be left? Would you know who you are?
- Does your life feel like it has a clear sense of meaning and direction, or are you mostly just getting through each day?

The Spiral

- Can you trace a pattern where one struggle feeds another? (For example: poor sleep → sugar cravings → weight gain → shame → stress → worse sleep)
- Have you been fighting the same battles for years without making real progress—not because you're lazy, but because nothing seems to stick?
- Do you ever feel like something is fundamentally "off," even when your life looks fine on the outside?

A Word Before You Continue

If these questions surfaced some uncomfortable truths, good. That discomfort is the beginning of honesty—and honesty is the doorway to change.

But hear this clearly: *Your answers don't define your worth.* You are not your struggles. You are not your symptoms. You are not the sum of your worst habits or your lowest moments.

You are the beloved. And the God who loves you is not standing at a distance with arms crossed, waiting for you to get your act together. He's already walking toward you—through the smoke, through the confusion, through the mess—ready to lead you somewhere better.

The chapters ahead will give you a map and the tools to use it. But maps only help people who know they're lost.

Now you know. Let's find the way home.

4

THE WILDERNESS

"He restores my soul; He guides me in the paths of righteousness for the sake of His name."
—Psalm 23:3

The Wilderness We All Enter

If you've ever watched a movie that moved you—*The Lord of the Rings*, *The Shawshank Redemption*, *Rocky*, even *Finding Nemo*—you've experienced something storytellers have known for thousands of years: Every great story follows the same basic pattern.

Joseph Campbell, a scholar who spent his life studying myths and stories from every culture on earth, called it "the hero's journey." Here's the pattern: An ordinary person is living their ordinary life. Then something happens—a call, a crisis, a disruption—that pulls them out of their comfort zone and into the unknown. They face trials. They meet guides. They're tempted to quit. But if they press through, they're transformed. They return home changed, carrying something valuable for others.

Now here's what most people miss: *You* are the hero of your story.

Not because you're special in some ego-inflating way, but because this pattern isn't just how stories work—it's how *life* works. It's how God has always worked with His people. And it's almost certainly how He's working with you right now.

Every hero's journey begins the same way, with a call that disrupts everything they thought they knew about their life.

Sometimes that call comes as a dream, a vision, or a burning bush. Sometimes it comes as a diagnosis, a crisis, or a moment when everything you've built starts to crumble. The form doesn't matter. What matters is this: The call always leads to the wilderness.

The Israelites experienced this. God didn't lead them from Egypt directly to the Promised Land—a journey that should have taken eleven days. Instead, He led them into the desert for forty years. Why? Because the people who left Egypt as slaves weren't ready to possess the land as conquerors. The wilderness wasn't punishment—it was preparation.

The desert strips away everything non-essential. It reveals who you really are when the comforts, distractions, and securities of the old life are gone. It teaches you to depend on God's provision rather than your own strength. It transforms slaves into warriors, victims into victors, followers into leaders.

But here's what most people miss: The Promised Land isn't a place to retire and get comfortable. It's a place to fulfill your calling. The wilderness prepares you not just to arrive somewhere better, but to become someone who can steward that better place well.

This is true in the spiritual realm, and it's true in the physical realm too.

If Chapter Three was the wake-up call to the modern epidemic we're all facing, this chapter is about what happens when that epidemic becomes personal. When the abstract becomes visceral. When the statistics become your story.

Because sooner or later, most of us will face our own health wilderness—a time when our bodies betray us, when conventional answers fail us, when we're forced to question everything we thought we knew about wellness, medicine, and our own mortality.

I'm not sharing my story because it's unique. I'm sharing it because it's universal. The details will be different, but the pattern is the same: comfort → crisis → wilderness → transformation → calling.

Most people get stuck in the crisis. They never enter the wilderness because they're too afraid of what they might find there. Or they enter but try to rush through, missing the lessons that only come through patient endurance.

But for those who embrace the wilderness journey, who allow God to use the breakdown to create a breakthrough—something profound happens. They don't just get their life back. They discover why they needed to lose it in the first place.

They become guides for others who are just entering their own wilderness seasons.

This is the story of how I learned to stop running from the wilderness and start listening to what it was trying to teach me.

My Journey into the Desert

The irony wasn't lost on me that my wilderness began in what should have been paradise.

There was a time when life felt nearly perfect. I was the Chief Operating Officer of The Perfect Workout, married to my best friend, and a proud father of two young boys. We were thriving in Texas—raising our kids, building a business that helped people reclaim their health, and dreaming about our big move to Colorado. Nature, mountains, beauty, peace—it was supposed to be our family's next great adventure.

We were finally making the move. Everything was aligned. Everything was working.

And that's exactly when the wilderness called.

It started on a trip to Crested Butte, Colorado—a ski vacation that should have been the preview of our new life. The first two days were magical. Crisp air, fresh powder, my boys laughing and learning to ski. I felt like I was exactly where God wanted me to be.

Then, out of nowhere, I felt wrecked. Nausea. Vertigo. Crushing fatigue. I figured it was altitude sickness even though I'd skied and hunted in Colorado for years without issue. This would pass.

But it didn't pass. Even after we returned to Texas, I was trapped in a miserable fog. Constant nausea. Dizzy spells. Memory issues. Pain that seemed to move around my body with no clear source. And worst of all—insomnia. My Oura Ring, a device that measures sleep quality, showed twenty minutes of deep sleep … on a good night.

I'll never forget sitting at the zoo on my son's birthday, watching him run and play, and feeling completely detached. I wasn't present. I was drowning in anxiety and despair, gripped by a thought that would haunt me for years: "You're sick. You're dying. You won't be here to watch your boys grow up."

That's what the wilderness does. It strips away your sense of control, your confidence in your plans, your illusion that you can manage life through willpower and good intentions. Suddenly, the COO who had helped build a successful fitness company couldn't even manage his own body.

Looking back, I can see that this was exactly what needed to happen.

When Paradise Becomes Prison

The full weight of my condition hit me a few months later during what should have been another perfect moment—a trip to Costa Rica to celebrate a friend's fortieth birthday.

On paper, it was paradise: a sprawling cliffside villa with six bedrooms, an infinity pool, and panoramic views of the ocean. Every morning, we woke to the sound of tropical birds, monkeys, and waves crashing against the rocks below. The trip was packed with everything I loved—deep-sea fishing, hikes to waterfalls, wildlife tours, gourmet meals, and belly laughs with old friends.

But I was miserable.

The entire trip, I was caught in a haze of nausea, dizzy spells, bloating, and brain fog so thick I felt like I was viewing life through a dirty window. It was like my body had become a prison I couldn't escape—even in paradise. I was surrounded by beauty, adventure, and people I loved, yet I couldn't enjoy a second of it.

I remember sitting in that infinity pool one evening, looking out at the orange sky melting into the sea—the kind of moment that should inspire awe and gratitude—and feeling nothing but numb despair. No wonder. No joy. Just a low-grade panic buzzing beneath my skin, whispering the same thought on loop: *How many more trips like this do I even have left?*

If you've ever experienced deep, unexplained illness—especially the kind that chips away at your personality, your joy, your connection to life itself—you know exactly what I mean. It wasn't just that I felt sick. It was that I couldn't see a way out. I couldn't imagine feeling normal again.

That's what chronic symptoms do. They make you question everything—your memories, your future, your sanity. I kept thinking, *if this is how I feel in my thirties, what are my forties going to look like? Fifties? Will I even get there? Will I still be me if I do?*

This is why health span matters infinitely more than lifespan. It's not about how many years you live—it's about how many years you feel truly alive. Able to show up for your family. To laugh without anxiety. To take in beauty without pain. To be present instead of pretending.

In my wilderness, I learned that all the success in the world meant nothing if I didn't have the health to enjoy it.

The Gauntlet of Dead Ends

What followed was a gauntlet that will be familiar to anyone who's ever dealt with chronic, unexplained illness: eight different specialists, countless tests, and a parade of dismissals.

ENTs looked in my ears and said everything was fine. Neurologists ran CT scans and found nothing. Gastroenterologists ordered blood work that came back "normal." Almost all of them eventually chalked it up to the same thing: anxiety.

But I knew it was something deeper. Yes, I felt anxious—but not in the way they meant. I wasn't panicked about work or overwhelmed by life circumstances. In fact, I was doing everything "right." I meditated. I journaled. I took cold showers and spent hours in the sauna. I cut out gluten, then all carbs. I went strict keto. I tried intermittent fasting. I spent thousands on specialty supplements and even something called deuterium-depleted water.[13]

Nothing worked. And worse—I started to question my own sanity.

This is one of those gaps in the modern medical wilderness: the gaslighting. When your labs come back "normal" but you feel terrible, the implicit message is that the problem is in your head. That you're weak, anxious, or attention-seeking. That you need to try harder, think more positively, or just accept that this is what aging feels like.

But here's what I learned: Normal lab ranges are based on a sick population. When eighty-eight percent of adults are metabolically unhealthy, "normal" doesn't mean optimal—it means average. And average, in our society, is sick.

I refused to accept that this was my new normal. Even when I wanted to give up, something deeper kept pushing me forward. Now I understand what that something was: God was using my desperation to drive me toward the answers I needed—not just for my own healing, but for my future calling as a guide for others.

The wilderness has a way of making you relentless in pursuit of truth.

Understanding Lab Reference Ranges

Here's what I learned in the wilderness: Not all "normal" is created equal—and understanding the difference could save your health.

When you get blood work done, the lab report comes back with your results plotted against "reference ranges"—those little brackets showing what's considered normal. Most people glance at the report, see everything falls within the lines, and assume they're fine.

But here's what most people don't realize: Those reference ranges aren't one-size-fits-all, and they're not all created equal. Some are rock-solid medical standards. Others are moving targets that shift with population health. And still others are so wide that you can be "normal" while feeling terrible.

Let me break this down, because understanding this changed everything for me.

The Ranges That Shift: Population-Based Standards

Some reference ranges aren't based on what's *optimal* for human health—they're based on what's *average* in the current population. And when eighty-eight percent of American adults are metabolically unhealthy, "average" isn't a target to aim for—it's a warning sign to avoid.

The clearest example is testosterone.

In the 1980s, the reference range for total testosterone in men was roughly 500-1500 ng/dL. Today? Most labs use a range of 250-1000 ng/dL—with some going as low as 200 for the bottom end. The range literally shifted downward as population testosterone levels declined.

This isn't because men evolved to need less testosterone. Multiple studies, including a landmark 2007 study in the *Journal of Clinical Endocrinology & Metabolism*, found that men's testosterone levels have declined by roughly one percent per year since the 1980s.[14]

A sixty-year-old man in 1987 had significantly higher testosterone than a sixty-year-old man today. The reasons are complex—obesity, endocrine disruptors, sedentary lifestyles, stress—but the result is that what was considered "low" in your grandfather's era might now be labeled "normal."

So, when a doctor tells a man with testosterone of 280 ng/dL that he's "within normal range," technically that's true. But compared to healthy men from previous generations? That same level would have triggered concern.

This is the gaslighting I experienced: Labs that came back "normal" while my body was screaming that something was wrong.

The Wide Ranges: Normal vs. Optimal

Other reference ranges aren't shifting over time, but they're so broad that "normal" covers everything from barely functional to thriving.

Vitamin D is the perfect example. Most labs report a reference range of 30-100 ng/mL (or sometimes 20-100). Anything in that range technically counts as normal.

But here's what the research shows: Levels below 40 ng/mL are associated with increased risk of autoimmune disease, depression, cardiovascular issues, and poor immune function. Dr. Michael Holick, one of the world's leading vitamin D researchers, argues that optimal levels for most people fall between 40-60 ng/mL, with some research suggesting benefits up to 60-80 ng/mL. [15]

So it happens that someone with a vitamin D level of 32 ng/mL gets a report saying they're "normal"—when they might be significantly below optimal for immune function, mood, and disease prevention.

The same applies to other markers. Fasting insulin reference ranges typically span 2.6-24.9 uIU/mL—but research suggests that optimal metabolic health correlates with levels below 10, ideally below 5. Ferritin (iron storage) ranges from roughly 20-400 ng/mL, but optimal function for most people sits between 50-150.

You can be "normal" on paper and still have significant room for optimization.

The Ranges That Are Definitive: Pass/Fail Markers

Not all reference ranges are subject to this kind of drift or interpretation. Some markers have clear, clinically established thresholds where being outside the range indicates genuine disease or immediate concern.

Blood glucose is a good example. A fasting glucose above 126 mg/dL on two separate occasions indicates diabetes—that's not a moving target based on population averages. Severe electrolyte imbalances (sodium, potassium) have narrow ranges because being significantly outside them can be immediately life-threatening.

Similarly, certain markers like creatinine (kidney function) and liver enzymes (ALT, AST) have thresholds that indicate organ damage or disease. These aren't about optimization—they're about identifying pathology.

The challenge is knowing which type of marker you're looking at. Your doctor may treat all reference ranges the same, but they're not.

The Ranges That Mean Nothing Alone: Context Is Everything

Here's something that frustrated me for years: Certain lab values are nearly useless unless viewed in context with other markers.

Total testosterone is the classic example. A man could have a total testosterone of 600 ng/dL—solidly "normal"—and still have symptoms of low testosterone. Why? Because what matters isn't just the total amount, but:

- **Free testosterone**: How much is available for your body to use (most testosterone is bound to proteins and inactive).
- **Sex Hormone Binding Globulin (SHBG)**: High SHBG binds up testosterone, leaving less available.
- **Estrogen levels**: Elevated estrogen can create symptoms even with adequate testosterone.
- **Thyroid function**: Thyroid problems can cause symptoms that mimic low testosterone.

A complete picture requires multiple markers viewed together, often alongside symptoms. This is what good functional medicine practitioners do well; they look at patterns and systems, not isolated numbers.

The same principle applies to thyroid health. TSH (thyroid stimulating hormone) is often the only thyroid marker checked in standard blood work. But TSH can be "normal" while free T3 (the active thyroid hormone), free T4, reverse T3, and thyroid antibodies tell a completely different story. I've seen people with textbook "normal" TSH levels who were profoundly hypothyroid when the full picture was examined.

The Danger of Going Too Far: When "More" Becomes Toxic

Now, here's the other side of the coin—and I need you to hear this clearly. Just because "normal" might not be optimal doesn't mean "more is always better."

Some nutrients and hormones have what's called a "U-shaped" or "J-shaped" relationship with health. Too little causes problems. The right amount promotes health. But too much swings back around to causing problems again.

Vitamin D itself is a perfect example. While many people are deficient, pushing levels above 100 ng/mL can lead to hypercalcemia—too much calcium in the blood—causing nausea, kidney problems, and even cardiac issues. The sweet spot for most people is 40-80 ng/mL, not "as high as possible."

Vitamin A is even more dramatic. Someone I knew was told that vitamin A might help with a health issue he was experiencing. Since it seemed like a harmless vitamin, he started taking mega doses daily thinking you can't get too much of a good thing.

He ended up in the hospital with liver failure, literally on his deathbed.

Vitamin A is fat-soluble, meaning it accumulates in your body rather than being excreted like water-soluble vitamins. Chronic high-dose supplementation can cause severe liver toxicity, neurological symptoms, and even death. Once he stopped the vitamin A and his body recovered, he went on to live a healthy life—but that near-miss illustrates why supplementation without guidance can be dangerous.

Iron is another common offender. Many people supplement iron without testing their levels first. But iron overload (hemochromatosis) damages organs, promotes oxidative stress, and increases the risk of heart disease and cancer. You should *never* supplement iron without confirming you're truly deficient.

Even water—the most essential nutrient—can kill you if you drink too much too quickly (hyponatremia). Everything exists on a spectrum.

The Bottom Line: You Need More Than a Normal/ Abnormal Report

What do you do with all this?

First, don't assume that "normal" means "optimal." If you're experiencing symptoms despite normal labs, keep investigating. Trust your body. Sometimes the labs need to catch up to what you already know.

Second, understand which type of marker you're looking at. Is it a population-based range that might have shifted? A wide range where optimal is narrower? A definitive pass/fail threshold? A marker that only makes sense in context with others?

Third, consider working with practitioners who look at the full picture—functional medicine doctors, integrative physicians, or forward-thinking primary care providers who understand the difference between pathology detection and health optimization.

And fourth, never assume that if a little is good, more is better. Supplementation without testing is gambling with your health. The goal isn't to push every marker to the extreme—it's to find *your* optimal range, which might be different from someone else's.

This is wisdom-based stewardship: knowing enough to ask good questions, partnering with knowledgeable practitioners, and always remembering that the body is a complex, interconnected system—not a collection of isolated numbers on a page.

The Breadcrumbs Begin

Looking back, I can see how God was dropping breadcrumbs long before I was ready to pick them up.

Two years before that ski trip in Colorado, on our fifth wedding anniversary trip to the Dominican Republic, I came down with one of the worst illnesses of my life—fever, vomiting, diarrhea, and dehydration that lasted for days. When I got home, I couldn't shake the aftermath: chronic gut issues, loose stool, bloating. I was told it was just "traveler's IBS." Nothing to do but live with it, they said.

Spoiler: It wasn't IBS. It was a parasite—a ticking time bomb that had begun disrupting my gut microbiome, slowly unraveling my health from the inside out.

What started as "just a bug" had burrowed deeper than anyone realized. Over time, that parasite triggered a chain reaction. My gut, once strong, became inflamed and permeable. Foods I used to love suddenly caused bloating, nausea, and pain. My energy tanked. My mind was trapped in a fog I couldn't shake.

At the time, I didn't connect the dots. I was too focused on managing symptoms to investigate root causes. I was treating my body like a machine that needed quick fixes rather than a complex ecosystem that needed careful restoration.

This is where most people get stuck. They chase symptoms instead of systems. They want the quick solution, the magic bullet, the one thing that will make it all go away. But the wilderness teaches you patience. It teaches you that real healing is a process, not an event.

Still, I refused to give up. I devoured every book I could find on gut health, chronic illness, and neuroinflammation. I listened to hundreds of hours of podcasts. I attended conferences across the country, desperate for someone to say something that would connect the dots.

The Lightning Bolt Moment

Eventually, my relentless search led me to a Paleo Health Conference in Austin, Texas. I wasn't there to network or socialize. I was there because I was out of conventional answers, and somewhere deep down, I still believed unconventional ones might exist.

I wandered the vendor booths, half-present, still dizzy and nauseous from what had become my daily reality. Between lectures on fermented foods and ancestral movement, I crossed paths with Dr. Michael Ruscio.

I didn't expect much—just another smart guy with supplements and theories. But in a brief, almost passing conversation, I rattled off my symptoms: vertigo, insomnia, brain fog, gut pain, the mysterious rollercoaster of energy and inflammation. He listened carefully, then said something that would change everything: "Sounds like you might have histamine intolerance."

That sentence hit me like a lightning bolt.

I didn't even know what histamine intolerance was, but the moment he said it, something clicked. It was the first time in years that anyone had put my symptoms together in a way that made sense. Not a label to dismiss me. Not a prescription to mask symptoms. A potential root cause.

I went home and dove headfirst into research. What I found was astonishing: Histamine intolerance can look like everything and nothing all at once. Anxiety. Insomnia. GI distress. Skin issues. Brain fog. It wasn't just a food allergy—it was a systemic overload. My body wasn't breaking down histamine properly, and my gut—the very place where this breakdown is supposed to happen—was so damaged it had lost the ability to keep up.

Suddenly, the symptoms made sense. The sleepless nights. The weird reactions to leftovers and aged foods. The fact that alcohol made me feel awful. The rollercoaster days where I'd feel okay one minute and wrecked the next. It was all connected.

That clue cracked open a door I didn't even know existed. For the first time in years, I didn't feel crazy. I felt seen. And I had a direction.

In the wilderness, hope is the difference between despair and perseverance. Sometimes one conversation, one insight, one person who truly listens can provide the hope you need to keep going.

Moving to the Mountain

We soon moved to Fort Collins, Colorado—one of those moves you make hoping geography can provide what's missing in your life. I was still struggling daily with my health, exhausted by the trial-and-error loop of diets, doctors, and dead ends.

But God, in His grace, cracked open another door. At a local church where I played drums, I met someone who worked for a functional medicine doctor. Briefly, functional medicine is a patient-centered approach that identifies and treats underlying root causes rather than simply managing symptoms.[16]

That connection was divine timing. This doctor didn't dismiss me. She didn't hand me a brochure for anxiety or write prescriptions and rush me out the door. She listened—really listened. She asked questions no one had ever asked before. And then she ordered labs—actual labs. Not the standard blood panel that looks for disease, but comprehensive testing that looks for optimal function: stool analysis, breath tests, genetic reports, urine metabolites, micronutrient panels, inflammation markers.

The diagnosis came back like a detailed map of everything that had been hiding beneath the surface: SIBO (small intestinal bacterial overgrowth), leaky gut, nutrient deficiencies, histamine intolerance, immune activation, and chronic systemic inflammation. My gut wasn't just "off"—it was under siege. It was a war zone.

I teared up when I saw the results. Not because I was afraid—but because I finally had proof that something was actually wrong. I wasn't crazy. My symptoms had real, measurable, treatable causes.

But even then, the path wasn't straight. One of the first results came back with a red flag that stopped my heart: My thyroid levels were so high that my doctor was convinced I might have thyroid cancer. She told me she'd never seen levels that elevated without a cancer diagnosis.

If you've ever waited for a possible cancer diagnosis, you know the unique hell of that limbo. That week felt like a year.

But after CT scans, iodine uptake tests, and a battery of follow-ups, the results came in: I didn't have cancer. My thyroid was functioning perfectly. The real culprit? My gut.

Because of SIBO and a leaky gut lining, my immune system was responding to certain foods by releasing antigens that mimicked TSH (thyroid-stimulating hormone), artificially spiking my thyroid levels. This immune confusion explained everything—the unexplained weight loss, the anxiety, the relentless insomnia.

For the first time, I had a complete picture of what was happening in my body. More importantly, I had a roadmap for healing.

The Long Road to Restoration

What followed wasn't a miracle turnaround—it was a slow, methodical reconstruction. There were no shortcuts. No quick fixes. Just protocol after protocol: antimicrobial herbs, gut repair powders, binders, probiotics, antifungals, enzymes, low FODMAP (Fermentable Oligosaccharides, Disaccharides, Monosaccharides, and Polyols) diets, low-histamine phases.[17]

I slept more. I walked more in nature. I stopped drinking alcohol entirely. I took cold showers and saunas. I prioritized breathwork, fasting, and prayer. And slowly—painfully slowly—my body began to respond. The fog began to lift. The cramps faded. I could think again. Sleep again. Laugh again.

But just as I was turning the corner, the world turned upside down. COVID hit.

The timing was brutal. We had just bought our dream property—a rustic cabin nestled in the Northern Colorado mountains, surrounded by pine trees and silence. It was meant to be a sanctuary, a symbol of a new chapter for our family.

But six months later, in the middle of COVID, the largest wildfire in state history tore through our land. We were forced to evacuate twice. The second time, it destroyed our twelve acres. Our home office went up in flames. Keepsakes. Journals. Furniture we had built by hand. Gone. Our neighbor's home was reduced to ash. The entire forest was blackened.

I remember standing at the edge of the driveway days later, staring at the charred skeletons of trees in despair. It felt like I was cursed—first my health, now my home, my sanctuary, my symbol of new beginnings.

At the same time, The Perfect Workout lost half its revenue. Studios were closed. Trainers were scared. Half our clients vanished overnight. I was asked to step in as CEO, tasked with saving a business, guiding hundreds of employees, and serving thousands of members—all while battling my own trauma and the lingering effects of years of dysregulation.

I could barely hold it together.

At home, we were raising three kids with a fourth on the way. Homeschooling during a pandemic. Navigating fear and uncertainty. Trying to stay positive while watching the world fall apart.

But inside? I was unraveling again.

The Dark Night of the Soul

This is where the wilderness gets truly dangerous—not at the beginning, when the crisis is acute and you're motivated to fight, but in the middle, when you're exhausted from fighting and the end is nowhere in sight.

I turned to coping mechanisms I thought I had left behind. Alcohol to numb the stress. Sugar to boost my mood. Late-night eating to fill the emotional void. I told myself I was managing, that I was functional, that everyone was struggling, and this was just survival mode.

But deep down, I knew. I wasn't healing anymore. I was just surviving. Barely holding on.

Eventually, I hit a wall. The SIBO supplements weren't working anymore. The strict diet wasn't enough. I was still fighting my body every day just to feel "okay." I stopped reading health books. Stopped trying new protocols. Stopped caring.

I was spiritually burned out, physically exhausted, and completely disillusioned with God. The prayers felt empty. The Bible felt distant. The whole idea of a loving Father felt like a cruel joke when everything I cared about seemed to be falling apart.

This is the darkest part of the wilderness—when you can't see the point of the journey anymore. When you wonder if God has forgotten you, abandoned you, or worse, is actively working against you.

But that's also when the real transformation begins.

The Breakthrough

Here's the thing about giving up: It doesn't work.

I had tried it. I'd stopped reading health books, stopped experimenting with protocols, stopped caring. I told myself I was done fighting. But my body didn't get the memo. The symptoms didn't politely exit just because I'd mentally checked out. If anything, they got worse—because now I was dealing with the original problems *plus* the consequences of numbing out with alcohol, sugar, and late-night eating.

One night, lying awake at 2 a.m. with my mind spinning and my gut in knots, I had a thought that was equal parts desperation and dark humor: *Well, giving up isn't working either. Maybe I should try something else.*

It wasn't a lightning bolt of faith. It wasn't a dramatic moment of renewed hope. It was more like ... exhausted curiosity. A flicker of "what if" that hadn't quite died.

I started listening to podcasts again—cautiously, skeptically. And that's when I stumbled onto an episode where Dr. Ruscio was talking about SIBO. But he wasn't saying the things everyone else was saying. In fact, he was directly contradicting the conventional wisdom I'd been following for months. Where most practitioners emphasized killing the overgrown bacteria with round after round of antimicrobials, he was suggesting something radically different.

That got my attention. Not because I was suddenly optimistic, but because I was curious enough to wonder: *What if the approach I've been taking is exactly wrong?*

I reached back out to Dr. Ruscio.

Unlike most practitioners, he didn't just repeat old protocols. He was humble, curious, open to new data. He listened to where I was—not where I had been months earlier—and proposed something completely different.

Instead of constantly trying to kill the bad bacteria in my gut, he suggested we flood it with good bacteria. High-dose, specific, multi-strain probiotics. A low-FODMAP diet to reduce fermentation. No antimicrobials. No killing. Just restoration.

It worked.

Within a few weeks of following the new protocol—faithfully, patiently—something profound began to shift.

The debilitating symptoms that had defined my days began to lose their grip. The brain fog lifted. The bloating faded. The heart palpitations that I'd mistaken for anxiety began to disappear. I was sleeping through the night again, waking with clarity, experiencing moments of energy I hadn't felt in years.

But what changed most wasn't just physical. I wasn't just healing—I was awakening.

It was as if I had been walking through life half-asleep, dulled by survival mode, numbed by coping mechanisms, addicted to distraction and noise. Now, for the first time in what felt like forever, I could feel again. I could see beauty. I could think clearly. I could play with my kids without being irritable or distracted. I could sit in stillness without wanting to escape.

And that's when it hit me: I hadn't just been sick—I had been lost.

What the Wilderness Teaches

Through illness, I had been brought to the edge of myself. Through addiction and coping mechanisms, I had stared into my own shadows. Through the literal fire that burned our home and the pandemic that tested our business, I had come to the end of my striving, my plans, my image of what life was supposed to be.

The old version of me—the one who powered through pain, who outworked problems, who wore achievement like armor—was gone. And in his place was someone who had learned to surrender, to listen, to trust a process bigger than himself.

This is what the wilderness does. It strips away everything you thought you needed to be strong, successful, or valuable. It rips apart whatever control you thought you had. It reveals the difference between who you are and who you thought you were. And in that revelation, it creates space for something new to emerge.

I learned that healing isn't just about fixing what's broken—it's about becoming who you were meant to be all along. The person who went into the wilderness as a successful but secretly fragile CEO emerged as someone who could guide others through their own dark valleys.

I learned that suffering isn't random or meaningless—it's preparatory. God doesn't waste anything. Every struggle, every setback, every moment of despair was preparing me for something I couldn't have imagined when the journey began.

Did I know at the time I was being prepared? No. That knowledge came later—through introspection, awareness, and faith.

I learned that the goal isn't to avoid the wilderness—it's to trust the One who leads you through it.

And most importantly, I learned that the Promised Land isn't a place of ease and comfort. It's a place of purpose. All the pain, all the confusion, all the years of searching and struggling weren't just about getting my health back. They were about preparing me to help others get theirs back too.

Becoming a Guide

God met me not in my strength, but in my surrender. Not with condemnation, but with compassion. He reminded me I was never alone—not in the hospital rooms, not in the ashes of our home, not in the boardroom trying to save a business, not in my tears of desperation.

He showed me that grace wasn't a theological concept—it was the invisible thread that had held everything together when I couldn't. It was the only reason I was still standing.

He restored my spirit. He renewed my purpose. He reawakened my calling—not as a performer who had to prove his worth, but as a vessel who could serve from my abundance.

We eventually moved back to Texas to be closer to family—to come home in more ways than one. Old wounds started to heal. Our marriage grew stronger. My joy returned. My laugh came back. We returned to the same church where Tiff and I had first met, and were now watching our story being used to serve others.

And The Perfect Workout? It didn't just survive—it grew. Even in a changed world, our team rallied. We innovated. We adapted. A new vision emerged that went far beyond our expectations. For the first time, I saw our mission with total clarity: It's not just about training bodies. It's about restoring lives.

This book you're reading isn't a theory. It's a testimony. I've lived the pain, fought the darkness, stumbled through confusion and doubt. I've questioned God, avoided mirrors, and begged for answers in hospital rooms and boardrooms and on my knees in the middle of the night.

And still—He never let me go.

Now I get to help others find their way through their own wilderness seasons. Not because I have all the answers, but because I've learned to listen to the right Guide.

Your Wilderness, Your Calling

Here's what I want you to understand: If you're reading this book, there's a good chance you're in your own wilderness right now. Maybe it's a health crisis like mine. Maybe it's burnout, depression, addiction, or just the slow realization that the life you've built isn't the life you want.

Whatever form your wilderness takes, I want you to know three things:

First, you're not alone. The same God who led the Israelites through the desert with a pillar of cloud by day and fire by night is leading you too. He hasn't abandoned you in your struggle—He's using your struggle to prepare you for something greater.

Second, your wilderness is not random. It's not punishment for past mistakes or evidence that God doesn't care about you. It's preparation for the calling He has on your life. The very struggles that feel like they're destroying you are forging you into the person who can fulfill your purpose.

Third, your healing is not just about you. Yes, God wants you healthy, whole, and thriving. But He also wants you to use your journey to help others who will face similar challenges. Your wilderness prepares you to be a guide for others who are just entering theirs.

The path forward isn't about avoiding difficulty—it's about learning to see difficulty differently. Not as an enemy to defeat, but as a teacher to learn from. Not as evidence of God's absence, but as a sign of His preparation.

You don't have to figure it all out at once. You don't have to be perfect or have complete faith. You just have to take the next step, trust the process, and remember that the One who called you into the wilderness is the same One who will lead you through it.

The Promised Land—your land of health and purpose—is waiting. But first, there are lessons to learn, character to build, and strength to develop that can only come through the wilderness journey.

This is what it means to be guided. This is what it means to trust the process. This is what it means to discover that sometimes the breakdown is actually the breakthrough in disguise.

Your wilderness is not your destination. It's your preparation for the calling that's waiting on the other side.

Before moving forward, take a moment to reflect on your own wilderness season. Where are you in the journey? What is God trying to teach you through your current struggles? What calling might He be preparing you for on the other side? The practical tools in the chapters ahead will be most effective when applied with this deeper understanding of your journey's purpose.

5

EXERCISE FIRST— THE FOUNDATION OF VITALITY

"Strength and dignity are her clothing, and she smiles at the future." — Proverbs 31:25

The First Domino

After walking through the wilderness of chronic illness and emerging on the other side, I learned something crucial: You can't separate the physical from the spiritual, the body from the mind, or your health from your calling.

They're all connected. And when you want to transform your life, you must start somewhere. You must push the first domino.

For me, that first domino is strength training.

Not because it's the only thing that matters, but because it's the thing that impacts everything else. Your hormones. Your sleep. Your mood. Your confidence. Your energy. Your ability to handle stress. Even your capacity to serve others.

I've seen this play out thousands of times: Someone starts getting stronger, and suddenly their whole life begins to change. They sleep better. They think more clearly. They carry themselves differently. They start believing different things about what's possible.

Strength training isn't just about building muscle—it's about building the foundation for everything else you want to accomplish.

And here's the beautiful irony: The most effective way to get strong is also the most efficient. You don't need to live in the gym. You don't need complicated programs. You don't need to become a fitness influencer.

You just need to understand what works—and then do it consistently.

The Problem: We've Forgotten What We're Made For

Picture this: You're 40 years old, sitting at your desk, and your back aches from hunching over a computer for eight hours. You get up to grab coffee and your knees creak like an old wooden ship. You catch a glimpse of yourself in the bathroom mirror and barely recognize the person staring back—you're soft where you used to be strong, tired where you used to be energetic.

When did this happen? When did you go from feeling capable and confident in your body to feeling like you're living in a meat suit that's betraying you?

Here's the brutal truth: We've become a generation of spectators in our own lives.

We watch our kids play at the park while we sit on benches, already exhausted. We hire people to move our furniture because we're afraid we'll hurt ourselves. We avoid activities we used to love because we "don't have the energy" or "might get injured."

We've confused comfort with health, convenience with power, and safety with vitality.

And it's killing us—slowly, quietly, but surely.

Muscle mass is the single greatest predictor of longevity. Not your cholesterol levels. Not your blood pressure. Not even whether you smoke. Perhaps read that first sentence in the paragraph again … Your strength today literally determines whether you'll be independent at 80 or dependent on others for basic tasks.

But here's what's even more sobering: This isn't just about your golden years. Your strength today determines how you show up for your family right now. How you handle stress. How confident you feel in your own skin. How much energy you have for the calling God has placed on your life.

The Science: Why Strength Training Changes Everything

Let me share something that will probably surprise you: Strength training is more effective than any medication ever created.

I'm not exaggerating. Here's what happens when you consistently challenge your muscles with progressive resistance:

Hormonal Optimization: Your testosterone increases (yes, for women too—you need it for bone density and energy). Growth hormone surges. Insulin sensitivity improves dramatically. Cortisol patterns normalize. You literally become a more hormonally optimized version of yourself.

Cardiovascular Health: Despite what you might have heard, strength training is incredibly effective for heart health. A 2022 study in the *British Journal of Sports Medicine* found that just thirty to sixty minutes of strength training per week reduced the risk of cardiovascular disease by forty to seventy percent. [18]

Brain Health: Resistance training increases BDNF (brain-derived neurotrophic factor), which Dr. John Ratey calls "Miracle-Gro for the brain." It literally grows new brain cells, improves memory, and reduces the risk of dementia. Here's the kicker: Strength training is more effective at preventing cognitive decline than any brain game or supplement on the market.

Mental Health: Multiple studies show strength training is as effective as antidepressants for treating depression and anxiety. When you consistently do hard things in the gym, you develop the mental resilience to handle hard things everywhere else.

Metabolic Health: Muscle tissue is metabolically active. The more you have, the more calories you burn even at rest. Strength training also creates something called EPOC (excess post-exercise oxygen consumption)—you continue burning calories for hours after your workout.

Bone Density—The Hidden Superpower: Here's where it gets really interesting. Your bones aren't static structures—they're living tissue that responds to stress. When you lift heavy weights, you create microscopic stress on your bones. Your body responds by depositing more calcium and phosphorus, making them denser and stronger.

But here's the fascinating part: Only heavy resistance triggers this response. Walking, swimming, and light yoga don't create enough stress to build bone. You need to lift weights heavy enough to challenge your muscles to failure. This is why astronauts lose bone density in space—not because of lack of calcium, but because of lack of gravitational stress.

Women especially need to understand this. After menopause, women can lose one to two percent of their bone density per year.

But studies show that postmenopausal women who strength train can *increase* (yes, increase) their bone density, even in their seventies and eighties.

The Muscle-Building Miracle: One of the most encouraging discoveries in exercise science is that muscle-building capacity doesn't decline with age as much as we thought. A groundbreaking study published in *Frontiers in Physiology* found that people in their seventies and eighties could build muscle at nearly the same rate as people in their twenties when following proper resistance training.

Think about that: an eighty-year-old who starts strength training can potentially double their muscle mass in the same timeframe as a twenty-five-year-old. The difference isn't in capacity—it's in whether you use it or lose it.

The Longevity Chasm: Perhaps most compelling is what researchers call the "strength-longevity chasm." People who maintain their strength throughout life don't just live longer—they live dramatically better. The difference between someone who strength trains consistently and someone who doesn't becomes a chasm by age sixty.

A study following over 80,000 adults for decades found that those in the strongest quartile had a forty-six percent lower risk of all-cause mortality (death from any cause) compared to the weakest quartile. But here's what's truly remarkable: The protective effect of strength training is cumulative and lasting. Every year you strength train adds compound benefits for decades to come.

Dr. Gabrielle Lyon, author of *Forever Strong*, puts it perfectly: "Muscle is the organ of longevity." It's not just about looking good—it's about functioning optimally in every area of your life.

The Messenger Molecules of Strength

There's one more reason strength training transforms every system in your body—and it's something most people have never heard of: myokines.

Myokines are tiny messenger proteins released by your muscles every time you train. Think of them as biochemical text messages that your muscles send throughout your body. Each rep you do literally talks to your brain, heart, immune system, and even your mood.

Scientists have identified more than six hundred different myokines, and new ones are still being discovered. Here's what some of the best-known ones do:

Irisin helps convert white fat (the kind that stores calories) into brown fat (the kind that burns calories), increasing metabolism and energy expenditure.

BDNF (Brain-Derived Neurotrophic Factor)—sometimes called Miracle-Gro for your brain—improves memory, mood, and neuroplasticity.

IL-6, released during muscle contractions, reduces systemic inflammation and helps regulate blood sugar and fat metabolism.

Myostatin inhibitors promote new muscle growth and tissue repair, slowing the aging process at a cellular level.

In other words, when you strength train, you're not just building muscle—you're triggering a hormetic cascade of signals that improve almost every aspect of health: lower inflammation, sharper thinking, better immunity, faster metabolism, and even reduced cancer risk.

Dr. Bente Pedersen, one of the world's leading researchers on myokines, calls muscle an endocrine organ—meaning it functions like a hormone-producing system in its own right. When your muscles move, they communicate healing, renewal, and resilience throughout the body.

And this is where the connection to faith comes alive.

When Scripture says, "You are fearfully and wonderfully made," it's not poetic exaggeration—it's biochemistry. God designed your muscles to speak life into the rest of your body. Movement literally sends messages of healing.

That means when you move your body, you're not just working out. You're activating God's design for vitality.

The Perfect Method: High-Intensity, Slow-Motion Strength Training

Now, here's where most people get it wrong. They think effective strength training requires two hours in the gym, six days a week, grunting and groaning through endless sets with perfect form and complicated periodization schemes.

That's not just unnecessary—it's counterproductive.

The most effective form of strength training is also the most efficient: High-intensity, slow-motion resistance training to muscle failure.

This isn't some fad or marketing gimmick. It's based on decades of research showing that muscles respond best to intense, focused effort—not necessarily volume or duration.

Here's the fascinating science: Your muscles can't tell the difference between a heavy weight and a light weight moved slowly. What they respond to is mechanical tension and time under tension. When you move slowly, you're eliminating momentum and forcing every muscle fiber to work throughout the entire range of motion.

Dr. Doug McGuff, author of *Body by Science*, explains it perfectly: "The muscle doesn't know or care how much weight is on the bar. It only knows the intensity of the stimulus it's receiving."

Here's how it works:

High Intensity: You work your muscles to momentary muscle failure—the point where you literally cannot complete another repetition with good form. This is the stimulus that forces adaptation and growth. Research shows that training to failure activates the maximum number of motor units and triggers the greatest adaptive response.

Slow Motion: Instead of throwing weights around, you move slowly and deliberately—typically five to ten seconds up, five to ten seconds down. This eliminates momentum, maximizes muscle fiber recruitment, and dramatically reduces injury risk. Studies show that slow-tempo training can produce strength gains up to fifty percent greater than traditional speed training.

Brief Duration: Workouts last twenty minutes max. Why? Because true high-intensity exercise depletes your muscles' energy stores (ATP and creatine phosphate) within sixty to ninety seconds. Once depleted, you're no longer training at high intensity—you're just going through the motions.

Infrequent Training: You train one to three times per week, with at least forty-eight hours between sessions. Here's why: Muscle growth doesn't happen during the workout—it happens during recovery. When you strength train to failure, you're actually creating microscopic tears in muscle fibers. Your body then repairs these tears with additional protein, making the muscle stronger and larger.

Training more frequently actually interferes with this adaptation process. It's like constantly picking at a scab—you prevent proper healing.

Multiple studies—including Carpinelli & Otto, 1998 and Fisher et al., 2011 have found that lower-volume, high-intensity resistance training can yield comparable or superior strength improvements to traditional, high-volume training, suggesting that more isn't always better when it comes to results. [19]

The Game-Changer: FastFit Isokinetic Technology

At our FastFit studios, we use something even more advanced than traditional slow-motion training: true isokinetic machines. These aren't your typical gym machines. They're motor-driven, computer-controlled devices that provide variable resistance throughout the entire range of motion, ensuring maximum muscle activation without the risk of injury.

Let me explain why this matters—and why it's fundamentally different from anything you've experienced.

The Problem with Traditional Weights

Here's what nobody tells you about traditional strength training: Every time you lift a weight, there's a weakest point in the movement where you're most vulnerable to injury. That's called your "sticking point."

Think about a chest press. At the bottom of the movement, your muscles are stretched and relatively weak. At the top, your muscles are contracted and relatively strong. But the weight stays the same throughout. This creates two problems:

> First, you're limited by your weakest point. You can't use enough weight to challenge your muscles at their strongest position because you couldn't move that weight through your weakest position.
>
> Second, you're forced to use momentum to get through the weak points. This is why people "bounce" at the bottom of exercises or use jerking movements—they're compensating for mechanical disadvantages. But momentum is precisely what causes injuries.

Traditional machines tried to solve this with weight stacks and pulleys, but they still have the same fundamental limitation: fixed resistance that doesn't match your body's natural strength curve.

The Isokinetic Solution

Isokinetic machines solve this problem completely through computer-controlled variable resistance.

Here's how it works: As you push or pull against the machine, motors inside adjust the resistance in real-time—every millisecond—to match your exact force output. When you're strong, the machine provides maximum resistance. When you reach a mechanically weaker position, it provides exactly the right amount of resistance to keep the movement smooth and controlled.

The result? You're working at one hundred percent of your capacity throughout the *entire* range of motion, not just at your strongest points.

Think of it like this: Imagine having a training partner who's infinitely strong and can perfectly match your force at every single moment of every single rep. When you're fresh and powerful, they push back hard. As you fatigue and approach muscle failure, they adjust instantly to keep you working at maximum safe intensity. That's what isokinetic training feels like.

The Science Behind the Technology

The research on isokinetic training is compelling. Studies show that isokinetic resistance training produces:

- **Greater strength gains** across the full range of motion compared to isotonic (traditional weight) training,
- **Significantly lower injury rates** because there's no momentum and the resistance automatically adjusts if you start to lose control,
- **More complete muscle fiber recruitment** because you're working at maximum capacity throughout the entire movement,
- **Faster recovery times** because there's no joint stress from impact or momentum.

But here's what makes it revolutionary for busy people: Because isokinetic training is so efficient at recruiting muscle fibers and creating the growth stimulus, you need even less volume and frequency than with traditional slow-motion training.

At FastFit, our workouts last exactly twenty minutes. You perform five to ten exercises, one set each, to complete muscle failure. That's it. And you only need to do this one to two times per week to see remarkable results.

What It Actually Feels Like

I'll be honest: The first time most people try an isokinetic machine, they're humbled.

You might bench press 200 pounds at a traditional gym and think you're strong. But on an isokinetic machine, you'll discover that your actual strength curve looks very different than you thought. You might be capable of 250 pounds at your strongest point but only 150 pounds at your weakest. The machine reveals the truth—and then it works with that truth to maximize your growth.

The sensation is unique. Because the resistance is always perfectly matched to your force output, you can't cheat. You can't use momentum. You can't recruit other muscles to help. It's just you and the targeted muscle group, working at absolute maximum capacity from the first inch of the movement to the last.

By the end of a set—typically sixty to ninety—your muscles are completely exhausted in a way that's hard to describe. It's not painful, but it's intensely demanding. And then you're done with that exercise. No second set. No third set. Just one perfect set that delivers the complete growth stimulus your muscles need.

Safety as a Feature, Not an Afterthought

Perhaps the most important aspect of isokinetic training is safety—especially for people who've been injured before or who are older and worried about getting hurt.

Because the resistance is controlled by motors rather than gravity and weight stacks, several things become true:

1. **No dropping weights.** The machine can't fall on you. Period.
2. **No momentum-based injuries.** You physically cannot jerk, bounce, or use momentum to move the resistance. The motors won't allow it.
3. **Automatic accommodation.** If you start to lose control or your form breaks down, the resistance automatically decreases to keep you safe.
4. **Perfect for rehabilitation.** Physical therapists have used isokinetic equipment for decades to rebuild strength after injuries because it's so precisely controllable and safe.

I've seen ninety-year-olds train safely on these machines. I've seen people recovering from joint replacements build strength without pain. I've seen former athletes with multiple injuries finally train hard again without fear.

The technology eliminates the risk that keeps many people from strength training in the first place.

My Personal Testimony: Ten Pounds of Muscle in Six Months

Now let me tell you what happened when I started using FastFit machines myself.

By the time we adopted this technology, I'd been training consistently for over a decade. I knew how to lift. I understood progressive overload and optimal recovery. I'd built a solid physique and considerable strength through traditional methods.

Because of my history, when we installed the first FastFit machines at our studios, I wasn't expecting dramatic personal results.

I figured maybe I'd see some marginal improvements, but I was already pretty optimized, right?

Wrong.

I started training on the FastFit machines three times a week, twenty minutes per session. I changed nothing else—same nutrition, same sleep, same stress levels, same supplements. The only variable that changed was switching from weight machines to the FastFit machines.

Six months later, I stepped on the DEXA scanner for my regular body composition assessment.

The results shocked me: I had gained ten pounds of pure muscle mass while my body fat percentage remained essentially unchanged.

Ten pounds. In six months. For someone who'd been training seriously for over a decade.

To put that in perspective: most well-trained individuals consider gaining two to three pounds of muscle per year a success. I gained more than three times that in half a year—and I wasn't even trying to bulk. I was just training efficiently.

But here's what was even more remarkable: I felt better. My joints didn't ache. I wasn't chronically sore. I had more energy for other activities because I wasn't spending six to eight hours per week in the gym. I was getting dramatically better results with less than half the time investment and none of the accumulated fatigue.

Your muscles don't care how long you spend in the gym. They care about the quality and intensity of the stimulus you provide. And isokinetic technology delivers that stimulus more precisely than any other method available.

Who This Is For

FastFit isokinetic training is ideal for:

- **Busy professionals** who can't spend eight to ten hours per week in the gym but still want excellent results,
- **Older adults** who want to maintain strength, bone density, and independence but worry about injury risk,
- **People recovering from injuries** who need safe, controlled resistance that won't aggravate old problems,
- **Athletes** who want to build strength without the accumulated fatigue that interferes with their sport,
- **Anyone who's tried traditional strength training and quit** because it was too time-consuming, too complicated, or too intimidating.

The only people who might not benefit are those who genuinely enjoy spending hours in the gym, who love the social atmosphere of traditional fitness facilities, or who are competitive strength athletes needing to practice specific movement patterns for their sport.

For everyone else? This is the most efficient path to getting—and staying—strong.

The Cardio Confusion: What You Think You Need vs. What Actually Works

I need to address something that stops countless people from getting started with strength training, the belief that they need "cardio."

I can't tell you how many times I've heard this objection, "Yeah, strength training sounds good, but I really need to focus on cardio first. My doctor said I need to improve my cardiovascular health."

"I'm trying to lose weight, so shouldn't I be doing more cardio?"

"Don't I need to do cardio for my heart?"

Here's the truth that might surprise you: you've been lied to about what "cardio" actually means.

What Cardio Really Is

Let's start with the basics. "Cardio" is short for "cardiovascular exercise"—exercise that strengthens your heart and circulatory system. It's not a specific type of exercise. It's an *effect* that exercise has on your body.

Your heart doesn't know the difference between running on a treadmill and doing a leg press. It only knows that it needs to pump blood to working muscles. Any exercise that elevates your heart rate and keeps it elevated is cardiovascular exercise.

The question isn't whether an activity counts as "cardio"—the question is: What's the most efficient way to strengthen your cardiovascular system?

The Cardiovascular Benefits of Strength Training

Here's what happens to your heart during a proper strength training session: When you work a muscle to complete failure using slow-motion, high-intensity training, your heart rate increases to 100-150 beats per minute—the same range you'd hit during moderate-intensity "cardio" like jogging or cycling.

But there's a crucial difference: Strength training creates this cardiovascular demand while simultaneously building muscle, strengthening bones, improving hormones, and burning calories for hours after your workout through EPOC (excess post-exercise oxygen consumption).

Traditional "cardio" gives you one benefit: improved cardiovascular endurance. Strength training gives you that *plus* everything else we've already discussed.

Let me say that again because it's worth emphasizing: **proper strength training provides cardiovascular benefits while simultaneously delivering benefits that traditional cardio cannot provide.**

The Research Proves It

Remember that 2022 study I mentioned earlier from the *British Journal of Sports Medicine*? It found that just thirty to sixty minutes of strength training per week reduced cardiovascular disease risk by forty to seventy percent.

That's not despite the lack of traditional cardio—that's *because* strength training is incredibly effective at improving cardiovascular health.

Other research has shown that:

- Resistance training lowers blood pressure as effectively as aerobic exercise,
- Strength training improves cholesterol profiles (increasing HDL, decreasing LDL),
- High-intensity resistance training improves VO_2 max[20] (the gold standard measure of cardiovascular fitness),
- Strength training reduces resting heart rate and improves heart rate variability.

Dr. Jurgen Giessing's research on high-intensity strength training found cardiovascular improvements equivalent to traditional endurance training—in a fraction of the time. [21]

Why People Think They Need Separate Cardio

So why does everyone believe they need hours of running, cycling, or elliptical work?

Partly, it's cultural momentum. For decades, we've been told that "cardio" means steady-state aerobic exercise. The image of cardiovascular fitness in most people's minds is someone jogging on a treadmill for forty-five minutes, not someone doing a leg press to failure.

Partly, it's the fitness industry's fault. Traditional gyms make money from memberships, not results. They want you to spend more time in the gym, not less. A twenty-minute strength workout doesn't fill membership hours the way rows of cardio equipment do.

And partly, it's because traditional strength training—the kind with long rest periods between sets, moderate effort, and lots of socializing—*doesn't* provide significant cardiovascular benefits. But that's a problem with the method, not with strength training itself.

The FastFit Cardiovascular Effect

When you train on our FastFit isokinetic machines using the protocol I'm about to describe, something remarkable happens to your cardiovascular system.

Within the first thirty seconds of a set, your heart rate begins climbing. By sixty seconds, you're in the cardiovascular training zone—heart pumping, breathing elevated, blood flowing to working muscles. When you finish one exercise and move immediately to the next (with minimal rest), your heart rate stays elevated throughout the entire twenty-minute session.

The result? You get a complete cardiovascular workout *embedded* within your strength training session.

But here's where it gets even better: Because you're using isokinetic resistance that perfectly matches your force output throughout the entire range of motion, you're able to work at a higher intensity than traditional training allows. This means your cardiovascular system is challenged more effectively in twenty minutes than many people achieve in an hour of traditional "cardio."

I've had clients who were skeptical about this—former runners, cyclists, people who'd spent years on treadmills and ellipticals. They'd ask, "But what about my heart health?" Then they'd try one session and understand.

By the end of twenty minutes, they're breathing hard, their heart is pounding, they're sweating, and every muscle in their body feels completely worked. They realize: "Wait... this *is* cardio. This is better than cardio."

What About Endurance Athletes?

Now, I'm not saying that strength training replaces all forms of cardiovascular exercise for everyone.

If you're training for a marathon, you need to run long distances. If you're preparing for a cycling race, you need to spend time on a bike. Specificity matters when you're training for a specific endurance event.

But here's what's fascinating: Even endurance athletes benefit dramatically from adding strength training to their programs. Research consistently shows that runners, cyclists, and swimmers who incorporate resistance training improve their performance in their sport get faster, more powerful, and more injury-resistant.

The reverse isn't true. Runners who only run don't typically see improvements in strength, bone density, or muscle mass. In fact, excessive endurance training without strength work often leads to muscle loss, decreased bone density, and increased injury risk.

For the Rest of Us

But let's be honest: Most people aren't training for endurance events. They're not aspiring Ironman triathletes or marathon runners.

Most people just want to:

- Lose weight and keep it off,
- Have energy to play with their kids,
- Feel confident in their body,
- Reduce their risk of heart disease and diabetes,
- Be able to climb stairs without getting winded,
- Maintain independence as they age.

For these goals—which represent ninety-five percent of the population—strength training isn't just sufficient. It's superior.

You don't need to spend an hour on the treadmill. You don't need to go to spinning classes. You don't need to force yourself through activities you hate in the name of "cardiovascular health."

You need twenty minutes of high-intensity strength training, one to three times per week. That's it.

The Metabolic Advantage

There's one more reason strength training beats traditional cardio for most people: the metabolic effect.

When you go for a thirty-minute jog, you burn calories during those thirty minutes. That's good. But when you finish, your metabolism returns to baseline relatively quickly. The calorie burn stops.

When you do high-intensity strength training to muscle failure, you burn calories during the workout, *and* your metabolism stays elevated for twenty-four to forty-eight hours afterward. This is the EPOC effect I mentioned earlier—your body continues burning extra calories as it repairs muscle tissue and adapts to the stress you created.

Plus, every pound of muscle you build increases your resting metabolic rate permanently. Muscle tissue burns calories even when you're sitting on the couch. More muscle equals higher metabolism equals easier weight management for the rest of your life.

Traditional cardio doesn't build muscle. In fact, excessive cardio can cause muscle loss, especially if you're not eating enough protein or if you're combining it with caloric restriction.

So for weight loss, for metabolism, for long-term health—strength training wins again.

The Bottom Line on Cardio

If you love running, cycling, swimming, or other endurance activities—keep doing them! Exercise you enjoy is exercise you'll do, and that's valuable.

But if you're forcing yourself through cardio workouts you hate because you think you need them for your heart health, I have good news: You don't.

High-intensity strength training will give you the cardiovascular benefits you need, plus all the additional benefits that traditional cardio can't provide—stronger muscles, denser bones, better hormones, improved body composition, and a metabolism that works for you instead of against you.

The next time you see your doctor and are told, "You've been doing cardio," you can smile and say, "I have. It's called strength training."

Overcoming the Excuses

I know what you're thinking. You've heard all this before. You know exercise is good for you. But somehow, you're still not doing it consistently. Why?

Let me address the real reasons people don't strength train:

"I don't have time." Allow me to repeat: this method requires twenty minutes, one to three times per week. That's less time than most people spend scrolling social media in a single day. You don't have time NOT to do this.

"I don't know what I'm doing." That's exactly why this approach works. There's no complicated programming, no need to learn dozens of exercises. Simple, guided movements that anyone can master.

"I'm afraid of getting hurt." Traditional weightlifting does carry injury risk. But slow-motion, controlled movements with proper supervision—especially on isokinetic machines—are incredibly safe. In fact, they're rehabilitative. They make you less likely to get injured in daily life.

"I've tried before and quit." Most people quit because they don't see results fast enough or because the time commitment is unsustainable. This method produces noticeable results within twelve weeks and requires minimal time investment.

"I'm too old/out of shape/weak to start." This is exactly who benefits most from strength training. Age is not a barrier to building muscle. Several studies have shown that even very old adults—people eighty to ninety-nine years old—can achieve large relative gains in strength over short periods of resistance training—especially when using careful protocols and beginning from a low baseline. For example, some programs in octogenarian and nonagenarian participants have produced strength improvements of twenty to eighty percent over eight to sixteen weeks.

I've personally worked with clients in their nineties who've doubled their strength in months. Your current fitness level doesn't matter—what matters is starting. In fact, the weaker you are when you start, the more dramatic your improvements will be.

The Biblical Case for Strength

Some Christians struggle with the idea of focusing on physical strength. Isn't that vanity? Shouldn't we focus on spiritual things instead?

This misses the point entirely.

Paul writes in 1 Corinthians 6:19-20: *"Or do you not know that your body is a temple of the Holy Spirit within you, whom you have from God, and that you are not your own? For you have been bought for a price: therefore glorify God in your body."*

Notice he doesn't say "honor God despite your body" or "honor God instead of your body." He says honor God *in* your body.

Your body is not a distraction from your spiritual life—it's an instrument of your worship. Taking care of it isn't vanity—it's stewardship.

Think about it this way: If someone gave you a million-dollar Stradivarius violin, would you let it sit in a corner collecting dust?

Would you ignore its maintenance and let it fall apart? Of course not. You'd tune it, protect it, and keep it in peak condition so it could produce the beautiful music it was designed to create.

Your body is infinitely more valuable than any violin. It's the instrument through which you love your family and fulfill your calling. Keeping it strong isn't selfish—it's essential.

The Proverbs 31 woman is "clothed with strength and dignity" and "can laugh at the days to come." That's not just metaphorical. Physical strength provides the foundation for the confidence, energy, and resilience needed to thrive in every area of life.

The Ripple Effect

Here's what happens when you get serious about strength training:

Week 1-2: You start sleeping better. Your posture improves. You carry yourself differently—with more confidence and dignity.

Week 3-4: People notice. Not just your appearance, but your energy. Your mood is more stable. You handle stress better. You have more capacity for work, family, and service.

Month 2-3: You're a different person. Your relationship with your body has fundamentally changed. You no longer see it as something that betrays you—you see it as something that serves you. You're proud of what you can do, not just how you look.

Month 6+: Strength becomes your foundation for everything else. You move through the world with confidence. You model health for your family. You have the physical capacity to serve others and pursue your calling without being limited by weakness or fatigue.

But here's what surprised me most after years of training both myself and hundreds of clients: The physical changes are just the beginning.

When you get strong, you start to believe different things about yourself. About what's possible. About what you deserve. About what you can handle.

You stop making excuses in other areas of your life because you've proven to yourself that you can do hard things consistently. You've learned to push through discomfort, to embrace challenge, to trust the process even when you can't see immediate results.

Getting strong teaches you how to be strong.

Your Strength-Training Blueprint

Alright, enough theory. Let's get practical. Here's exactly how to build a sustainable strength training practice that will transform your body and your life:

Phase 1: Foundation (Weeks 1-4)

Goal: Learn movement patterns and build the habit

Frequency: 1-2x per week (e.g., Monday and/or Thursday)

Duration: 20 minutes

Focus: Heavy resistance to muscle failure from day one

The Workout:

- Leg Press - 1 set to muscle failure
- Chest Press - 1 set to muscle failure
- Seated Row - 1 set to muscle failure
- Overhead Press - 1 set to muscle failure
- Lat Pulldown - 1 set to muscle failure

The Key: Choose a weight heavy enough that you reach muscle failure in three to six reps (about one to two minutes) using a twenty-second cadence—approximately ten seconds up, ten seconds down. If you can do more than six reps or last longer than two minutes, the weight is too light. Increase resistance until you hit muscle failure around the 1½-minute mark. Move as slowly as you can without stopping, and work to the point where you literally cannot complete another rep with good form.

Phase 2: Building (Weeks 5-12)
Goal: Progressive overload and strength gains
Frequency: 1-2x per week (e.g., Monday and/or Thursday)
Duration: 20 minutes
Focus: Continue heavy resistance, add exercises

Add exercises like:

- **Leg Curl**—This targets your hamstrings (the muscles on the back of your thigh). You bend your leg against resistance, like you're trying to kick your own backside. Strong hamstrings protect your knees and help you run, climb stairs, and get up from chairs without groaning.
- **Leg Extension**—The opposite movement. This works your quadriceps (the front of your thigh) by straightening your leg against resistance—think of it like a slow-motion kick. These are the muscles that power you up stairs and help you stand up from a seated position.
- **Hip Abduction/Adduction**—These work the muscles of your outer hips and inner thighs. Abduction means pushing your legs *apart* against resistance (like you're making room for someone to sit next to you). Adduction is the

opposite—squeezing your legs *together* against resistance. You've probably seen the machines at gyms where people sit with pads on the outside or inside of their knees. These movements strengthen the stabilizing muscles around your hips, which matter more than most people realize for balance, posture, and preventing injury.

- **Triceps Extension**—Your triceps are the muscles on the back of your upper arm—the ones that wave back at you if you're not careful. This exercise has you straighten your arm against resistance, which strengthens the muscles responsible for pushing movements and gives your arms that toned, firm look.
- **Biceps Curl**—The classic "make a muscle" movement. Your biceps are on the front of your upper arm, and you strengthen them by bending your elbow and curling weight toward your shoulder. Strong biceps help with any pulling motion—carrying groceries, lifting kids, opening stubborn doors.

The Key: Each week, try to increase resistance so you continue hitting muscle failure in that one to two minute window. This is called progressive overload, and it's the engine of adaptation. Never sacrifice the slow cadence or muscle failure for more weight.

Phase 3: Mastery (Month 3+)
Goal: Maximize strength gains and maintain long-term progress
Frequency: 2-3x per week
Duration: 20 minutes
Focus: Advanced techniques while maintaining the core methodology

At this point, you'll work with more sophisticated equipment and techniques, potentially including:

- Pre-exhaustion protocols
- Negative emphasis training
- Intensity extenders

The Key: Never abandon the fundamentals—heavy resistance, slow movement, muscle failure in one to two minutes. Consistency trumps perfection. It's better to train moderately for years than intensely for weeks.

The FastFit Advantage

While you can certainly start with basic equipment at home or a traditional gym, the most effective approach is training with proper isokinetic equipment under professional guidance.

At FastFit, we've perfected this methodology over decades. Our isokinetic machines provide:

- Perfect resistance matching throughout the entire range of motion,
- Low injury risk with computer-controlled safety mechanisms,
- Maximum efficiency with twenty-minute total-body workouts,
- Professional guidance to ensure proper form and progression,
- Measurable results with precise tracking of strength gains.

This isn't just marketing—it's the difference between guessing and knowing you're getting optimal results with minimal time investment.

The technology makes the difference. The efficiency is real. The results speak for themselves.

And after experiencing the difference firsthand—gaining ten pounds of muscle in six months as an already-trained individual—I can tell you with complete confidence: This is the future of strength training.

For more information, visit www.fastfit.com.

Beyond the Gym: Movement Throughout Life

While strength training is your foundation, it's not the only movement your body needs. You also want to incorporate:

Daily Movement (NEAT a/k/a Non-Exercise Activity Thermogenesis): Take walks, use stairs, park farther away, stand while working. This isn't structured exercise—it's just being a human being who moves regularly throughout the day.

But remember: Strength training is the foundation. Everything else is supplementary.

The Choice: Strength or Survival

Here's the truth: You're going to age. Your metabolism will slow. Your bones will become more fragile. Your balance will decline. Your energy will decrease.

That's not optional. That's biology.

But how much and how fast—that's up to you.

You can choose to age gracefully, maintaining your strength, independence, and vitality well into your later years. Or you can choose the path of least resistance and gradually become weaker, more dependent, and more fragile with each passing year.

The choice you make today determines the person you'll be at sixty, seventy, and eighty.

I want you to imagine two versions of your future self:

Version 1: You're seventy-five years old. You struggle to get out of a chair without help. Walking up a set of stairs leaves you winded. You've fallen twice in the past year because your balance isn't what it used to be. You rely on others for basic tasks. Your world has gotten smaller because your body can't keep up with your spirit.

Version 2: You're seventy-five years old. You move with confidence and grace. You can lift your grandchildren. You travel, serve in your community, and live independently. Your body is a tool that enables your purpose, not a limitation that restricts it.

Which version do you want to be?

The path to Version 2 starts with the choice to get strong. And that choice starts today.

Your Next Step

Don't wait for motivation. Don't wait for Monday. Don't wait for the perfect plan or the perfect time.

Just start.

If you have access to proper equipment and guidance, use it.

6

MENTAL HEALTH— THE SECOND DOMINO

" Finally, brothers and sisters, whatever is true, whatever is honorable, whatever is right, whatever is pure, whatever is lovely, whatever is commendable, if there is any excellence and if anything worthy of praise, think about these things."
— Philippians 4:8

The Invisible Battle

There's a moment that defined my entire health journey, though I didn't realize it at the time. I was lying in that infinity pool in Costa Rica, surrounded by everything that should have brought me joy—close friends, tropical paradise, the sound of waves crashing below—and I felt nothing but despair.

The physical symptoms were brutal enough: nausea that wouldn't quit, brain fog so thick I could barely follow conversations, fatigue that made every movement feel like I was walking through quicksand. But what nearly broke me wasn't happening in my body. It was happening in my mind.

A voice had taken up residence in my head, and it spoke with the authority of absolute truth: "You're broken beyond repair. This is your new normal. Your kids will remember you as the sick dad who couldn't be present. You'll never get better. You'll become a burden to everyone you love."

I believed every word.

That's when I learned something that would change everything: You can have the strongest body in the world, but if your thoughts are at war with you, you'll sabotage every good thing you try to build. Mental health isn't just another item on the wellness checklist—it's the lens through which you experience everything else.

This is why mental health is the second domino. Because no matter how disciplined you are with exercise, how perfect your nutrition becomes, or how many supplements you take, if you can't manage the battlefield between your ears, you'll stay stuck. I've seen it happen to countless people: They have all the knowledge, all the resources, and all the motivation in the world, but they never address the voice that tells them they can't do it.

The good news I wish someone had told me in that pool? That voice isn't you. And you don't have to believe everything it says.

The Modern Mental Health Crisis

Before we go deeper, we need to acknowledge something: We're living through the worst mental health crisis in recorded history.

The statistics are staggering. Depression is now the leading cause of disability worldwide. Anxiety disorders affect 40 million adults in the United States alone. Suicide rates have increased by thirty-five percent since 1999. These aren't just numbers—they represent millions of people who feel exactly like I felt in that pool: overwhelmed, isolated, and convinced that something is fundamentally wrong with them.

But here's what's truly sobering: This explosion in mental health issues has happened during the exact same period when we've had unprecedented access to mental health resources, medications, and therapeutic techniques. We know more about the brain than ever before, yet we're more anxious, depressed, and mentally fragile than previous generations.

What's Happening To Us?

Dr. Jean Twenge's research shows that the inflection point for teenage anxiety and depression wasn't gradual—it was dramatic and sudden, beginning around 2012. [22] That's when smartphone ownership crossed fifty percent and social media became ubiquitous. But it's not just teenagers. We've created a culture that's essentially designed to make us miserable: endless comparison through social media, chronic overstimulation, disconnection from nature and community, and the replacement of meaning with consumption.

Most people don't even realize they're fighting a mental health battle. They just think they're "stressed" or "overwhelmed" or "having a tough season." They've normalized feeling anxious, scattered, and emotionally reactive because that's what everyone around them is experiencing too. And when they do pause to look for a cause, they often misdiagnose it—either brushing it off as "just life" or, worse, blaming it all on "the devil" instead of facing the simple reality of their own choices.

But normal doesn't mean healthy. And it certainly doesn't mean inevitable.

Why Mental Health Determines Everything Else

Let me ask you something: How long does the confidence from a great workout last? If you're like most people, it starts strong but begins to fade the moment that familiar voice chimes in: "You still look the same. This isn't working. You'll probably quit in a few weeks like you always do."

This is why so many people start health programs with enthusiasm and abandon them within months. It's not because they don't know what to do—it's because they haven't learned to manage the internal critic that convinces them they can't do it.

Your thoughts don't just influence how you feel—they literally change your biology. Dr. Caroline Leaf, who I mentioned in Chapter Two, has spent decades studying this connection. Her research shows that seventy-five to ninety-five percent of mental, physical, and behavioral illness stems from our thought life. This isn't metaphorical—it's measurable. Toxic thoughts trigger the release of stress hormones that suppress immune function, disrupt sleep, and promote inflammation throughout the body.

When you're caught in patterns of negative thinking, you're not just hurting emotionally—you're creating a biological environment that makes healing harder and illness more likely. Conversely, when you learn to think in healthier patterns, you create the internal conditions that support physical healing and emotional resilience.

The strength training we talked about in Chapter Five gives you confidence to tackle mental strongholds. When you prove to yourself that you can do hard things in the gym, you start believing you can do hard things everywhere else. But you need specific tools to leverage that physical confidence into mental breakthroughs.

Understanding Your Two Minds

Before you can win the battle for your mental health, you need to understand how your mind works. Most people are fighting this battle with the wrong strategy because they don't realize they're dealing with two completely different systems.

Nobel Prize winner Daniel Kahneman revolutionized our understanding of human decision-making when he discovered that we essentially have two minds running simultaneously. In his landmark book *Thinking, Fast and Slow,* he describes these as System 1 and System 2.

System 1 is your automatic mind. It's fast, emotional, and operates below the level of consciousness. System 1 processes about eleven million bits of information per second and makes instant judgments based on past experiences, emotions, and ingrained patterns. This is the system that made me jump every time my phone buzzed during my illness, immediately assuming it was bad news.

System 2 is your deliberate mind. It's slow, logical, and requires conscious effort to engage. This is the part of your mind that can reason through problems, make thoughtful decisions, and choose responses rather than react automatically. System 2 is what you use when you consciously decide to reframe a negative thought or remember that God is in control even when circumstances feel chaotic.

Here's the problem: System 1 runs the show about ninety-five percent of the time. System 2 only engages when you deliberately activate it or when System 1 encounters something it can't handle automatically.

If you've been through trauma, chronic stress, or extended illness like I experienced, System 1 gets programmed for threat detection. It defaults to worst-case scenarios and interprets ambiguous situations as dangerous. This isn't a character flaw—it's a survival mechanism that's become overactive in an environment where most threats are psychological rather than physical.

During my sickest months, my System 1 was like a smoke detector with a dying battery—constantly going off even when there was no real danger. Every symptom meant I was dying. Every doctor visit would bring terrible news. Every day I didn't feel better proved I never would.

But here's the hope: System 2 can learn to override System 1. That's what saved my mental health, and it's what can transform yours.

The Neuroscience of Negative Thinking

Your brain has a built-in negativity bias that served our ancestors well but works against us in the modern world. Dr. Rick Hanson explains it this way: "The brain is like Velcro for negative experiences and Teflon for positive ones."[23]

This isn't a design flaw—it's a survival feature. For most of human history, missing a positive opportunity (like a particularly abundant berry patch) was disappointing. But missing a negative threat (like a predator) was fatal. Our brains evolved to pay more attention to, remember more vividly, and react more strongly to negative information.

Research shows that it takes five positive interactions to counteract the emotional impact of one negative interaction. One harsh criticism can undo the emotional benefit of ten compliments. One scary symptom can overshadow months of feeling well.

Understanding this helped me realize why my thoughts during illness were so catastrophic. My System 1 wasn't malfunctioning—it was doing exactly what it was designed to do. The problem was that in our modern world, most threats aren't physical. They're psychological, relational, or financial. But your brain can't tell the difference between a lion chasing you and a concerning lab result. Both trigger the same neurological alarm system.

The key insight that changed everything for me was this: Just because a thought *feels* urgent and true doesn't mean it *is* urgent and true. Your brain's threat detection system can be wrong. And when it is wrong, you can learn to correct it.

When Your Mind Becomes Your Prison

I remember the exact moment I realized I wasn't just battling physical symptoms—I was trapped by my thoughts about those symptoms. I was sitting in yet another doctor's office, receiving yet another "everything looks normal" report, when the physician said something that stopped me cold: "Kyle, I think your body is trying to heal, but your mind is convinced you're dying. That stress response is keeping you sick."

She was right. I had become so accustomed to catastrophic thinking that I couldn't imagine any other way to interpret what was happening to me. I was caught in what psychologists call "cognitive distortions"—systematic errors in thinking that make reality seem worse than it is.

The breakthrough came when I discovered that these thought patterns weren't truths—they were habits. And like any habit, they could be changed.

That's when I encountered cognitive behavioral therapy (CBT), and it literally saved my life. CBT is based on a simple but profound insight: Your thoughts create your emotions, which drive your actions, which determine your results.

Thoughts → Emotions → Actions → Results

This isn't positive thinking or wishful thinking—it's a recognition that the stories we tell ourselves about our circumstances often matter more than the circumstances themselves. Two people can face identical situations and have completely different experiences based on how they interpret what's happening.

During my darkest days, I was constantly telling myself stories that felt absolutely true but weren't based in fact: "I'll never get better" (predicting the future based on current feelings). "I'm letting everyone down" (taking responsibility for things outside my control). "If I can't figure this out, I'm a complete failure" (all-or-nothing thinking). "Everyone else my age is healthy and successful while I'm falling apart" (comparison based on limited information).

These narratives felt reasonable at the time. But when I learned to step back and examine them like a detective rather than believe them like gospel, I realized they were just stories. Not facts.

Common Mental Traps

Here are the most common cognitive distortions that keep people stuck:

All-or-Nothing Thinking: You see things in black and white categories. If you're not perfect, you're a total failure. I used to think that one bad day with my diet or one missed workout meant I might as well give up entirely.

Catastrophizing: You predict the worst possible outcome and treat it as inevitable. I convinced myself that if one treatment didn't work, nothing would work—despite having dozens of other options to explore.

Mind Reading: You assume you know what others are thinking, usually something negative about you. I was certain people were judging me for being weak when most were actually concerned and supportive.

Mental Filter: You focus on a single negative detail while ignoring everything positive. I would fixate on one lingering symptom while dismissing clear signs of improvement.

Discounting the Positive: You dismiss positive experiences as flukes or coincidences. When I had good days, I'd tell myself they didn't count because they were temporary.

Emotional Reasoning: You assume your feelings reflect reality. Just because you feel hopeless doesn't mean there's no hope. Just because you feel like a failure doesn't mean you are one.

Sound familiar? These patterns aren't signs of weakness—they're normal human responses to stress and uncertainty. The key is learning to recognize them and respond differently.

The Power of Better Questions

One of the most powerful discoveries in my healing journey was this: The quality of your life is determined by the quality of the questions you ask yourself.

For months, I was asking questions that led nowhere good: "Why is this happening to me?" "What if I never get better?" "Why can't I just be normal?"

These questions sent my brain searching for evidence of victimhood and hopelessness. And our brains are incredibly efficient at finding evidence for whatever we're looking for.

But what if I asked different questions? "What is this season teaching me?" "How might this struggle prepare me to help others?" "What's working that I might be taking for granted?" "What's one small step I can take today?"

Your brain will work just as hard to answer empowering questions as disempowering ones. The difference is where those answers take you.

It sort of reminds me of my all-time favorite quote by Henry Ford: "Whether you think you can or think you can't, you're right."

This isn't denial or toxic positivity. I wasn't pretending everything was fine. I was strategically directing my mental energy toward solutions instead of problems, toward possibilities instead of limitations.

The Shame That Keeps You Sick

There's one more enemy of mental health that we need to address directly: shame.

Shame almost kept me from getting the help I needed, and I see it derailing people's healing journeys every day. There's a crucial difference between guilt and shame that I wish I'd understood earlier: Guilt says, "I did something bad." Shame says, "I am bad."

Guilt can be helpful; it points toward specific behaviors that need to change. But shame is toxic because it attacks your identity rather than your actions.

When I was struggling, guilt might have said, "I made some choices that contributed to this situation." That would have been useful because it implies agency and the possibility of different choices.

But shame said, "I'm fundamentally broken. I'm weak. I'm a burden. If people really knew how much I'm struggling, they'd lose respect for me."

Shame convinced me to hide, to pretend I was fine when I wasn't, to avoid asking for help because that would prove I was weak. And shame has a particularly cruel way of targeting people of faith: "Good Christians don't struggle like this. Where's your faith? Why can't you just trust God and get better?"

The turning point came when I finally told a few close friends the complete truth about what I was experiencing—not just the physical symptoms, but the fear, the despair, the spiritual doubt. Instead of the judgment I expected, I found understanding. Instead of rejection, I found support. Several people shared their own struggles with anxiety and depression—struggles I never would have guessed from their outward appearance.

That's when I learned that shame loses its power when it's exposed to empathy and truth. The antidote to shame isn't perfection—it's vulnerability. It's discovering that your worst moments don't define your worth—a truth I first encountered through Brené Brown's work.

As Christians, we have a unique weapon against shame: The gospel reminds us that we are simultaneously broken and beloved. We don't have to pretend to be perfect because Jesus already paid the price for our imperfections. We can be honest about our struggles because our identity isn't based on our performance—it's based on God's grace.

Practical Tools for Mental Freedom

Here are the specific techniques that helped me win the battle between my ears:

The Evidence Gathering Technique: When you catch yourself believing a negative thought, become a detective. Ask yourself:

- What evidence supports this thought?
- What evidence contradicts it?
- What would I tell a good friend in this situation?
- What's a more balanced way to look at this?

For example, when I thought, "I'm never going to get better," the evidence against included: I felt good yesterday, my doctor said healing isn't linear, I'm still early in my treatment protocol, and I've overcome health challenges before.

The 5-4-3-2-1 Grounding Technique: When anxiety starts to spiral, interrupt the pattern by noticing:

- 5 things you can see,
- 4 things you can touch,
- 3 things you can hear,
- 2 things you can smell,
- 1 thing you can taste.

This pulls you out of your head and into the present moment, giving your rational mind a chance to engage.

The Best Friend Test: When your inner critic starts attacking, ask yourself: "Would I say this to my best friend if they were in this situation?" The answer is almost always no. We're our own harshest critics while being far more compassionate toward others.

Daily Gratitude Practice: Every night, write down three specific things you're grateful for and why. This trains your brain to notice what's going right instead of fixating on what's wrong. Gratitude isn't denial—it's choosing to see the whole picture instead of just the problems.

Morning Pages: Spend ten to fifteen minutes each morning writing stream-of-consciousness thoughts. This clears mental clutter and helps you process emotions before they build up throughout the day.

Biblical Wisdom for Mental Health

Scripture has profound insight into managing our minds, and much of it aligns perfectly with what modern psychology has discovered:

Philippians 4:8 isn't just spiritual advice—it's practical psychology. Paul is instructing us to direct our attention toward thoughts that build us up rather than tear us down. This is cognitive behavioral therapy, written 2,000 years before CBT was invented.

2 Corinthians 10:5 describes exactly what modern therapy teaches: "...we are taking every thought captive to the obedience of Christ." This is the practice of catching unhelpful thoughts and replacing them with truth.

Matthew 6:34 addresses anxiety directly: "Do not worry about tomorrow, for tomorrow will worry about itself." Jesus is calling us back to the present moment—the only place where we have any power to act.

Romans 12:2 calls us to be "transformed by the renewing of your mind." The Greek word for "renewing" implies a continuous process. Your mind can be renovated, but it requires ongoing work.

Mental Health as Spiritual Warfare

Here's something that might change how you think about your mental health struggles: The battle for your mind is spiritual, not just psychological.

Ephesians 6:12 reminds us that "…our struggle is not against flesh and blood, but against the rulers, against the powers, against the world forces of this darkness, against the spiritual forces of wickedness in the heavenly places." The enemy's primary weapon isn't temptation—it's deception. He wants to convince you that God doesn't love you, that you're beyond help, that your situation is hopeless.

During my darkest days, I was bombarded with thoughts that felt true but weren't: "God is punishing you." "You'll never be useful again." "Your family would be better off without you."

When I started recognizing these as spiritual attacks rather than personal truths, everything shifted. I began responding to them not with analysis but with authority.

"That thought is not from God. I reject it." "God says I am beloved, chosen, and redeemed." "I choose to believe God's truth over this lie."

This isn't magical thinking—it's spiritual discipline. You're training your mind to align with truth rather than deception.

When I first read *Psycho-Cybernetics* by Dr. Maxwell Maltz, I realized how much of my life had been shaped by the story I told myself about who I was.

Maltz, a plastic surgeon, noticed that changing a person's face didn't always change how they felt about themselves. The breakthrough was that self-image, not outward appearance or circumstances, drives nearly everything—confidence, performance, even happiness. That hit me hard. I saw how often I was living out of old labels or failures, letting my past dictate my potential.

What I learned is that the mind works like a goal-seeking machine: If you program it with negative instructions ("I'm not enough." "I always fail"), that's where it will aim. But if you deliberately feed it new pictures—truth, faith, possibility—your subconscious begins to move you toward them almost automatically.

For me, this wasn't about "positive thinking" in a cheesy sense. It was about upgrading my self-image to align with the identity God gave me and learning that true change happens when I see myself differently first.

The Choice Before You

Your thoughts are not facts. Your emotions are not commands. Your past does not determine your future. You have far more power over your mental state than you realize.

This doesn't mean pretending everything is fine when it's not. It doesn't mean spiritual bypassing or toxic positivity. It means developing the skills to navigate life's inevitable challenges without being destroyed by them.

The voice in your head will never be completely quiet. But you can learn to be its manager instead of its victim. You can train it to be your ally instead of your enemy.

Your mind is the second domino. Get this right, and everything else becomes possible. Get this wrong, and everything else becomes exponentially harder.

I thought my mind was broken beyond repair. But healing taught me something profound: God doesn't waste our struggles. He uses them to shape us into the people He's calling us to be.

The mental tools I learned during my illness didn't just help me survive—they equipped me to help others navigate their own dark valleys. The thought patterns I had to overcome made me more compassionate toward others who struggle. The community that supported me taught me how to support others.

Your wilderness season is preparing you for your calling. But first, you must win the battle between your ears.

The choice is yours. Will you remain a prisoner of your thoughts, or will you step into the mental freedom that God has made available to you?

Your calling depends on your answer.

Recap & Actions

Scripture to Reflect On: "Finally, brothers and sisters, whatever is true, whatever is honorable, whatever is right, whatever is pure, whatever is lovely, whatever is commendable, if there is any excellence and if anything worthy of praise, think about these things."—Philippians 4:8

Science-Backed Truth: Your thoughts create your emotions, which drive your actions, which determine your results. You have two thinking systems—automatic and deliberate—and you can train the deliberate system to override destructive automatic patterns. Cognitive distortions are learned habits that can be unlearned with practice.

Ready, Willing, Able Actions:

Ready (You can do this right now):

- Practice the 5-4-3-2-1 grounding technique when anxiety strikes,
- Write down three specific things you're grateful for and why,
- Apply the Best Friend Test to one self-critical thought.

Willing (You can do this within a week):

- Start a nightly gratitude journal with three specific entries.
- Identify your most common cognitive distortions.
- Begin asking empowering questions: "What can I learn?" instead of "Why me?"

Able (You can do this within a month):

- Establish a morning pages practice to clear mental clutter.
- Share your real struggles with trusted friends or a counselor.
- Consider professional help if needed—therapy is stewardship, not weakness.

Remember: Your thoughts are not facts, your emotions are not commands, and your past does not determine your future. You have the power to retrain your brain for resilience, peace, and purpose. You can take rest in this. And speaking of rest…

7

SLEEP, REST, AND RECOVERY—THE THIRD DOMINO

"It is futile for you to rise up early, to stay up late, to eat the bread of painful labor; this is how He gives to His beloved sleep.
— Psalm 127:2

The Night I Stopped Sleeping

There's a particular kind of despair that comes at 3 a.m. when you've been lying awake for hours, knowing you need sleep but unable to find it. Your body is exhausted, but your mind is wired. You're tired enough to cry but too anxious to rest. Every minute that passes feels like another piece of tomorrow's energy slipping away.

For over a year during my health crisis, this was my nightly reality. According to my Oura Ring, I was getting an average of eighteen minutes of deep sleep per night. Eighteen minutes. For context, healthy adults need sixty to ninety minutes of deep sleep to function optimally. I was getting less deep sleep than most people get during a brief afternoon nap.

Night after night, I would lie in bed feeling like my brain was trapped in a washing machine on the spin cycle. Thoughts racing between worry about my symptoms, anxiety about tomorrow's responsibilities, and despair about whether I'd ever feel normal again. My heart would pound and skip beats for no apparent reason. My body felt simultaneously exhausted and electric.

I tried everything the internet suggested: melatonin, magnesium, chamomile tea, meditation apps, white noise machines, blackout curtains, weighted blankets. Nothing worked. If anything, the pressure to sleep made the insomnia worse.

During the day, I was a zombie. Simple decisions felt overwhelming. Healthy foods tasted like cardboard, so I craved sugar and caffeine just to function. My mood was a constant rollercoaster. I snapped at my kids over nothing. Work that used to energize me felt draining.

I was caught in a vicious cycle: Poor sleep made all my other symptoms worse, which made me more anxious about my health, which made sleep even more elusive. I began to understand why sleep deprivation is used as a form of torture. It doesn't just make you tired—it slowly dismantles your ability to cope with life itself.

But when my health finally began to improve and my sleep started to normalize, it was like someone had handed me a cheat code for everything else. Suddenly, eating well felt effortless. Exercise became enjoyable again. My mood stabilized. Problems that had seemed insurmountable became manageable. I could think clearly for the first time in a long time.

Sleep is the foundation that makes everything else possible. And in our culture that glorifies exhaustion and treats rest as weakness, we've forgotten something our ancestors knew instinctively: Sleep is not a luxury—it's a necessity as fundamental as food and water.

The Foundation That Changes Everything

What if I told you there was one thing you could do tonight that would make you stronger tomorrow, smarter next week, and healthier for the rest of your life—without buying a single supplement, joining a gym, or changing what you eat?

That one thing is sleep. Quality sleep will do more for your health than most people's entire wellness routine. It's free, it feels good, and your body is literally designed to do it automatically. Yet we're terrible at it.

We treat sleep like an inconvenience rather than an investment. We wear exhaustion like a badge of honor and brag about how little sleep we got last night. We'll spend thousands on supplements and recovery gadgets while ignoring the most powerful recovery tool we already own.

Dr. Matthew Walker, one of the world's leading sleep researchers and author of *Why We Sleep* puts it bluntly: "The shorter your sleep, the shorter your life." But this isn't just about longevity—it's about the quality of every day you're alive. [24]

While you sleep, your body doesn't just rest—it rebuilds. Your brain doesn't just turn off—it cleans house. Your immune system doesn't just maintain—it strengthens. Every system in your body depends on quality sleep to function optimally.

Here's what happens during those eight hours when you're unconscious:

Memory Consolidation: Your brain transfers information from short-term to long-term memory, literally rewiring itself based on what you learned that day. Students who sleep after studying retain forty percent more information than those who stay awake. All those all-nighters you pulled in college? They were sabotaging the very thing you were trying to accomplish.

Brain Detoxification: During deep sleep, your brain cells shrink by up to sixty percent, creating space for cerebrospinal fluid to flush out metabolic waste—including the toxic proteins associated with Alzheimer's disease. Dr. Maiken Nedergaard's research shows this glymphatic system is sixty percent more active during sleep than when awake. Miss sleep, and the trash literally accumulates in your brain. [25]

Hormonal Reset: Sleep is when your body produces growth hormone for muscle repair, testosterone for energy and vitality, and leptin to regulate appetite. Men who sleep five hours per night for just one week have testosterone levels equivalent to someone ten to fifteen years older. Women experience similar disruptions in hormones that regulate mood, metabolism, and reproductive health.

Immune Strengthening: Your immune system essentially goes to boot camp while you sleep. Natural killer cells—your body's cancer-fighting warriors—increase by seventy percent after a full night's rest. Meanwhile, just one night of poor sleep can reduce your vaccine response by fifty percent. Sleep isn't just recovery—it's your first line of defense against disease.

Metabolic Regulation: Sleep controls the hormones that manage hunger and satiety. When you're sleep-deprived, ghrelin (the hunger hormone) spikes while leptin (the satiety hormone) plummets. This is why you crave donuts after a bad night's sleep—your body thinks it's starving. People who sleep less than six hours per night are thirty percent more likely to become obese than those who sleep seven to nine hours.

Emotional Regulation: Sleep deprivation hijacks your amygdala (the brain's alarm system) while shutting down your prefrontal cortex (the rational decision-maker). You're essentially walking around with a hair-trigger emotional response and no voice of reason to calm it down. This is why everything feels more dramatic when you're tired.

Sleep isn't a break from life—it's what makes life possible. It's not time lost—it's an investment that pays dividends in every other area.

The Hidden Epidemic

Most sleep problems aren't actually sleep problems. They're anxiety problems that show up at bedtime.

When your head hits the pillow and the distractions of the day finally quiet down, your mind often starts racing. All the worries you managed during the day become overwhelming in the darkness. The what-ifs and worst-case scenarios that you kept at bay with busyness suddenly demand attention.

This was my experience during my health crisis. My sleep-onset insomnia wasn't about sleep—it was about anxiety. The moment I tried to rest, my mind would spiral into catastrophic thinking about my symptoms, my future, my family's security. Rest felt impossible when my nervous system was convinced I was in danger.

There are three types of insomnia, each with different underlying causes:

Sleep-onset insomnia (can't fall asleep) is usually anxiety-driven. Your mind races with worries about the future or replays of the day's stresses. You're physically tired but mentally wired.

Sleep-maintenance insomnia (can't stay asleep) is often related to stress hormones or blood sugar instability. You fall asleep fine but wake up in the middle of the night feeling anxious or wired for no apparent reason.

Early-morning awakening (wake up too early and can't get back to sleep) is frequently associated with depression or elevated cortisol levels. You wake up at 4 a.m. feeling simultaneously exhausted and unable to return to sleep.

I experienced all three during my illness, and each one taught me something different about what my body was trying to communicate. The insomnia wasn't the enemy—it was the messenger, alerting me to deeper issues that needed attention.

This is why sleeping pills rarely provide long-term solutions. They're like unplugging the smoke detector instead of putting out the fire. They might provide temporary relief, but they don't address the underlying causes of sleep disruption.

The Biblical Wisdom of Rest

Before we dive into practical strategies, we need to address something our culture has completely forgotten: *Rest is sacred.*

Rest isn't just a biological necessity—it's a spiritual discipline.

Look at Psalm 127:2 again: "It is futile for you to rise up early, to stay up late, to eat the bread of painful labor; this is how He gives to His beloved sleep." This isn't just poetic language—it's a profound truth about human design. God grants sleep to those He loves. That means sleep is a gift, not a weakness. Rest is worship, not laziness.

Our culture tells us that sleep is for the weak, that rest is unproductive, that burning the candle at both ends is admirable. But God's design says the exact opposite: Rest is how we acknowledge our limitations and trust in His provision.

Jesus Himself modeled this. Even amid intense ministry demands, He regularly withdrew to quiet places to rest and pray (Luke 5:16). If the Son of God needed rest, what makes us think we don't?

There's something beautifully humbling about sleep. For eight hours every night, you must surrender control. You can't check your phone, answer emails, or solve problems. You have to trust that the world will keep spinning without your constant management.

Sleep is practice for trust. Rest is rehearsal for surrender. And both are essential for the kind of life God is calling you to live.

The Sleep Foundation: Getting the Basics Right

After years of struggling with sleep and working with clients who battle insomnia, I've realized that most sleep problems can be solved by addressing a few fundamental factors. I didn't come to this overnight—it's been a mix of trial and error, late-night experiments, and lessons drawn from countless books and podcasts on sleep science. What I discovered is that the best solutions aren't complicated biohacks or expensive interventions—they're simple changes that create the conditions your body already needs for quality rest.

Consistency: Your Circadian Rhythm's Best Friend Your body loves predictability. Going to bed and waking up at roughly the same time every day—yes, even on weekends—helps regulate your internal clock.

This is harder than it sounds in our culture of flexible schedules and Netflix binges. But your circadian rhythm doesn't care about your social calendar. It responds to consistency. Even a one-hour deviation from your normal bedtime can disrupt your sleep quality for several days.

Darkness: Protecting Your Circadian Rhythm Even small amounts of light can disrupt melatonin production. We're talking about the light from your phone charger, your alarm clock, or the streetlamp outside your window. Your bedroom should be cave-dark.

Light exposure tells your brain it's time to be awake and alert. Even if you fall asleep with light in the room, your sleep architecture will be compromised. Your body won't cycle through the deep sleep and REM stages as effectively.

Blackout curtains aren't optional—they're essential. And here's something most people aren't aware of: Light exposure through your skin can also affect circadian rhythms. If you can see your hand in front of your face in your bedroom, it's not dark enough.

Morning Sunlight: Nature's Wake-Up Call Just as darkness at night protects your circadian rhythm, sunlight in the morning anchors it. Getting natural light—especially direct sunlight into your eyes within the first thirty to sixty minutes of waking—signals your brain to shut down melatonin production and ramp up cortisol in a healthy, energizing way. This sets your body's internal clock, making it easier to fall asleep at night and wake up refreshed the next morning. You don't need hours outside—just five to ten minutes on a sunny day (or twenty to thirty minutes if it's cloudy) can make a measurable difference. Step outside, skip the sunglasses for a few minutes, and let your body sync with the natural rhythm it was designed for.

Temperature: Your Body's Sleep Signal Your core body temperature needs to drop by two to three degrees Fahrenheit to initiate sleep. This is why a hot bath or sauna before bed can help—the rapid cooling afterward triggers sleepiness. Keep your bedroom between 65 and 68°F. It might feel chilly at first, but your sleep quality will improve dramatically.

This temperature drop is one of the strongest signals your body receives that it's time to sleep. When your bedroom is too warm, you're fighting against this natural process. You might eventually fall asleep, but your sleep will be fragmented and less restorative.

Blue Light: The Modern Sleep Killer Blue light from screens suppresses melatonin production for up to three hours after exposure. That "quick" scroll through social media at 9 p.m. just guaranteed you won't feel sleepy until midnight, regardless of how tired your body is.

The solution isn't necessarily expensive blue light glasses (though they can help). It's avoiding screens (including television) for two hours before your intended bedtime. Read a book. Take a bath. Have an actual conversation. Pray. Journal. Engage in activities that help your nervous system downshift rather than ramp up.

The Caffeine Curfew Caffeine has a half-life of six to eight hours. That means if you have coffee at 2 p.m., a quarter of that caffeine is still circulating in your system at 10 p.m. You might be able to fall asleep, but your sleep quality will suffer significantly.

Cut off caffeine by noon if you're sensitive, 2 p.m. if you're not. And remember: caffeine is hiding in chocolate, tea, some pain medications, and even decaffeinated coffee (which still contains fifteen to thirty percent of the caffeine found in regular coffee).

Alcohol: The Sleep Saboteur Alcohol might make you feel drowsy initially, but it's one of the worst things you can do for sleep quality. It suppresses REM sleep—the stage crucial for memory consolidation and emotional processing—and fragments your sleep architecture throughout the night.

Dr. Matthew Walker describes alcohol as "sleep's arch enemy." Even small amounts can reduce REM sleep by twenty to thirty percent and cause you to wake up multiple times without realizing it. You might think you slept for eight hours, but you didn't get eight hours of quality sleep.

If you're going to drink alcohol, do it earlier in the day and ensure it's completely metabolized before bedtime—roughly one hour per drink for most people.

Rest Beyond Sleep: The Art of Active Recovery

Sleep is the foundation of recovery, but it's not the only form of rest your body and mind need. In our productivity-obsessed culture, we've forgotten how to truly rest while awake. We've confused rest with entertainment, recovery with distraction.

True rest involves creating space for your nervous system to downshift throughout the day. It's about moving from the sympathetic nervous system (fight-or-flight) to the parasympathetic nervous system (rest-and-digest) before you're completely exhausted.

The Power of Presence Most of us spend our days in a state of chronic partial attention—constantly multitasking, always slightly distracted, never fully present to any one thing. This creates a low-level stress response that accumulates throughout the day and interferes with our ability to rest at night.

Learning to be fully present to one activity at a time is a form of rest. When you're eating, just eat. When you're having a conversation, put away your phone. When you're walking, notice your surroundings rather than planning your next task.

This kind of presence requires practice in our hyperconnected world, but it's essential for mental and emotional recovery.

Meditation: Training Your Mind to Rest I used to think meditation was too mystical or "New Age" for Christians. But then I realized I'd been practicing it my whole life—I just called it prayer.

Meditation is simply the practice of focused attention. When you pray, you're meditating on God's character and promises. When you read Scripture contemplatively, you're training your mind to focus on truth rather than anxiety.

Research shows that just ten minutes of daily meditation can reduce cortisol levels by twenty-three percent, improve sleep quality, and increase your ability to focus and regulate emotions. But more importantly for believers, it creates space to hear God's voice above the noise of daily life.

The Digital Sabbath Here's a practice that transformed my mental health: taking regular breaks from technology. Not just putting your phone down for a few minutes but completely disconnecting from digital input for extended periods.

Start with a digital sunset—no screens after 8 p.m. Work up to one morning per week without checking email or social media. Eventually, consider a full twenty-four-hour digital sabbath once a week.

What happens when you disconnect? You remember what it feels like to be human. You notice things. You have deeper conversations. You think original thoughts instead of reacting to other people's content. You discover that you exist beyond your online persona.

Your nervous system gets a chance to reset. Your dopamine receptors become more sensitive. Your attention span increases. You reconnect with activities that restore you rather than just entertain you.

Recovery: Listening to Your Body

The recovery industry has exploded in recent years, with companies selling everything from $300 heart rate variability monitors to sophisticated apps that track seventeen different metrics. But here's what the research shows: The most accurate indicator of your recovery status isn't your HRV (Heart Rate Variability), your sleep score, or your resting heart rate.

It's how you feel.

What is heart rate variability? Your heart doesn't beat like a metronome—and that's a good thing. Heart rate variability measures the tiny fluctuations in time between each heartbeat. If your heart beats sixty times per minute, those beats aren't perfectly spaced one second apart. There might be 0.9 seconds between one beat and 1.1 seconds before the next. This variation is controlled by your autonomic nervous system—the same system that manages your stress response and recovery.

Here's the counterintuitive part: *Higher* variability is better. When your HRV is high, it means your nervous system is flexible and responsive, able to shift smoothly between "go mode" and "rest mode." When HRV is low, it often signals that your body is under stress, fighting illness, under-recovered, or stuck in a chronic stress state. Think of it like a rubber band—a healthy one stretches and rebounds easily, while a worn-out one is stiff and brittle. Athletes, researchers, and clinicians now consider HRV one of the best objective markers of overall resilience and recovery capacity.

Dr. Shona Halson's research on elite athletes found that subjective measures of recovery—how tired, sore, or energetic you feel—are often more predictive of performance than objective metrics.[26] Your body has been giving you recovery feedback for your entire life through fatigue, soreness, mood, energy levels, and motivation.

These aren't primitive signals that need to be overridden by technology. They're sophisticated biofeedback systems that evolved over millions of years to help you optimize your health and performance.

The Problem with Gadget Obsession

I love data. I wear an Oura Ring, track my sleep, and find the metrics fascinating. But I've learned something important: Data without wisdom is just noise.

I've watched people become slaves to their recovery scores—feeling anxious when their HRV is low or forcing themselves to work out when their body is begging for rest because their app says they're "recovered."

The goal isn't to optimize your numbers—it's to optimize your life. And sometimes your life requires you to push through fatigue to serve others, or to rest even when your metrics suggest you're recovered.

The Simple Recovery Assessment

Instead of relying primarily on gadgets, try this daily check-in:

Physical: How does my body feel? Am I sore, energetic, or sluggish? Do I feel strong or weak? Is there any pain or unusual tension?

Mental: How's my cognitive function? Am I sharp or foggy? Motivated or resistant? Can I focus easily or am I scattered?

Emotional: What's my mood like? Am I patient or irritable? Optimistic or anxious? Do I feel resilient or fragile?

If you're feeling good in all three areas, you're likely well-recovered and can handle more intensive activities. If you're struggling in one or more areas, prioritize rest and recovery over intensity.

The Recovery Hierarchy If you want to optimize recovery, here's the order of importance:

1. **Sleep** (seven to nine hours of quality sleep trumps any recovery device),
2. **Stress management** (chronic stress blocks recovery regardless of everything else),
3. **Nutrition** (your body can't repair without proper fuel),
4. **Movement** (gentle movement enhances recovery; intense movement requires it),
5. **Everything else** (saunas, ice baths, massage, supplements are helpful but not essential).

Notice what's not high up on that list? Expensive gadgets, complicated protocols, or special techniques. The fundamentals work—and they're mostly free.

Active Recovery: The Gentle Movement Principle

Recovery doesn't mean being sedentary. In fact, gentle movement often enhances recovery by increasing blood flow, reducing muscle stiffness, and promoting the circulation of lymphatic fluid.

A twenty-minute walk after an intense workout does more for recovery than lying on the couch for two hours.

The key word is gentle. Active recovery should feel restorative, not depleting. If you're breathing hard or feeling fatigued, you've crossed the line from recovery into training.

The Cultural Lie We Must Reject

Our culture promotes a lie that's destroying our health and our souls and that lie says that rest is earned through productivity. You can relax once you've checked everything off your list, answered all your emails, and solved all your problems.

But this is backwards. Rest isn't a reward for productivity—it's a requirement for it. You don't earn the right to sleep by working hard enough. You don't deserve recovery only after you've pushed yourself to exhaustion.

The most productive people aren't those who work the most hours—they're those who work the most strategically. They understand that their brain needs downtime to process information, their body needs recovery to adapt to stress, and their spirit needs stillness to connect with what matters most.

Think about it this way: A violin string that's too tight snaps. A violin string that's too loose makes no music. The beautiful sound comes from the right tension—and the spaces between the notes.

Your life needs the same rhythm: periods of intensity balanced with periods of rest. Work balanced with play. Effort balanced with ease. This isn't just practical wisdom—it's biblical wisdom.

Even God rested on the seventh day, not because He was tired, but because He was modeling a pattern essential for human flourishing. Rest is woven into the fabric of creation itself.

Sleep as Spiritual Discipline

When you choose sleep over late-night productivity, you're saying, "I trust that God can handle what I can't get done today." When you prioritize rest over endless scrolling, you're declaring that your worth isn't tied to your output.

This is why insomnia often gets worse during stressful periods. It's not just that stress makes sleep difficult—it's that sleep requires a level of trust that stress makes feel impossible.

But here's the beautiful paradox: The more you practice the surrender of sleep, the easier it becomes to surrender in other areas of your life. Rest teaches trust. Sleep schools you in faith.

When you prioritize sleep, you're acknowledging that you are not God. You're admitting that you need restoration, that you have limits, that you're designed to work within rhythms rather than operate as a machine.

This humility isn't weakness—it's wisdom. It's the recognition that sustainable effectiveness comes from working with your design rather than against it.

A Practice for Better Sleep

Before you go to bed tonight, try this simple routine: Spend five minutes reviewing the day with gratitude. What went well? What are you thankful for? This helps shift your nervous system from stress to appreciation.

Pray or meditate briefly, releasing the day's worries to God. You might pray: "God, I give You this day—the successes and failures, the completed tasks and unfinished business. I trust You with my loved ones, my work, and my concerns. Thank You for the gift of rest. Help me surrender to Your care and wake refreshed for whatever You have planned tomorrow."

Then turn off your phone, close your eyes, and let yourself be held by the One who never sleeps so that you can.

Your Recovery Revolution

Let me paint you a picture of what your life could look like with proper sleep and recovery: You wake up naturally, without an alarm, feeling refreshed and ready for the day. Your mind is clear and focused. You have energy for your morning activities, patience for your family, and creativity for your work.

Throughout the day, you handle stress with resilience instead of reactivity. You make decisions from wisdom rather than fatigue. You're present in conversations instead of distracted by mental fog.

You go to bed at a reasonable hour, not because you're forced to, but because you value what sleep gives you more than what late-night productivity promises. You fall asleep easily, trusting that tomorrow's challenges will meet a well-rested version of yourself.

This isn't fantasy—it's what your body and brain are designed for. You just have to give them the conditions they need: consistent sleep, strategic rest, and genuine recovery.

The benefits compound over time. One good night's sleep makes the next day easier, which makes that night's sleep better, which makes the following day even more productive. Conversely, one bad night starts a downward spiral that can last for days or weeks.

The question isn't whether you can afford to prioritize rest. The question is whether you can afford not to.

Your Sleep Experiment

Instead of trying to overhaul your entire routine overnight, pick one area to focus on for the next week:

Week 1: Temperature—make your bedroom two to three degrees cooler and track how you feel.

Week 2: Darkness—invest in blackout curtains or a quality eye mask.

Week 3: Consistency—go to bed and wake up at the same time every day, including weekends.

Week 4: Digital sunset—no screens for two hours before bed.

Pay attention to which change makes the biggest difference for you. Everyone's sleep needs are slightly different, but everyone's sleep needs are real.

Remember: This isn't about becoming a perfect sleeper. It's about becoming a person who values rest enough to protect it. Because when you're well-rested, you become available for everything God is calling you to do.

The world needs the well-rested version of you—the one with energy to serve, wisdom to lead, and peace to share. That version is available every morning, but only if you give them what they need to exist: quality sleep, genuine rest, and strategic recovery.

Sleep well. Your calling depends on it.

Recap & Actions

Scripture to Reflect On: "It is futile for you to rise up early to stay up late, to eat the bread of painful labor; this is how He gives to His beloved sleep." —Psalm 127:2

Science-Backed Truth: Sleep isn't downtime—it's when your brain detoxifies, your body repairs, and your hormones reset. Quality sleep improves every area of health and performance, while poor sleep undermines everything else you're trying to accomplish. Most recovery gadgets can't improve on the fundamentals: adequate sleep, stress management, and listening to your body.

Ready, Willing, Able Actions:

Ready (You can do this right now):

- Make your bedroom two to three degrees cooler tonight.
- Put your phone in another room before bed.
- Take ten slow, deep breaths, focusing on extending your exhale.
- Practice five minutes of gratitude before sleep.

Willing (You can do this within a week):

- Establish a consistent bedtime and wake time, even on weekends.
- Create a two-hour digital sunset routine.
- Try a simple meditation or prayer practice for five to ten minutes daily.
- Implement one fundamental sleep improvement (darkness, temperature, or consistency).

Able (You can do this within a month):

- Transform your bedroom into a sleep sanctuary with proper darkness, temperature, and minimal electronics.
- Develop a wind-down routine that signals your nervous system it's time to rest.
- Practice the daily recovery check-in: assess physical, mental, and emotional states before planning your day's intensity.
- Experiment with a weekly digital sabbath or extended break from technology.

Remember: Rest isn't earned through productivity—rest enables productivity. Sleep isn't a luxury—it's the foundation that makes everything else in your health and calling possible.

8

NUTRITION—THE FOUNDATION THAT FUELS EVERYTHING

"So whether you eat or drink or whatever you do, do it all for the glory of God." — 1 Corinthians 10:31

The Great Fruit Experiment

I need to tell you about one of the most ridiculous chapters of my health journey—the time I decided to eat nothing but fruit for three months.

I was in my twenties, convinced I had discovered the secret to perfect health through a book (*The 80/10/10 Diet*) that promised miraculous results from a "fruitarian" diet. The author claimed that humans were designed to eat only fruit, that cooking food was unnatural, and that this way of eating would unlock boundless energy and perfect health.

So I did what any enthusiastic young person would do: I went all in. For three months, I ate nothing but raw fruit. Bananas for breakfast. Apples for lunch. Dates and berries for dinner. I was convinced I was eating like Adam and Eve in the Garden of Eden.

The first few weeks felt incredible—probably because I had dramatically reduced my total calorie intake and eliminated all processed foods. I lost weight quickly and felt energetic. I thought I had found the answer to everything.

But by month two, things started falling apart. My energy crashed. My sleep became erratic. My mood swung wildly between euphoria and despair. My digestion was a disaster. And perhaps most concerning, I was constantly thinking about food—specifically, food that wasn't fruit.

By month three, I was miserable. My body was crying out for protein, healthy fats, and nutrients that simply aren't abundant in fruit. I had inadvertently created massive nutrient deficiencies while destabilizing my blood sugar and wreaking havoc on my gut microbiome.

When I finally abandoned the experiment and returned to eating a balanced diet, I felt like I was recovering from a bout of malnutrition—which, in many ways, I was.

This experience taught me something crucial about nutrition: Extremes feel compelling, but they rarely lead to lasting health. The most profound truths about eating well aren't found in revolutionary new theories or ancient dietary secrets. They're found in understanding a few fundamental principles and applying them consistently over time.

The Problem with Nutrition Today

If you're confused about nutrition, you're not alone. We're living through the most information-rich and simultaneously most confusing era in the history of human nutrition.

Every day brings a new study, a new superfood, a new dietary villain, or a revolutionary eating plan that promises to solve all your health problems. Carbs are evil—except when they're essential. Fat makes you fat—unless it's the good kind that makes you thin. Meat causes cancer—or maybe it prevents it. Vegetables are healing—except for the ones that are toxic.

The nutrition space has become more like religion than science, with passionate believers on every side claiming to have discovered the one true way to eat. Keto. Paleo. Vegan. Carnivore. Mediterranean. Intermittent fasting. Each camp has compelling testimonials, cherry-picked studies, and influencers with impressive physiques promoting their approach as the answer to everything.

But here's what I learned after years of cycling through every diet imaginable: Most of this complexity is noise. The fundamentals of healthy eating haven't changed much in the past century. What's changed is our ability to overcomplicate simple truths and our willingness to ignore basic principles in favor of the latest trend.

The worst part is that all this confusion keeps people from taking action. They're so overwhelmed by conflicting information that they either give up entirely or spend years jumping from one extreme to another, never giving any approach enough time to work.

I know this pattern intimately because I lived it for years. Fruitarianism was just one stop on a much longer journey through nearly every dietary philosophy you can imagine. I was a chronic yo-yo dieter, always searching for the perfect plan that would finally give me the energy, physique, and health I wanted.

What I didn't realize at the time was that all this dietary chaos was actually making me sicker. Every time I dramatically changed my eating patterns, I was disrupting my gut microbiome, stressing my digestive system, and creating new nutritional imbalances. My sleep problems, mood swings, and eventual gut health crisis weren't just random bad luck—they were partly the result of years of nutritional extremism.

The 80/20 Principle: Focus on What Actually Matters

After years studying nutrition research, I've come to believe in the 80/20 principle: 80 percent of your results come from 20 percent of your efforts. This principle applies to every area of life, but it's especially relevant to nutrition.

Most people spend 80 percent of their energy obsessing over details that might contribute 20 percent of their results: whether to eat organic versus conventional, the perfect macro ratios, the ideal meal timing, or which supplements might give them a slight edge. Meanwhile, they ignore the 20 percent of fundamentals that drive 80 percent of their outcomes.

Here's what the 20 percent looks like for nutrition:

1. **Energy balance** (eating the right amount of total calories)
2. **Protein adequacy** (getting enough high-quality protein)
3. **Food quality** (choosing whole foods over processed foods most of the time)
4. **Hydration** (drinking enough water)
5. **Consistency** (following a sustainable approach long-term)

That's it. Master these five fundamentals, and you'll be healthier than 90 percent of the population. Everything else—meal timing, specific macro ratios, supplement protocols, elimination diets—belongs in the remaining 20 percent.

This doesn't mean the details never matter. For some people, in specific circumstances, optimizing the 20 percent can provide meaningful benefits. But for most people, most of the time, focusing on the fundamentals will deliver far better results than chasing the latest nutritional optimization strategy.

The Great Calorie Debate (Spoiler: It's Not Actually a Debate)

One of the most frustrating conversations in nutrition is the debate between those who believe "calories in, calories out" is all that matters and those who insist that food quality trumps quantity. This is like debating whether you need both oxygen and water to survive—the answer is obviously both.

Let's start with the uncomfortable truth about calories: The average American now consumes approximately 3,600 calories per day. To put that in perspective, that's enough energy to fuel a marathon runner in heavy training. But most Americans aren't marathon runners—they're sedentary office workers who *might* burn 2,000 to 2,400 calories per day.

This massive caloric excess is one of the primary drivers of our obesity epidemic, which now affects over 70 percent of American adults. Excess calories don't just make you fat—they create a metabolic burden that contributes to diabetes, heart disease, fatty liver, and chronic inflammation.

Dr. Kevin Hall's metabolic ward studies—the gold standard for nutrition research because they control every variable—consistently show that when calorie intake is tightly controlled, people lose weight regardless of whether those calories come from low-carb, low-fat, or balanced diets. Energy balance isn't just important—it's fundamental.[27]

But—and this is crucial—not all calories are created equal when it comes to how they affect your hunger, energy, hormones, and long-term health.

One hundred calories from a Snickers bar will have dramatically different effects on your body than one hundred calories from salmon and vegetables. The candy will spike your blood sugar, trigger insulin release, get stored as fat more easily, and leave you hungry again within an hour. The salmon and vegetables will provide stable energy, promote satiety, support muscle maintenance, and keep you satisfied for hours.

So yes, total calories matter for weight management. And yes, food quality matters for everything else—energy, mood, sleep, hormonal health, disease prevention, and long-term vitality.

The smartest approach addresses both: Eat the right amount of high-quality calories.

The Protein Priority: Why It Should Be Your First Focus

If I could only give someone one piece of nutritional advice, it would be this: Prioritize protein at every meal.

Protein is the most metabolically active macronutrient. It requires more energy to digest (thermic effect), promotes greater satiety (the feeling of fullness) per calorie, and is essential for maintaining muscle mass as you age. Yet most people dramatically under-consume it.

The current Recommended Dietary Allowance (RDA) for protein is 0.8 grams per kilogram of body weight per day. This recommendation was established to prevent deficiency diseases, not to optimize health. Dr. Gabrielle Lyon, author of *Forever Strong*, points out that this is like watering a garden with just enough to keep the plants from dying, rather than what they need to bloom.[28] The RDA tells you the minimum to avoid deficiency—not the amount your body needs to build muscle, support your immune system, maintain bone density, and thrive as you age.

Recent research suggests that most adults should consume 1.2—2.4 grams of protein per kilogram of body weight, with higher intakes for older adults, active individuals, and those trying to lose fat while preserving muscle. For a 150-pound person, that's roughly 80-135 grams of protein per day—significantly more than the RDA's recommendation of 55 grams.

Here's why protein should be your nutritional priority:

Muscle Preservation: After age thirty, you lose approximately three to five percent of your muscle mass per decade if you don't actively work to maintain it. Adequate protein intake, combined with resistance training, can prevent or even reverse this decline.

Metabolic Advantage: Protein has the highest thermic effect of all macronutrients—your body burns twenty to thirty percent of protein calories just during digestion, compared to five to ten percent for carbs and zero to three percent for fats.

Satiety and Appetite Control: Protein is the most filling macronutrient. People who eat adequate protein at breakfast consume an average of 400 fewer calories throughout the day without conscious effort.

Blood Sugar Stability: Protein slows the absorption of carbohydrates, preventing the blood sugar spikes and crashes that lead to energy fluctuations and cravings.

Hormonal Health: Many hormones are made from amino acids (the building blocks of protein). Inadequate protein intake can disrupt hormone production and signaling.

Immune Function: Your immune system is largely made of proteins. Without adequate intake, your body can't produce enough antibodies, enzymes, and other immune molecules to function optimally.

The best sources of protein are animal foods—meat, fish, eggs, and dairy—because they contain all nine essential amino acids in the right proportions for human needs. Plant proteins can also contribute significantly, but they often require combining different sources to achieve a complete amino acid profile.

For most people, aiming for twenty-five to forty grams of protein per meal is a practical target that will ensure adequate daily intake while promoting satiety and stable energy throughout the day.

Carbohydrates: Not the Enemy, But Context Matters

Let's address one of the most contentious topics in nutrition: carbohydrates.

Carbs aren't evil. They're not inherently fattening. They don't automatically cause diabetes or inflammation. In fact, many of the longest-lived populations in the world consume significant amounts of carbohydrates from whole food sources.

The problem isn't carbohydrates themselves—it's the type, amount, and context in which most Americans consume them.

The average American gets about fifty to sixty percent of their calories from carbohydrates, with much of that coming from refined sources: white bread, pasta, rice, cereals, snack foods, and added sugars. When you're eating 3,600 calories per day and fifty percent of those are carbohydrates, you're consuming roughly 450 grams of carbs daily—equivalent to eating thirty slices of bread.

This massive carbohydrate load, especially from refined sources, creates several problems:

Insulin Resistance: Chronic high carbohydrate intake forces your pancreas to produce large amounts of insulin repeatedly throughout the day. Over time, your cells become less responsive to insulin, requiring even higher levels to achieve the same effect. This is the pathway to type 2 diabetes.

Energy Instability: Refined carbohydrates cause rapid spikes and crashes in blood sugar, leading to the energy rollercoaster that leaves you reaching for more carbs or caffeine every few hours.

Increased Hunger: High-carb meals, especially those low in protein and fiber, leave you hungry again quickly, promoting overeating.

Fat Storage: When insulin levels are chronically elevated, your body preferentially stores energy as fat rather than burning it.

But here's the key insight: These problems are largely solved when you eat appropriate amounts of carbohydrates from whole food sources in the context of adequate protein and overall caloric balance.

If you're eating 2,000-2,400 calories per day (appropriate for most people), prioritizing protein (100-150 grams), and including adequate healthy fats (70-90 grams), you'll naturally end up with a moderate carbohydrate intake (100-200 grams) that won't overwhelm your metabolic capacity.

This level of carb intake allows you to include nutrient-dense sources like vegetables, fruits, potatoes, brown rice, and even some grains without creating the metabolic chaos associated with the standard American diet.

Training Day vs. Rest Day Strategy

One practical approach is to eat more carbohydrates on days when you exercise and fewer on days when you don't. Your muscles can absorb and utilize glucose much more effectively after resistance training or intense physical activity.

On training days, aim for the higher end of your carbohydrate range and time most of your carb intake around your workouts. On rest days, focus more heavily on protein and vegetables, with minimal starchy carbs.

This approach optimizes both performance and body composition while maintaining metabolic flexibility—your body's ability to efficiently use both carbs and fats for fuel.

Fats: Essential, Not Optional

For decades, dietary fat was vilified as the cause of heart disease and obesity. We now know this was based on flawed research and has led to one of the most damaging nutritional recommendations in history.

Fat isn't just okay to eat—it's essential. Your body requires certain fats that it cannot produce on its own. Fat is necessary for hormone production, brain function, vitamin absorption, and cellular health.

The key is choosing the right types and amounts of fat while avoiding the ones that can cause problems.

Healthy Fats to Emphasize:

- **Monounsaturated fats:** Olive oil, avocados, nuts, and the fat in animal foods,
- **Saturated fats:** Found in animal foods, coconut oil, and dairy (despite decades of fearmongering, saturated fat from whole foods doesn't cause heart disease in healthy people),
- **Omega-3 fatty acids:** Fatty fish, walnuts, flax seeds, and algae.

Fats to Minimize:

- **Highly processed vegetable oils:** While recent research suggests that seed oils aren't the dietary villain some make them out to be, there's little reason to consume large amounts of highly processed oils when better options exist.
- **Trans fats:** Still found in some processed foods and linked to cardiovascular disease.

For most people, seventy to ninety grams of fat per day (about twenty-five to thirty-five percent of calories) provides adequate essential fatty acids while leaving room for protein and carbohydrates.

The Quality Question: Whole Foods vs. Processed Foods vs. Ultra-Processed Foods

While calories and macronutrients form the foundation of healthy eating, food quality matters tremendously for how you feel and function day to day.

The human body evolved eating whole foods—plants and animals in their natural forms. We're exceptionally well-adapted to extracting nutrients from meat, fish, eggs, vegetables, fruits, nuts, and seeds. We're much less well-adapted to processing the highly refined, chemically altered foods that now make up 70 percent of the average American's diet.

Before we go further, let's clear up some terminology that gets thrown around carelessly in nutrition conversations.

Almost everything we eat is processed to some degree. Cooking is processing. Freezing is processing. Fermenting, drying, grinding, pasteurizing—all processing. A protein shake is highly processed. So is Greek yogurt, canned tuna, and frozen broccoli. And these foods are perfectly fine—sometimes even more convenient and nutritious than their "whole food" alternatives.

The problem isn't processing itself. The problem is a specific category that researchers call **ultra-processed foods** (or highly processed foods)—and the distinction matters.

Ultra-processed foods aren't just foods that have been through more steps in a factory. They're foods that have been *engineered*. They contain industrial ingredients you'd never find in a home kitchen: emulsifiers, flavor enhancers, hydrogenated oils, high-fructose corn syrup, and additives designed to extend shelf life or manipulate texture. More importantly, they're formulated by food scientists to hit what the industry calls the "bliss point"—that perfect combination of salt, sugar, and fat that lights up your brain's reward center and makes you want to keep eating long after you're full.

Here's the key difference: **A protein shake is processed to deliver nutrition efficiently. A Dorito is engineered to override your body's satiety signals and make you consume more.**

One serves your biology. The other exploits it.

Ultra-processed foods are typically:

- **Hyper-palatable**: Designed to be almost irresistibly tasty,
- **Easy to overconsume**: You can eat 1,000 calories of chips without feeling full, but try eating 1,000 calories of chicken breast,
- **Nutrient-poor**: High in calories, low in the vitamins, minerals, protein, and fiber your body needs,
- **Quickly absorbed**: They bypass the normal digestive signals that tell your brain you've eaten enough.

This is why Dr. Kevin Hall's study found that people eating ultra-processed foods consumed 500 more calories per day without trying—even when the diets were matched for protein, fat, carbs, sugar, sodium, and fiber.[29] The processing itself changed how people ate.

When I say, "minimize processed foods," I'm not talking about your post-workout protein shake or the frozen vegetables in your freezer. I'm talking about the foods designed in laboratories to make you eat more than you need—the ones that come in crinkly bags, have ingredients lists longer than this paragraph, and somehow leave you hungrier an hour after eating them.

This is why focusing on whole foods is so powerful. When you eat mostly minimally processed foods, it becomes much easier to maintain appropriate calorie intake without constantly battling hunger and cravings.

The 80/20 Rule for Food Quality

Aim to get eighty percent of your calories from whole, minimally processed foods: meat, fish, eggs, vegetables, fruits, nuts, seeds, and simple starches like potatoes and rice. The remaining twenty percent can come from more processed foods without significantly impacting your health.

This approach is sustainable because it allows for flexibility and enjoyment while ensuring that the majority of your nutrition comes from high-quality sources.

The Great Diet Debate: Cutting Through the Noise

Let's address some of the most contentious dietary philosophies and separate fact from fiction:

The Carnivore Extreme The carnivore diet—eating only animal products—has gained popularity recently, with proponents claiming it can cure everything from autoimmune diseases to depression. While some people do experience significant improvements on this approach, especially those coming from a highly processed diet, there's no compelling evidence that eliminating all plant foods is necessary or optimal for most people.

The benefits people experience on carnivore diets are likely due to eliminating processed foods, stabilizing blood sugar, increasing protein intake, and removing potential food sensitivities—not because plants are inherently harmful.

The Vegan Extreme On the other end of the spectrum, vegan advocates claim that all animal products are harmful and that plant-based diets are superior for health, longevity, and disease prevention. While well-planned vegan diets can certainly be healthy, they require careful attention to nutrients that are difficult to obtain from plants alone—vitamin B12, iron, zinc, omega-3 fatty acids, and complete proteins.

The longest-lived populations in the world (the Blue Zones) do eat predominantly plant-based diets, but they also include fish, dairy, or meat. Pure veganism is a modern experiment with limited long-term data.

The Daniel Diet Misunderstanding Many Christians have embraced the "Daniel Diet" based on Daniel 1:8-16, where Daniel and his friends eat vegetables and water instead of the king's rich food and wine. They often interpret this as biblical endorsement of vegetarianism.

But this misses the context entirely. Daniel's dietary choice wasn't about optimal nutrition—it was about avoiding food sacrificed to idols and maintaining religious purity in captivity. The story demonstrates faithfulness to God, not ideal dietary composition.

Moreover, Daniel's diet was temporary (twenty-one days in one instance), and the text doesn't suggest it was continued long-term. Using this passage to promote permanent vegetarianism ignores both the historical context and the broader biblical narrative that includes God providing animal foods and Jesus eating fish.

The most defensible position, based on current research, is that humans thrive on diets that include both plants and animals. The optimal ratio varies by individual, but completely eliminating either category seems unnecessary for most people.

The Hydration Foundation

Let's talk about something so basic that we often overlook its importance: water.

Your body is approximately sixty percent water. Every cellular process, every chemical reaction, every transport system in your body depends on adequate hydration. Yet most people spend their days in a state of chronic mild dehydration without realizing it.

The old "eight glasses a day" recommendation is overly simplistic. Your water needs depend on your size, activity level, climate, and overall health. A more practical approach is to aim for roughly half your body weight in ounces per day as a starting point, adjusting up for exercise, heat, or illness.

But here's what many people don't realize: Hydration isn't just about drinking water. It's about maintaining proper electrolyte balance. Water without electrolytes can dilute your blood sodium levels, leading to fatigue, headaches, and poor cellular function.

The Electrolyte Equation

We've all heard "drink more water" so many times it's become background noise. But here's something most people don't realize: You can drink *too much* water—and the consequences can be serious.

Every year, marathon runners collapse not from dehydration, but from the opposite problem. It's called hyponatremia, and it happens when you drink so much water that you dilute the sodium in your blood to dangerous levels. Your cells start swelling. Your brain presses against your skull. In severe cases, it can be fatal. These runners did exactly what they were told—"stay hydrated!"—and it nearly killed them.

This isn't meant to scare you away from water. It's meant to introduce a crucial concept: **Hydration isn't just about water volume. It's about the balance between water and electrolytes.**

What Are Electrolytes, Exactly?

Electrolytes are minerals that carry an electrical charge when dissolved in water. That might sound like chemistry class, but here's why it matters: Your body runs on electricity. Every nerve signal, every muscle contraction, every heartbeat depends on electrical impulses—and electrolytes are what make those impulses possible.

The major electrolytes your body needs are:

- **Sodium**: Regulates fluid balance, blood pressure, and nerve function. It's the one most people know about—and the one most affected by excessive water intake.
- **Potassium**: Works alongside sodium to regulate fluid balance, but also critical for muscle contractions (including your heart) and nerve transmission. Most Americans are severely deficient.

- **Magnesium**: Involved in over 300 enzymatic reactions in your body, including muscle relaxation, sleep quality, and stress response. Another widespread deficiency.
- **Calcium**: Beyond bone health, calcium is essential for muscle function, nerve signaling, and blood clotting.
- **Chloride**: Partners with sodium to maintain fluid balance and is a key component of stomach acid.

These minerals work together like instruments in an orchestra. Too much or too little of any one throws off the whole system.

Why Plain Water Isn't Always Enough

When you sweat, you don't just lose water—you lose electrolytes, especially sodium and potassium. If you replace only the water without replacing the minerals, you dilute what's left in your bloodstream. This is why athletes who drink only water during long events can end up in worse shape than those who drink nothing at all.

But it's not just athletes who face this problem. If you're drinking large amounts of water throughout the day—especially if you're eating a low-sodium whole foods diet, exercising regularly, using a sauna, or living in a hot climate—you may be chronically diluting your electrolytes without realizing it.

Signs of electrolyte imbalance include:

- Fatigue that doesn't improve with rest,
- Muscle cramps or twitches,
- Headaches (often mistaken for dehydration),
- Brain fog or difficulty concentrating,
- Dizziness or lightheadedness,
- Heart palpitations,
- Feeling "off" despite drinking plenty of water.

Sound familiar? Many people experiencing these symptoms drink *more* water, which only makes the problem worse.

The Modern Electrolyte Problem

Here's the irony: The modern diet is high in sodium (from processed foods) but low in potassium and magnesium (found in whole foods like vegetables, fruits, and nuts). We've got the ratio completely backwards.

Our ancestors consumed far more potassium than sodium—some estimates suggest a ratio of 4:1 or higher. Today, most Americans consume twice as much sodium as potassium. This imbalance contributes to high blood pressure, poor cellular function, and chronic dehydration even when water intake seems adequate.

Practical Hydration Strategy

What do you do with this information?

First, stop thinking about hydration as just "drinking water." Think about it as maintaining fluid and mineral balance.

For everyday hydration:

- Add a pinch of high-quality sea salt or Himalayan pink salt to your water (about 1/8 teaspoon per 16 ounces). It shouldn't taste salty—just slightly more satisfying.
- Eat potassium-rich foods daily: avocados, bananas, potatoes, leafy greens, and fish.
- Consider a magnesium supplement, especially if you exercise regularly, experience stress, or have trouble sleeping. Magnesium glycinate is well-absorbed and gentle on the stomach.

For exercise or heavy sweating:

- Use an electrolyte supplement or drink that contains sodium, potassium, and magnesium without excessive sugar. Look for products with at least 500-1000mg sodium, 200-400mg potassium, and some magnesium per serving.
- Avoid drinks that are mostly sugar with token amounts of electrolytes (most commercial sports drinks fall into this category).

For sauna use or hot climates:

- Pre-load with electrolytes before your session or before extended time in the heat.
- Replenish afterward with both water and minerals.

The goal isn't to obsess over electrolyte ratios. It's to recognize that water alone isn't the complete picture—and that many of the symptoms we attribute to "not drinking enough water" are actually signs that we're missing the minerals that make hydration work.

The modern diet, which is high in sodium but low in potassium and magnesium, creates electrolyte imbalances that make proper hydration more difficult. Adding a pinch of high-quality sea salt to your water or eating water-rich foods like fruits and vegetables can improve hydration more effectively than drinking plain water alone.

Signs of optimal hydration include:

- Pale yellow urine (clear urine often indicates overhydration),
- Stable energy throughout the day,
- Absence of afternoon headaches,
- Good skin elasticity,
- Rare feelings of thirst.

The Smart Approach to Supplementation

The supplement industry is a $40 billion behemoth filled with bold claims, minimal regulation, and enormous profit margins. Most supplements are unnecessary, some are helpful, and a few are essential for most people.

Here's my evidence-based approach to supplementation:

1. The Foundation Four These supplements have strong research support for most people:

2. High-Quality Probiotic: Your gut microbiome affects everything from immune function to mood regulation. Years of antibiotic use, stress, and processed food consumption have disrupted most people's gut health. A multi-strain probiotic with research-backed organisms can help restore balance.

3. Multivitamin/Mineral: Even people eating whole foods diets often have micronutrient gaps due to soil depletion, food storage, and preparation methods. A high-quality multivitamin provides insurance against deficiencies.

4. Omega-3 Fatty Acids: Most people don't eat enough fatty fish to get adequate EPA and DHA. These fats are crucial for brain health, inflammation regulation, and cardiovascular function.

5. Vitamin D3: Unless you live near the equator and spend significant time outdoors with skin exposed, you're probably deficient in vitamin D. This isn't just about bone health—vitamin D functions more like a hormone, affecting immune function, mood, and disease risk.

Everything Else Beyond these foundations, supplementation should be individualized based on specific needs, health conditions, and laboratory testing. Taking random supplements because you heard they might help is expensive and potentially counterproductive.

Work with a knowledgeable healthcare provider who can assess your individual needs through proper testing and recommend targeted interventions when appropriate.

A Historical Perspective: What We Can Learn from the Past

Sometimes the best way to understand our current nutritional problems is to look at what changed.

In 1850, the average American consumed about 2,500-2,800 calories per day and worked physically demanding jobs. Obesity was rare, type 2 diabetes was virtually unknown, and heart disease was uncommon before age seventy.

What did their diet look like? Meat, fish, eggs, dairy, vegetables, fruits, nuts, and simple grains prepared at home. They ate seasonally, locally, and stopped eating when food wasn't available. They didn't snack constantly or drink their calories.

The massive changes in our food environment over the past 150 years help explain our current health crisis:

- **Caloric density increased:** We engineered foods to pack more calories into smaller packages.
- **Processing intensified:** We moved from simple preservation methods to chemical alteration of food structure.
- **Variety exploded:** We went from seasonal eating to having every food available year-round.
- **Convenience prioritized:** We outsourced food preparation to companies focused on profit rather than health.
- **Portion sizes expanded:** What used to be considered a meal for two is now a single serving.

The solution isn't to return to 1850, but we can learn from what worked: eating mostly whole foods, preparing meals at home, consuming appropriate portions, and stopping when we're satisfied rather than stuffed.

Your Practical Nutrition Plan

Here's how to implement everything we've discussed:

Phase 1: Foundation (First 30 Days) Focus only on the 80/20 fundamentals:

1. **Track your total calorie intake** for one week without changing anything—just awareness.
2. **Prioritize protein** at every meal—aim for twenty-five to forty grams per meal.

3. **Hydrate properly**—half your body weight in ounces of water daily.
4. **Eat whole foods** 80 percent of the time—if it has more than five ingredients or ingredients you can't pronounce, limit it.
5. **Establish consistent meal times**—three meals per day at roughly the same times.

Phase 2: Optimization (Days 31-60) Once the foundations are solid, add:

1. **Adjust total calories** based on your goals and tracking data.
2. **Time carbohydrates** around training if you exercise regularly.
3. **Add the foundation supplements**—probiotic, multivitamin, omega-3, vitamin D3.
4. **Experiment with meal prep** to make healthy choices easier.
5. **Create a sustainable twenty percent** for foods you enjoy but aren't optimal.

Phase 3: Personalization (Days 61+) Fine-tune based on your individual response:

1. **Get laboratory testing** if you want to optimize further.
2. **Work with a functional medicine practitioner** if you have specific health concerns.
3. **Adjust macronutrient ratios** based on your goals and how you feel.
4. **Add targeted supplements** only if indicated by testing.
5. **Focus on consistency** rather than perfection.

Sample Daily Framework Here's what a day of eating might look like following these principles:

Breakfast (400-500 calories):

- 3 eggs cooked in olive oil
- 1 cup sautéed vegetables
- 1/2 avocado
- 1 piece of fruit

Lunch (400-500 calories):

- 6 oz lean protein (chicken, fish, lean beef)
- Large salad with olive oil dressing
- 1/2 cup sweet potato or brown rice (more on training days)

Dinner (400-500 calories):

- 6 oz protein
- 2 cups cooked vegetables
- Small amount of healthy fat (nuts, olive oil, etc.)
- Snack if needed (100-200 calories):
- Greek yogurt with berries
- Nuts and fruit
- Protein smoothie

This framework provides roughly 1,400-1,700 calories with adequate protein (100-120g), moderate carbs (75-150g), and healthy fats (70-90g).

The Biblical Perspective on Food

"Therefore, whether you eat or drink, or whatever you do, do all things for the glory of God." —1 Corinthians 10:31

This verse isn't just about saying grace before meals—it's about approaching food with intentionality, gratitude, and wisdom.

Throughout Scripture, food is seen as both a necessity and a gift. God provides food for our nourishment and enjoyment, but He also calls us to stewardship and self-control. The goal isn't to make food an idol (in either direction—obsession or neglect), but to use it as fuel for the purposes He's called us to.

When you eat in a way that supports your health, energy, and longevity, you're better equipped to serve others, pursue your calling, and be present for your family. When you eat in a way that leaves you sluggish, sick, or distracted by food thoughts, you're limiting your capacity to live out your calling.

This perspective frees you from both guilt and extremism. You don't have to eat perfectly to honor God, but you should eat intentionally. You can enjoy food as one of God's good gifts while also recognizing your responsibility to steward your body well.

The Long View: Nutrition as a Lifetime Practice

The goal of good nutrition isn't to achieve some perfect state and then coast. It's to develop a sustainable relationship with food that serves you well over decades.

This means:

- **Prioritizing progress over perfection**—consistent good choices trump occasional perfect days.
- **Building systems rather than relying on motivation**—make healthy eating easier than unhealthy eating.
- **Planning for real life**—include strategies for travel, stress, celebrations, and unexpected challenges.
- **Staying curious rather than dogmatic**—be willing to adjust as you learn and as your needs change.
- **Focusing on how you feel**—energy, mood, sleep, and vitality are better metrics than just weight or appearance.

Remember: You'll eat roughly 1,000 meals per year for the rest of your life. The patterns you establish now will compound over time into either vitality or disease, energy or fatigue, clarity or brain fog.

The choice is yours, one meal at a time.

Recap & Actions

Scripture to Reflect On: "Therefore, whether you eat or drink, or whatever you do, do all things for the glory of God." —1 Corinthians 10:31

Science-Backed Truth: The 80/20 principle applies to nutrition—Eighty percent of your results come from mastering five fundamentals: energy balance, adequate protein, food quality, hydration, and consistency. Both total calories and food quality matter. Protein should be prioritized at every meal, carbs aren't evil in appropriate amounts, and whole foods are superior to processed foods for satiety and health.

Ready, Willing, Able Actions:

Ready (You can do this right now):

- Track everything you eat and drink for three days without changing anything—just awareness.
- Add twenty to thirty grams of protein to your next meal.
- Drink sixteen ounces of water with a pinch of sea salt.
- Plan your next meal around a protein source, then add vegetables and healthy fats.

Willing (You can do this within a week):

- Calculate your approximate daily calorie needs and compare to your current intake.
- Prioritize protein at every meal—aim for twenty-five to forty grams per meal.
- Replace one processed food with a whole food option each day.
- Establish consistent meal timing—three meals at roughly the same times daily.

Able (You can do this within a month):

- Implement the complete nutrition framework: appropriate calories, adequate protein, whole foods eighty percent of the time.
- Add the foundation four supplements after consulting with a healthcare provider.
- Meal prep two to three days' worth of healthy options to make good choices easier.
- Create your sustainable twenty percent—identify which less-optimal foods you want to include occasionally.

Remember: Nutrition isn't about perfection—it's about establishing patterns that fuel your body and support your calling. Focus on the fundamentals, be consistent over time, and adjust based on how you feel and function.

9

ANTI-FRAGILE—THE POWER OF GOOD STRESS

"Consider it all joy, my brothers and sisters, when you encounter various trials, knowing that the testing of your faith produces endurance." — James 1:2-3

The Sauna

I need to tell you about a conversation that fundamentally changed how I think about stress, discomfort, and human resilience.

I was sitting in a business mastermind group when my mentor and health coach, Dan Miller, started talking about something that seemed completely unrelated to business strategy: a Finnish study on saunas.[30] Dan has this way of connecting seemingly random dots that always end up being profound, and this was no exception.

"There's this incredible research," he said, "showing that people who use saunas regularly have a forty percent reduction in all-cause mortality. Forty percent. That's not from a drug or a surgery—that's from sitting in heat."

At the time, I was in the middle of my health crisis, desperately trying everything to feel better. The idea of adding more heat to my already inflamed system seemed counterintuitive. But Dan explained something that stuck with me: "The sauna isn't supposed to feel comfortable. It's supposed to stress your body in a way that makes it stronger."

That phrase—stress that makes you stronger—planted a seed that would eventually revolutionize my understanding of health and healing.

Over the following weeks, as I forced myself to return to that uncomfortable heat, something remarkable happened. Not only did I start tolerating the sessions better, but I began feeling more resilient in other areas of my life. My sleep improved. My mood stabilized. My energy increased. It was as if my body was learning how to handle stress more effectively, both in the sauna and outside of it.

Years later, I discovered the science behind what I was experiencing. The sauna wasn't just helping me relax—it was triggering a biological process called hormesis, where controlled stress actually strengthens the body's adaptive systems.

This principle extends far beyond saunas. It's the foundation of what Nassim Taleb calls "anti-fragility"—the idea that some systems don't just withstand stress, they become stronger because of it.[31]

And that's exactly what the human body is designed to do.

Understanding Anti-Fragility

Most people think about health in terms of avoiding stress and protecting themselves from anything uncomfortable. Rest is good, stress is bad. Comfort promotes healing, discomfort causes damage. But this binary thinking misses something crucial about human physiology.

Your body is an anti-fragile system. Unlike fragile systems that break under stress, or resilient systems that simply withstand stress, anti-fragile systems actually improve when exposed to the right kind of controlled stress.

Think about your muscles. When you lift weights, you're literally creating microscopic tears in muscle fibers. This is stress—controlled, purposeful stress. Your body responds by repairing those tears with additional protein, making the muscle stronger than it was before. The stress didn't just break you down—it built you up.

This same principle applies to nearly every system in your body: Your cardiovascular system gets stronger when challenged with exercise. Your bones get denser when subjected to load-bearing activities. Your immune system becomes more robust when exposed to mild challenges. Even your brain forms new neural pathways more readily when faced with novel, challenging experiences.

The key insight is that there are two fundamentally different types of stress: chronic stress that depletes and breaks down (distress) and acute stress that challenges and builds up (eustress).

Chronic stress—the kind most people experience daily through work pressure, relationship conflicts, financial worry, poor sleep, and constant digital stimulation—is indeed harmful. It elevates cortisol, suppresses immune function, promotes inflammation, and accelerates aging.

But acute stress—brief, intense challenges followed by adequate recovery—triggers powerful adaptive responses that make you healthier, stronger, and more resilient.

The problem is that modern life has inverted this relationship. We're chronically stressed by things that shouldn't stress us (traffic, emails, social media) while avoiding the acute stresses that would actually make us stronger (cold, heat, physical exertion, occasional hunger).

The solution isn't to eliminate all stress. It's to minimize chronic stress while strategically introducing beneficial acute stress.

This is the foundation of anti-fragile health: Using controlled discomfort to build extraordinary resilience.

The Sauna: Heat Shock Proteins and Cardiovascular Magic

Let's start with the intervention that has the most compelling research: sauna use.

The data on regular sauna use is nothing short of extraordinary. Dr. Jari Laukkanen's landmark Finnish studies, following over 2,300 men for decades, found that people who used the sauna four to seven times per week had a forty percent reduction in all-cause mortality compared to those who used it once per week.[32]

Again ... forty percent! That's the kind of mortality benefit you'd expect from a revolutionary miracle drug, not from sitting in a hot room.

But the benefits go far beyond longevity. Regular sauna use has been shown to:

- Reduce cardiovascular disease risk by twenty-seven to fifty percent,
- Lower stroke risk by sixty-one percent,
- Reduce Alzheimer's disease risk by sixty-six percent,
- Improve depression and anxiety symptoms,
- Enhance athletic performance and recovery,
- Boost growth hormone production by 200-500 percent,
- Improve insulin sensitivity,
- Reduce inflammation markers, and
- Enhance immune function.

How does sitting in heat create such profound health benefits? The answer lies in heat shock proteins (HSPs)—molecular chaperones that are produced when your body is exposed to elevated temperatures. These proteins serve as your cellular repair crew, fixing damaged proteins, protecting against oxidative stress, and maintaining cellular function under challenging conditions.

When you heat stress your body in a sauna, you're essentially training your cellular repair mechanisms to work more efficiently. The heat shock proteins produced during sauna sessions continue working long after you've cooled down, providing ongoing protection and repair throughout your body.

Sauna use also triggers cardiovascular adaptations similar to moderate exercise. Your heart rate increases to 100-150 beats per minute, your blood vessels dilate, and your cardiac output increases. Regular sauna users develop improved cardiovascular fitness, lower resting blood pressure, and enhanced blood flow.

The sweet spot for sauna benefits appears to be 174-194°F (79-90°C) for fifteen to twenty minutes, four to seven times per week. This is hot enough to trigger the heat shock response but not so extreme as to be dangerous for healthy individuals.

Practical Sauna Guidelines:

- Start with ten to fifteen minutes at lower temperatures and gradually work up.
- Stay hydrated before, during, and after sessions.
- Listen to your body—if you feel dizzy or nauseous, exit immediately.
- Cool down gradually after each session.
- Avoid alcohol before or during sauna use.
- Consult your physician if you have cardiovascular conditions.

If you don't have access to a traditional sauna, infrared saunas can provide some similar benefits, though the research is less extensive. The key is consistent exposure to heat stress that challenges your system without overwhelming it.

Cold Therapy: The Hormetic Power of Discomfort

If heat stress builds resilience, what about cold stress?

Cold exposure—whether through cold showers, ice baths, or winter swimming—triggers a completely different but powerful set of adaptive responses.

When you expose your body to cold, several remarkable things happen:

Norepinephrine Release: Cold exposure triggers a release of norepinephrine, which improves focus, attention, and mood while reducing inflammation. Some studies show increases of 200-300 percent that can last for hours after the cold exposure ends.

Brown Fat Activation: Cold stress activates brown adipose tissue, a special type of fat that burns calories to generate heat. People with more active brown fat have better metabolic health and find it easier to maintain healthy body weight.

Improved Circulation: Regular cold exposure enhances your circulatory system's ability to rapidly adjust blood flow, improving cardiovascular health and recovery.

Enhanced Immune Function: Moderate cold stress has been shown to increase white blood cell count and improve immune system responsiveness.

Mental Resilience: Perhaps most importantly, regularly doing something that's acutely uncomfortable builds mental toughness that transfers to other areas of life.

Dr. Susanna Soberg's research suggests that eleven minutes of cold exposure per week (spread across multiple sessions) is sufficient to trigger most of these adaptations. This could be as simple as ending your daily shower with two to three minutes of cold water.

Cold Therapy Guidelines:

- Start gradually—thirty seconds of cold water at the end of your shower.
- Work up to two to three minutes of cold exposure.
- Aim for water temperature around 50-59°F (10-15°C).
- Focus on controlled breathing during the exposure.
- Don't do cold therapy immediately after strength training—it can blunt the muscle-building response.
- Avoid if you have certain heart conditions or are pregnant.

The key with cold therapy is finding the minimum effective dose. You want the discomfort that triggers adaptation without creating excessive stress that impairs recovery.

Some people become obsessed with extreme cold exposure—sitting in ice baths for twenty-plus minutes or taking frigid outdoor swims. While this can be safe for experienced practitioners, it's not necessary for health benefits and can actually become counterproductive if it creates more stress than benefit.

The goal isn't to torture yourself. It's to provide a controlled, brief stress that makes your body more resilient to all forms of stress.

Sunlight: The Original Biohack

Before we had expensive red light devices, humans had access to the most powerful light therapy tool ever created, the sun.

Sunlight exposure, particularly in the morning, provides benefits that go far beyond vitamin D production:

Circadian Rhythm Regulation: Morning sunlight exposure helps set your internal clock, improving sleep quality, hormone production, and energy levels throughout the day. Just ten to fifteen minutes of morning sunlight can significantly improve your sleep that night.

Mood Enhancement: Sunlight exposure increases serotonin production and helps regulate seasonal mood changes. This is why light therapy is an effective treatment for seasonal affective disorder.

Nitric Oxide Production: UV exposure triggers the release of nitric oxide from the skin, which helps lower blood pressure and improve cardiovascular health—benefits that occur independent of vitamin D.

Metabolic Benefits: Some research suggests that appropriate sun exposure can improve insulin sensitivity and metabolic health through mechanisms we're only beginning to understand.

The key is finding the balance between getting enough sun exposure for health benefits while avoiding the skin damage that comes from excessive UV radiation.

Smart Sun Exposure:

- Get ten to twenty minutes of morning sunlight on your skin and in your eyes (without looking directly at the sun).
- Build up your tolerance gradually—start with shorter exposures.
- Avoid burning—this negates the benefits and creates harmful inflammation.
- Consider your skin type and latitude when determining appropriate exposure time.
- Use sunscreen for extended outdoor activities, but don't fear brief, unprotected exposure.

For people living in northern latitudes or spending most of their time indoors, targeted light therapy devices can provide some similar benefits, though they're not a complete replacement for natural sunlight.

The Breath: Training Your Stress Response

One of the most accessible and immediate ways to practice antifragility is through breathwork.

Your breath is the bridge between your conscious and unconscious nervous systems. While you can't directly control your heart rate or hormone production, you can control your breathing—and through your breathing, you can influence almost every other system in your body.

Controlled breathing exercises create a mild, beneficial stress that trains your nervous system to respond more effectively to all forms of stress.

Box Breathing (4-4-4-4):

- Inhale for 4 counts,
- Hold for 4 counts,
- Exhale for 4 counts,
- Hold empty for 4 counts,
- Repeat for 5-10 cycles.

This technique helps activate your parasympathetic nervous system and improve your heart rate variability—a marker of resilience and recovery capacity.

Wim Hof Method[33]: This technique combines specific breathing patterns with cold exposure:

- Take 30-40 deep, controlled breaths.
- On the last exhale, hold your breath as long as comfortable.
- Take a deep breath and hold for 15 seconds.
- Repeat for 3-4 rounds.

This method can increase your tolerance for stress and improve your ability to maintain calm under pressure.

4-7-8 Breathing:

- Inhale for 4 counts,
- Hold for 7 counts,
- Exhale for 8 counts.

This technique is particularly effective for reducing anxiety and improving sleep quality.

The beauty of breathwork is that it's free, always available, and can be practiced anywhere. It's also one of the fastest ways to shift your physiological state when you're feeling overwhelmed or stressed.

Movement as Medicine: Beyond the Gym

We've already discussed strength training as a foundation, but there are other movement practices that provide unique hormetic benefits:

High-Intensity Interval Training (HIIT): Short bursts of intense exercise followed by recovery periods create powerful adaptations in cardiovascular health, mitochondrial function, and metabolic efficiency. Just ten to fifteen minutes of HIIT can provide benefits similar to much longer periods of moderate exercise.

Zone 2 Cardio: Low-intensity, steady-state exercise that you can maintain while still holding a conversation improves mitochondrial health and fat-burning capacity. This is the type of exercise that builds your aerobic base and enhances recovery.

Natural Movement: Activities that challenge your body in varied, unpredictable ways—hiking on uneven terrain, climbing, swimming in open water, playing sports—provide movement stresses that improve coordination, balance, and adaptability.

The key is variety. Your body adapts quickly to repeated stresses, so mixing different types of movement challenges keeps your systems responsive and growing.

The Biblical Perspective on Beneficial Stress

James 1:2-3 tells us to "consider it all joy, my brothers and sisters, when you encounter various trials, knowing that the testing of your faith produces endurance."

This isn't masochism or a call to seek out suffering for its own sake. It's recognition of a profound truth: We grow stronger through appropriate challenges, not in spite of them.

The same God who designed our bodies to become stronger through physical stress also designed our spirits to grow through trials and testing. Both require the same elements: a challenge that stretches us beyond our comfort zone, followed by adequate recovery and support.

When you choose to sit in a sauna, take a cold shower, or push through a difficult workout, you're not just building physical resilience—you're practicing the spiritual discipline of doing hard things. You're training yourself to say yes to discomfort when it serves a greater purpose.

This doesn't mean seeking out stress for its own sake or ignoring wisdom about rest and recovery. It means becoming more intentional about the types of stress you allow into your life, choosing beneficial stress over harmful stress, and trusting that your body and spirit are designed to grow stronger through appropriate challenges.

The Practical Anti-Fragile Protocol

Here's how to implement anti-fragile practices into your weekly routine:

Daily Foundations:

- 10-15 minutes morning sunlight exposure
- 2-3 minutes cold exposure (end of shower)
- 5-10 minutes breathwork practice
- Some form of physical movement

Weekly Additions:

- 3-4 sauna sessions (15-20 minutes each)
- 1-2 HIIT workouts (10-15 minutes)
- 1-2 longer Zone 2 cardio sessions (30-45 minutes)

Monthly Challenges:

- Try a new movement practice
- Increase the duration or intensity of one practice slightly
- Take on a mental or physical challenge outside your comfort zone

Seasonal Variations:

- Adapt practices based on season, schedule, and life circumstances
- Focus on consistency over perfection
- Allow for periods of reduced intensity during high-stress life events

The key is building these practices gradually and sustainably. Start with one or two interventions, master them over several weeks, then add others as they become routine.

Remember: the goal isn't to maximize discomfort—it's to optimize adaptation. You want to provide enough stress to trigger beneficial changes without overwhelming your recovery capacity.

The Compound Effect of Anti-Fragility

What makes these practices so powerful isn't just their individual benefits—it's how they compound and reinforce each other.

When you regularly expose yourself to controlled stress, you don't just adapt to that specific stressor. You build general resilience that helps you handle all forms of stress more effectively.

The person who takes cold showers doesn't just become more tolerant of cold—they become more emotionally regulated, more focused under pressure, and more willing to tackle other uncomfortable but beneficial challenges.

The person who uses the sauna regularly doesn't just get cardiovascular benefits—they sleep better, recover faster from workouts, and have improved stress resilience in daily life.

The person who practices breathwork doesn't just improve their lung capacity—they gain a tool for managing anxiety, improving focus, and enhancing performance in any situation.

Over time, these practices create an upward spiral of resilience, energy, and capability that extends far beyond the specific interventions themselves.

Anti-Fragile vs. Optimization Obsession

An important distinction: anti-fragile practices are about building resilience, not achieving perfect optimization.

The wellness industry is full of people obsessing over the perfect protocol—exactly the right temperature, duration, timing, and frequency for maximum benefit. They turn beneficial stress into another source of anxiety and perfectionism.

This misses the point entirely.

The goal isn't to find the perfect sauna temperature or the ideal cold exposure duration. It's to regularly challenge your system in ways that build strength and resilience over time.

A 15-minute sauna session is better than no sauna session. Two minutes of cold water is better than avoiding discomfort entirely. Ten minutes of morning sunlight is better than staying indoors all day.

Progress, not perfection. Consistency, not optimization. Building the habit matters more than maximizing the variables.

Your Anti-Fragile Journey

As we wrap up this exploration of beneficial stress, I want you to remember something important: *you are designed for this.*

Your body isn't fragile. Your spirit isn't weak. You have within you the capacity to not just survive challenges but to emerge stronger because of them.

The modern world has convinced us that comfort equals health and that stress equals danger. But your physiology tells a different story. You are an anti-fragile system, designed to adapt, grow, and thrive when faced with appropriate challenges.

The practices in this chapter aren't about adding more stress to your already stressful life. They're about replacing random, chronic stress with purposeful, beneficial stress. They're about taking control of your adaptation rather than leaving it to chance.

When you step into that sauna, you're not just sweating—you're training your cellular repair systems. When you turn the shower cold, you're not just being uncomfortable—you're building mental and physical resilience. When you practice controlled breathing, you're not just oxygenating your blood—you're learning to remain calm under pressure.

These small acts of chosen discomfort compound into extraordinary resilience over time. They prepare you not just for the specific stresses you've practiced with, but for whatever challenges life might bring.

Your calling requires you to be anti-fragile. The world needs people who can handle stress without breaking, who can face uncertainty without panicking, who can endure discomfort while maintaining their purpose and peace.

The practices in this chapter will help you become that person—not through avoiding stress, but through engaging with it wisely.

Start small. Be consistent. Trust the process. Your body knows how to adapt—you just need to give it the right signals.

Recap & Actions

Scripture to Reflect On: "Consider it all joy, my brothers *and sisters,* when you encounter various trials, knowing that the testing of your faith produces endurance." —James 1:2-3

Science-Backed Truth: Anti-fragile systems get stronger through controlled stress rather than breaking down. Hormetic stressors—brief, intense challenges followed by recovery—trigger beneficial adaptations including heat shock proteins, improved cardiovascular health, enhanced immune function, and increased resilience to all forms of stress.

Ready, Willing, Able Actions:

Ready (You can do this right now):

- End your next shower with 30-60 seconds of cold water.
- Step outside for 10 minutes of morning sunlight (no sunglasses).
- Practice 5 minutes of box breathing (4-4-4-4 pattern).
- Take the stairs instead of the elevator when possible.

Willing (You can do this within a week):

- Build up to 2-3 minutes of cold water exposure at the end of daily showers.
- Establish a morning sunlight routine of 10-15 minutes.
- Try one sauna session if you have access (start with 10-15 minutes).
- Practice breathwork daily for stress management and focus.

Able (You can do this within a month):

- Incorporate 3-4 weekly sauna sessions (15-20 minutes each) if accessible.
- Add 1-2 HIIT workouts per week (10-15 minutes each).
- Create a weekly routine that includes multiple hormetic stressors with adequate recovery.

Remember: The goal isn't to maximize discomfort—it's to optimize adaptation. Start with practices that challenge you without overwhelming you, build consistency over time, and trust that your body is designed to grow stronger through appropriate stress.

10

MEASURE WHAT MATTERS— THE ART OF WISE STEWARDSHIP

"For which one of you, when he wants to build a tower, does not first sit down and calculate the cost, to see if he has enough to complete it?" — Luke 14:28

The Scale That Lied

I've seen this scenario play out countless times at our studios. A motivated client starts strength training, determined to finally get healthy after years of yo-yo dieting and feeling exhausted. They're religious about their workouts, follow nutrition guidance, prioritize sleep, and feel stronger and more energetic than they have in years. Their clothes fit better, their posture improves, and people comment that they look healthier.

But then they step on the scale.

They've gained weight.

I've had clients come to me in tears, convinced they're failing. "I'm doing everything right," they say, "but I'm gaining weight. Nothing works for me."

This is when I ask them to come in for a body composition scan. The results consistently tell a completely different story: They've gained muscle and lost fat. Their body fat percentage has dropped significantly. Their hip-to-waist ratio has improved.

What the scale registers as "failure" is actually remarkable success. Their bodies are transforming exactly as they should—adding vital muscle tissue that will boost metabolism, strengthen bones, and improve quality of life for decades to come.

This is why I've learned that what and how you measure matters. If you measure the wrong things, you'll get discouraged by progress. If you measure the right things, you'll be encouraged by transformation that might otherwise go unnoticed.

The parable Jesus told about counting the cost before building a tower wasn't just about construction projects—it was about the wisdom of measuring what matters. And when it comes to your health, measuring what matters can mean the difference between sustainable transformation and giving up in frustration.

The Problem with How We Think About Health

Most people have a completely distorted view of what health actually looks like, and it's not their fault. We've been conditioned by fitness magazines, social media influencers, and Hollywood to believe that health means looking like a professional athlete or fitness model.

But here's the reality: Extremely low body fat percentages aren't just unnecessary for health—they're often incompatible with optimal health, especially long-term.

The fitness models you see with eight to twelve percent body fat (men) or sixteen to nineteen percent body fat (women) are often in unsustainable competition conditions. They've used extreme diets, dehydration, and sometimes dangerous substances to achieve those levels temporarily. Many of them experience hormonal disruption, mood problems, and obsessive relationships with food.

True health lies in a much more reasonable range.

For Men:

- Essential fat: 2-5 percent
- Athletes: 6-13 percent
- **Fitness/Healthy: 14-17 percent**
- **Average/Acceptable: 18-24 percent**
- Obese: 25 percent+

For Women:

- Essential fat: 10-13 percent
- Athletes: 14-20 percent
- **Fitness/Healthy: 21-24 percent**
- **Average/Acceptable: 25-31 percent**
- Obese: 32 percent+

Notice that "healthy" and "average" are different categories. The average American is metabolically unhealthy, so average isn't a target—it's what we're trying to improve from.

But even within the healthy ranges, there's significant variation based on genetics, age, and personal goals. A forty-five-year-old father of three doesn't need the same body fat percentage as a twenty-five-year-old personal trainer. A woman in her fifties doesn't need to maintain the same composition as someone half her age.

The goal isn't to achieve some arbitrary aesthetic standard. It's to reach and maintain a level of body composition that supports energy, strength, hormonal health, and disease prevention.

Why the Scale Deceives

The bathroom scale might be the most misleading health metric ever invented, yet it's what most people use to judge their progress.

Here's why the scale fails as a health indicator:

Muscle vs. Fat Density: Muscle tissue is approximately eighteen percent denser than fat tissue. When you start strength training, you'll likely gain muscle faster than you lose fat initially. This is actually ideal—muscle is metabolically active tissue that burns calories, improves insulin sensitivity, and provides the foundation for long-term health.

Water Weight Fluctuations: Your body weight can fluctuate two to five pounds daily based on hydration, sodium intake, carbohydrate consumption, hormonal cycles, stress levels, and bathroom timing. These fluctuations have nothing to do with fat loss or muscle gain.

Inflammation Changes: When you start exercising, your muscles often retain extra water as part of the repair process. This temporary inflammation can mask fat loss on the scale while your body composition is actually improving.

Hormonal Factors: Women especially experience significant weight fluctuations throughout their menstrual cycle due to hormonal changes affecting water retention and bloating.

I've watched countless people abandon effective health programs because the scale didn't move quickly enough, even as their bodies were transforming in remarkable ways.

This story isn't unique. During the first two to three months of strength training, it's common to see:

- Scale weight stay the same or increase slightly,
- Body fat percentage decrease significantly,
- Muscle mass increase substantially,
- Clothes fit better and energy improve dramatically.

If you're only measuring scale weight, you'll miss the most important changes happening in your body.

Body Composition: The Metrics That Actually Matter

Instead of obsessing over total weight, focus on these more meaningful measurements:

Body Fat Percentage This tells you what percentage of your body is fat versus lean tissue (muscle, bone, organs, water). Two people can weigh exactly the same but have completely different body compositions and health profiles.

Lean Muscle Mass This is often the most important metric to track, especially as you age. After thirty, you lose three to five percent of your muscle mass per decade unless you actively work to maintain it. Maintaining and building muscle mass is crucial for metabolism, bone health, hormone production, and longevity.

Hip-to-Waist Ratio Divide your waist measurement by your hip measurement. This ratio indicates where you carry fat, which matters more for health than how much fat you carry. Abdominal fat (apple shape) is more metabolically dangerous than hip/thigh fat (pear shape).

For health, aim for:

- Men: 0.85 or lower
- Women: 0.80 or lower

Waist-to-Height Ratio Your waist circumference should be less than half your height. This is one of the strongest predictors of metabolic health and disease risk.

How to Measure Body Composition There are several methods available, each with different levels of accuracy and cost:

DEXA Scan (Gold Standard): The most accurate method available to consumers. Measures bone density, lean mass, and fat mass with precision. Costs $100-200 but provides comprehensive data.

Prism AI/3D Body Scanning: We use this technology at The Perfect Workout and FastFit studios. It's quick, non-invasive, and provides detailed body composition data plus visual comparisons over time.

Bioelectrical Impedance (BodPod, InBody): Less accurate than DEXA and Prism but easily accessible. *Can be easily influenced by hydration status.

Circumference Measurements: Simple tape measure assessments of waist, hips, arms, and thighs. Not as precise but free and trackable at home.

Progress Photos: Visual documentation of changes that might not show up in numbers. Take photos in consistent lighting, poses, and clothing every two to four weeks.

The key is choosing one method and sticking with it for consistency. Don't jump between different measurement techniques and expect the numbers to match perfectly.

Strength: The Ultimate Health Metric While body composition tells you about your current state, strength progression tells you about your trajectory. Are you getting stronger and more capable, or are you losing ground?

Muscle mass is the organ of longevity, and that muscle strength is equally important. You can have impressive muscle mass but poor strength due to neurological factors, training methods, or health issues.

Why Track Strength:

- Strength gains indicate that your nervous system, muscles, and recovery are all functioning well.
- Progressive strength improvement means you're building the foundation for long-term independence and vitality.
- Strength tracking provides objective feedback on your training effectiveness.

What to Track: You don't need to measure every exercise. Focus on a few key movements that represent different movement patterns:

- **Upper Body Push:** Chest press or push-ups
- **Upper Body Pull:** Seated row or pull-ups
- **Lower Body:** Leg press, squat, or deadlift variation

How to Track: Record the weight and the time under load (time to failure) for your key exercises every four to six weeks. At The Perfect Workout, we track every session because our slow-motion, high-intensity protocol makes precise measurement possible.

VO2 Max: Your Cardiovascular Foundation

VO2 max is the maximum amount of oxygen your body can use during intense exercise. It's considered one of the strongest predictors of longevity and health span—more predictive than blood pressure, cholesterol, or even smoking status.

Research shows that people in the top twenty-five percent of VO2 max for their age have a fifty percent lower risk of all-cause mortality compared to those in the bottom twenty-five percent. The difference between the top 2.5 percent and bottom twenty-five percent is even more dramatic—a 400 percent reduction in mortality risk.

Why VO2 Max Matters:

- Indicates cardiovascular efficiency and mitochondrial health,
- Predicts your ability to perform daily activities as you age,
- Reflects your body's ability to deliver oxygen to working muscles,
- Strongly correlated with brain health and cognitive function.

Normal VO2 Max Ranges (ml/kg/min):

Men:

20-29 years: 35+ (fair), 45+ (good), 50+ (excellent)

30-39 years: 33+ (fair), 43+ (good), 48+ (excellent)

40-49 years: 31+ (fair), 41+ (good), 46+ (excellent)
50-59 years: 29+ (fair), 38+ (good), 43+ (excellent)
60-69 years: 26+ (fair), 35+ (good), 40+ (excellent)
70-79 years: 23+ (fair), 32+ (good), 37+ (excellent)

Women:
20-29 years: 28+ (fair), 36+ (good), 42+ (excellent)
30-39 years: 27+ (fair), 34+ (good), 40+ (excellent)
40-49 years: 25+ (fair), 32+ (good), 37+ (excellent)
50-59 years: 23+ (fair), 30+ (good), 35+ (excellent)
60-69 years: 21+ (fair), 27+ (good), 32+ (excellent)
70-79 years: 19+ (fair), 24+ (good), 29+ (excellent)

How to Measure VO2 Max: Gold Standard: Laboratory testing with mask and equipment during progressive exercise test. Most accurate but requires specialized facility.

Fitness Trackers: Many modern wearables estimate VO2 max based on heart rate data during exercise. Less accurate but convenient for tracking trends.

Field Tests: Twelve-minute run test or step test can provide rough estimates using established formulas.

I recommend getting your VO2 max tested once per year, either through formal testing or consistent use of a quality fitness tracker. The goal is to maintain or slowly improve your score as you age, rather than accepting the typical eight to ten percent decline per decade.

Advanced Blood Work: Looking Beyond the Basics

Most annual physicals include basic blood work that's designed to catch serious disease, not optimize health. Standard panels often use reference ranges based on sick populations rather than optimal health targets.

Companies like Function Health and InsideTracker (one of our partners) are changing this by offering comprehensive panels with optimization-focused ranges and personalized recommendations.

Beyond Basic Labs While your annual physical might check ten to fifteen markers, comprehensive health panels can assess fifty to one hundred-plus biomarkers including:

Advanced Lipid Panels: Beyond total cholesterol, these look at particle size, oxidized LDL, and inflammatory markers that better predict cardiovascular risk.

Hormone Comprehensive: Testosterone, estrogen, progesterone, thyroid (TSH, T3, T4, reverse T3), cortisol patterns, and insulin sensitivity markers.

Inflammatory Markers: hs-CRP, ESR, homocysteine, and other indicators of systemic inflammation.

Nutrient Status: B vitamins, vitamin D, magnesium, omega-3 index, and other markers that affect energy and health.

Metabolic Health: Fasting glucose, insulin, HbA1c, and markers of liver function and detoxification capacity.

The Optimization vs. Reference Range Difference Standard lab ranges are often too wide to be useful for optimization. For example:

Vitamin D:

- Standard range: 30-80 ng/ml
- Optimal range: 40-60 ng/ml

Testosterone (men):

- Standard range: 250-1000 ng/dl
- Optimal range: 500-800 ng/dl

TSH (thyroid):

- Standard range: 0.5-5.0 mIU/L
- Optimal range: 1.0-2.5 mIU/L

Getting comprehensive labs once or twice per year allows you to:

- Identify problems before they become diseases,
- Optimize nutrients and hormones for better energy and performance,
- Track the impact of lifestyle changes on biomarkers,
- Make informed decisions about supplementation.

A Word of Caution More data isn't automatically better. It's possible to become obsessed with optimizing every biomarker while missing the bigger picture of how you feel and function.

Use advanced testing as a tool for insight and optimization, not as a source of anxiety or perfectionism. Work with knowledgeable practitioners who can help interpret results in the context of your overall health and goals.

Gut Health: The Foundation Beneath Everything

We'll dive deeper into functional medicine in a later chapter, but gut health deserves mention here because it affects every other system in your body.

Your gut houses seventy percent of your immune system, produces ninety percent of your serotonin, and communicates directly with your brain through the vagus nerve. Gut dysfunction can manifest as:

- Digestive issues (obviously),
- Mood and anxiety problems,
- Sleep disturbances,
- Skin conditions,
- Autoimmune symptoms, or
- Energy fluctuations.

Gut Health Testing Options: Comprehensive Stool Analysis: Looks at beneficial bacteria, pathogenic organisms, inflammation markers, and digestive function.

SIBO Testing: Breath tests that identify small intestinal bacterial overgrowth, a common cause of digestive symptoms.

Food Sensitivity Testing: While controversial, some tests can identify foods that trigger inflammatory responses.

Leaky Gut Assessment: Measures intestinal permeability, which can contribute to autoimmune and inflammatory conditions.

The key insight is that gut health affects everything else you're trying to measure and improve. If your gut is inflamed or imbalanced, it will be harder to build muscle, lose fat, improve energy, or optimize any other health marker.

The Wisdom of Intentional Measurement

Proverbs 27:23 says, "Know well the condition of your flocks, and pay attention to your herds." This ancient wisdom about livestock management applies perfectly to personal health stewardship.

You can't steward what you don't monitor. You can't improve what you don't measure. But you also can't become obsessed with measurement to the point where it becomes another source of stress.

The goal is wise, intentional monitoring that helps you:

- Catch problems early before they become serious,
- Track progress that might not be visible day-to-day,
- Make informed decisions about interventions,
- Stay motivated by seeing objective improvement.

The Measurement Hierarchy Not all metrics are equally important. Here's how I prioritize:

Daily Awareness (subjective):

- Energy levels,
- Sleep quality,
- Mood and mental clarity,
- Physical comfort/pain, and
- Stress levels.

Weekly Tracking:

- Strength progression,
- Body measurements (waist, hips),
- Progress photos, and
- Exercise performance.

Monthly Assessments:

- Body composition (DEXA, Prism, or consistent scale + measurements) and
- Overall life satisfaction and goal progress.

Quarterly/Annual:

- Comprehensive blood work,
- VO2 max testing, and
- Complete health assessment with healthcare provider.

This hierarchy ensures you're paying attention to what matters most (how you feel and function daily) while also gathering objective data on longer-term trends.

Building Your Personal Dashboard

Think of these measurements as your personal health dashboard—a collection of indicators that provide insight into how your body is responding to your lifestyle choices.

Like a car's dashboard, you don't need to stare at every gauge constantly, but you should check them regularly enough to catch problems early and track progress over time.

Your Basic Health Dashboard:

1. **How you feel and function** (daily awareness)
2. **Body composition** (monthly measurement)
3. **Strength progression** (workout tracking)
4. **Cardiovascular fitness** (annual VO2 max)
5. **Biomarkers** (annual comprehensive labs)
6. **Gut health** (as needed based on symptoms)

Making It Simple The key to sustainable measurement is making it as simple as possible while still being effective:

- Choose one body composition method and stick with it.
- Track two to three key strength exercises consistently.
- Use a fitness tracker for cardiovascular trends.
- Schedule annual comprehensive testing like you would any other important appointment.
- Focus on trends over individual data points.

Remember: The goal isn't to have perfect numbers—it's to ensure you're moving in the right direction and catch any concerning trends early.

The Compound Effect of Measurement

Here's what I've observed over years of working with clients: People who track the right metrics consistently get dramatically better results than those who don't track anything or who track the wrong things.

This isn't because measurement itself creates change—it's because measurement provides:

Feedback loops that help you understand what's working and what isn't,

Motivation when you can see objective progress even if you don't feel different,

Early warning systems that catch problems before they become serious, and

Accountability to yourself and your health goals.

But perhaps most importantly, measurement helps you develop "body literacy"—the ability to understand and respond to your body's signals rather than just hoping for the best.

When you track your strength consistently, you learn to recognize when you're recovered and ready for intensity versus when you need more rest. When you monitor your energy and mood, you can identify patterns related to sleep, stress, or nutrition. When you check your body composition regularly, you can make adjustments before small problems become big ones.

This body literacy becomes increasingly valuable as you age. The people who maintain vitality into their seventies and eighties aren't just genetically lucky, they're typically people who paid attention to their bodies and made adjustments throughout their lives rather than ignoring problems until they became crises.

The Balance: Measurement Without Obsession

As we wrap up this exploration of health metrics, I want to address an important balance: the difference between wise stewardship and neurotic optimization.

Measurement should serve you, not enslave you. The goal is to gather enough information to make wise decisions about your health without becoming obsessed with perfect numbers or optimal ranges.

Some people take measurement too far and become prisoners of their data. They check their weight multiple times per day, obsess over every biomarker, and lose the joy of living in pursuit of perfect optimization.

Others avoid measurement entirely and remain clueless about their health until problems become serious. They're surprised by diabetes diagnoses, shocked by heart disease, and confused about why they feel terrible despite "eating healthy."

The wise path lies between these extremes: paying attention without becoming obsessed, tracking progress without losing perspective, and using data to enhance life rather than control it.

Your health is too important to ignore, but it's also too precious to reduce to a collection of numbers. Measure what matters, track your progress, and use the data to make wise decisions. But remember that the ultimate goal isn't perfect metrics—it's a life well-lived in service to God and others.

When you're strong, energetic, and healthy, you're better equipped for whatever calling God has placed on your life. That's worth measuring, tracking, and protecting.

Recap & Actions

Scripture to Reflect On: "For which one of you, when he wants to build a tower, does not first sit down and calculate the cost, to see if he has enough to complete it?" —Luke 14:28

Science-Backed Truth: What gets measured gets managed. Health isn't about extreme body fat percentages or perfect numbers—it's about tracking meaningful metrics that indicate strength, vitality, and disease prevention. Body composition matters more than scale weight; strength progression indicates trajectory; and comprehensive biomarkers provide early warning systems for optimization.

Ready, Willing, Able Actions:

Ready (You can do this right now):

- Take baseline measurements: waist, hips, calculate waist-to-hip ratio.
- Take progress photos in consistent lighting and clothing.
- Track your next workout: weights, reps, and how you felt.
- Schedule annual comprehensive blood work (Function Health, InsideTracker, or similar).

Willing (You can do this within a week):

- Get baseline body composition measurement (DEXA scan, BodPod, or consistent method).
- Start tracking two to three key strength exercises consistently.
- Calculate your estimated VO2 max using a fitness tracker or field test.
- Put your scale away and commit to measuring body composition monthly instead of daily weigh-ins.

Able (You can do this within a month):

- Create your personal health dashboard with the metrics that matter most to you.
- Schedule VO2 max testing or establish consistent cardiovascular fitness tracking.
- Complete comprehensive blood work with optimization-focused ranges.
- Establish quarterly measurement routine for body composition, strength, and biomarkers.

Remember: The goal isn't perfect numbers—it's wise stewardship. Track enough to make informed decisions, but don't become enslaved by data. Focus on trends over individual measurements, and use metrics to enhance your life rather than control it.

11

ACTION—WHERE THE RUBBER MEETS THE ROAD

"The mind of a person plans his way, but the Lord directs his steps."
— Proverbs 16:9

The Myth of One-Size-Fits-All

Over the years at our studios, I've observed a pattern that initially puzzled me. Two people with seemingly identical circumstances—similar ages, goals, schedules, and resources—would start the same program on the same day. Six months later, their results would be completely different.

One person would thrive with structured meal prep and rigid workout schedules, losing weight consistently and gaining significant strength. They'd follow protocols precisely, never missing sessions, motivated completely by measurable progress and clear guidelines.

Another person with the exact same program would struggle. They'd start strong but gradually become inconsistent. The meal prep would feel overwhelming, especially with travel demands. The rigid workout times would conflict with unpredictable work schedules.

Despite having the same knowledge and resources, they'd feel like they were failing.

This happened over and over again, and I began to realize something important: These people didn't need the same approach, even though they had similar goals and circumstances. What worked brilliantly for one was completely wrong for the other—not because of laziness or lack of commitment, but because they had different biological, psychological, and social needs.

This is where most health programs fail. They assume that if the science is sound and the program is effective, everyone should be able to follow it. But human beings aren't lab rats in controlled environments. We're complex creatures with different personalities, life circumstances, stress levels, support systems, and motivation triggers.

The key to lasting transformation isn't finding the perfect program—it's finding the approach that works for your unique situation and gradually building from there.

Understanding Your Biopsychosocial Needs

The concept of biopsychosocial health comes from Precision Nutrition's groundbreaking research on why people succeed or fail with health changes.[34] Instead of focusing solely on what to do, they studied who people are and how that affects their ability to implement change.

Every person operates within three interconnected systems:

Biological: Your genetics, metabolism, hormones, sleep patterns, stress response, and physical capabilities,

Psychological: Your personality, motivations, relationship with food, stress management skills, and mental health, and

Social: Your family dynamics, work environment, cultural background, financial resources, and support systems.

Most health advice ignores two of these three systems. It gives you biological solutions (eat this, exercise that way) without considering your psychological makeup or social reality. No wonder so many people fail—they're trying to force themselves into approaches that fundamentally conflict with who they are and how they live.

The Biological Reality Let's start with biology because it's the most straightforward—and the most ignored.

Some people are naturally morning people; others are night owls. Some feel great on higher carbohydrate intake; others function better with more fats and proteins. Some can handle intermittent fasting easily; others get irritable and lose focus when hungry.

These aren't character flaws or excuses—they're biological realities that should inform your approach rather than being bulldozed by generic advice.

During my own health journey, I learned this the hard way. I spent months fighting my natural tendency to prefer evening workouts because I'd read that morning exercise was "optimal." I forced myself to do high-intensity cardio because it "burned more calories," even though it left me exhausted and craving sugar. I tried intermittent fasting even though it made me irritable and affected my protein intake.

It wasn't until I started working with my biology instead of against it that everything became easier. I scheduled workouts for late afternoon when my energy naturally peaked. I focused on strength training that energized rather than depleted me. I ate in a pattern that supported my energy levels rather than fighting them.

The result? Better results with less willpower.

The Psychological Component Your personality and psychological makeup dramatically affect which approaches will work for you.

Some people are what researchers call "abstainers"—they find it easier to give something up completely than to moderate. For abstainers, "I don't eat sugar" is easier than "I eat sugar in moderation." They prefer clear rules and boundaries.

Others are "moderators"—they rebel against strict rules and do better with flexible guidelines. For moderators, completely eliminating foods feels restrictive and often leads to backlash. They prefer balanced approaches with room for treats and exceptions.

Some people are motivated by tracking and data—they love seeing progress in numbers, charts, and measurements. Others find tracking stressful and prefer to gauge progress by how they feel and function.

Some people need external accountability—classes, trainers, or workout partners. Others prefer the autonomy of exercising alone and resent feeling pressured by others.

During my fruititarian phase, I was operating as a classic abstainer without realizing it. The extreme simplicity of "only fruit" felt easier than making complex decisions about balanced nutrition. But as a moderate in other areas of life, the rigidity eventually became unsustainable.

Understanding your psychological tendencies allows you to choose strategies that work with your nature instead of requiring you to become someone you're not.

The Social System Your environment and social context might be the most important factor of all—and the most overlooked.

If your spouse isn't supportive of healthy changes, if your friends center all social activities around food and alcohol, if your work culture glorifies overwork and poor self-care, if you lack the financial resources for fresh food and gym memberships—these aren't excuses. They're real barriers that need to be addressed strategically.

I've watched people with incredible knowledge and motivation fail because they tried to implement changes that conflicted with their social reality. The executive who tried to meal prep when she traveled three weeks per month. The mother of young children who attempted 6 a.m. workout classes. The person with a tight budget who tried to follow expensive supplement protocols.

Success requires either changing your environment or adapting your approach to work within your current constraints.

The Ready, Willing, Able Framework

Instead of trying to change everything at once, successful transformation happens when you match your actions to your current capacity in three areas:

Ready: What are you prepared to do right now, today, with no additional resources or preparation?

Willing: What could you do this week with minimal planning and adjustment?

Able: What could you accomplish this month with more significant preparation and commitment?

This framework, developed by Precision Nutrition, recognizes that your capacity for change varies based on your current life circumstances, stress levels, and available resources.

When You're Ready During high-stress periods—job transitions, family crises, major life changes—your capacity for new habits is limited. This is when you focus on maintaining basics rather than pursuing optimization.

Ready actions require no planning, minimal time, and work within your current routine:

- Add a ten-minute walk to your existing schedule.
- Drink a glass of water before each meal.
- Take three deep breaths when you feel stressed.
- Go to bed fifteen minutes earlier.
- Add protein to meals you're already eating.

The goal isn't dramatic transformation—it's maintaining momentum without adding stress to an already overwhelming situation.

When You're Willing During moderate stress periods—normal work demands, stable family life, manageable challenges—you can implement small changes that require some planning and adjustment.

Willing actions might require weekly preparation or slight schedule modifications:

- Meal prep basics every Sunday.
- Schedule three, twenty-minute workouts per week.
- Establish a wind-down routine before bed.
- Practice stress management techniques daily.
- Track key metrics weekly.

When You're Able During lower stress periods—things are stable, you have energy and motivation, life feels manageable—you can pursue more significant changes that require preparation, resources, and commitment.

Able actions might require significant planning, new resources, or major routine changes:

- Complete nutrition overhaul with detailed meal planning.
- Establish comprehensive fitness routine with multiple components.
- Work with healthcare providers for optimization
- Implement advanced tracking and measurement systems.
- Address underlying health issues through functional medicine.

The key insight is that you don't stay at one level permanently. Your capacity changes based on life circumstances, and successful people adjust their approach accordingly rather than abandoning it entirely.

During my health crisis, I was barely in "Ready" mode for most activities. Trying to implement "Able" level changes would have created additional stress and guaranteed failure. But as my health improved and life stabilized, I gradually moved into more comprehensive approaches.

The Science of Small Changes

Most people fail because they try to change too much too fast. They go from sedentary to daily workouts, from poor nutrition to perfect meal prep, from no self-care to elaborate wellness routines—all at once.

But research on behavior change shows that sustainable transformation happens through small, consistent actions that compound over time.

Dr. BJ Fogg's research at Stanford shows that tiny habits—behaviors so small they feel almost silly—are more likely to stick than dramatic changes.[35] His "Tiny Habits" method focuses on making new behaviors:

- Small (easy to do),
- Anchored to existing routines, and
- Immediately rewarded.

Instead of "exercise for an hour," start with "do two push-ups after brushing my teeth." Instead of "eat perfectly," start with "add vegetables to one meal per day." Instead of "manage stress better," start with "take three deep breaths after sitting down at my desk."

These micro-habits feel insignificant, but they create something more valuable than immediate results—they establish neural pathways and identity shifts that make bigger changes possible later.

The Compound Effect in Action I've seen this principle play out countless times with our clients. People come to us feeling overwhelmed and exhausted, wanting dramatic changes—lose forty pounds, start working out daily, completely overhaul their nutrition. They've tried dramatic transformations before and always burned out within weeks.

Instead of encouraging complete lifestyle overhauls, we've learned to start with one tiny habit. Maybe it's drinking a glass of water immediately upon waking. That's it.

After two weeks, when that feels automatic, we might add a five-minute walk during lunch break.

Two weeks later: adding protein to breakfast.

Two weeks later: going to bed fifteen minutes earlier.

Each change feels almost pointlessly small. But over six months, these tiny habits compound into remarkable transformations. People lose significant weight, develop consistent workout routines, and gain energy they haven't felt in years. More importantly, they feel confident in their ability to maintain these changes because the behaviors have become part of who they are, not something they're forcing themselves to do.

The Habit Loop: Understanding What Really Drives Behavior

To create lasting change, you need to understand how habits work. Charles Duhigg's research in *The Power of Habit* reveals that every habit follows the same neurological loop.[36]

Cue: The trigger that initiates the behavior

Routine: The behavior itself

Reward: The benefit you get from the behavior

Your brain automates this loop to conserve mental energy. Once a habit is established, the cue triggers the routine without conscious decision-making.

Most people focus only on the routine—trying to force themselves to exercise, eat better, or sleep more. But without addressing the cue and reward, willpower eventually fails.

Designing Better Cues

Make good behaviors more obvious and bad behaviors less obvious.

Instead of relying on motivation to remember to work out, lay out your gym clothes the night before. Instead of hoping you'll choose healthy snacks, put fruits and vegetables at eye level in your refrigerator and hide the processed foods.

I learned this principle during my recovery when I started putting my supplements next to my coffee maker. The visual cue of seeing them every morning as I made coffee created an automatic habit without requiring willpower.

Optimizing Rewards

Make good behaviors immediately satisfying and bad behaviors immediately unsatisfying.

Most health behaviors have delayed rewards—you don't feel the benefits of a workout immediately; you don't see the results of healthy eating for weeks. But your brain craves immediate gratification.

Create immediate rewards for healthy behaviors: Listen to your favorite podcast only while walking; buy yourself something small after a week of consistent workouts; use beautiful containers for meal prep to make healthy eating feel special.

Identity-Based Habits

The most powerful approach to behavior change is focusing on identity rather than outcomes.

Instead of "I want to lose twenty pounds," think "I am someone who takes care of my body." Instead of "I want to get stronger," think "I am someone who prioritizes movement." Instead of "I want to eat healthier," think "I am someone who nourishes my body with quality food."

Every time you perform a healthy behavior, you're casting a vote for this new identity. Eventually, the identity becomes self-reinforcing—you do healthy things because that's who you are, not because you're trying to become someone else.

In his book, *Atomic Habits*, James Clear offers a way to build new habits by stacking them on top of one you already have.[37] Your existing habit becomes a cue to act on the new ones.

For example:

- After I take off my work shoes (an existing habit), I will put on my workout clothes.
- After I put on my workout clothes, I will work out for fifteen minutes.

When Habits Aren't Enough: The Role of Functional Medicine

Sometimes, despite your best efforts with lifestyle changes, something deeper is blocking your progress. You're doing everything right—exercising consistently, eating well, managing stress, prioritizing sleep—but you still feel terrible. This is where functional medicine becomes essential.

During my own health crisis, I spent months implementing every lifestyle strategy imaginable. I changed my diet multiple times, tried various supplements, modified my exercise routine, and worked with traditional doctors who consistently told me everything looked "normal" on standard tests.

But I didn't feel normal. I felt like my body was failing me despite my best efforts to support it.

That's when I found Dr. Michael Ruscio, the functional medicine practitioner I mentioned earlier, who approached my health completely differently than any previous doctor.

What Makes Functional Medicine Different

Traditional medicine is designed to diagnose and treat diseases. If your labs fall within "normal" ranges and you don't have a clear diagnosis, you're often told nothing is wrong—even if you feel terrible.

Functional medicine looks for the root causes of symptoms and dysfunction, often long before they become diagnosable diseases. It views the body as an interconnected system rather than a collection of separate organs.

Instead of asking "What disease does this person have?" functional medicine asks, "Why has this person lost health?" and "What can we do to restore optimal function?"

The Functional Medicine Advantage

What sets functional medicine apart from other alternative approaches is that functional medicine doctors have the same rigorous medical training as conventional physicians—they're usually MDs, DOs, or nurse practitioners with additional specialized training in root cause analysis and systems thinking.

This is crucial because:

- They can order and interpret comprehensive lab work.
- They understand when conventional treatments are necessary.
- They can prescribe medications when appropriate.
- They have the medical knowledge to address serious conditions safely.

But unlike conventional doctors who are trained to focus on single symptoms or organ systems, functional medicine practitioners are trained to:

- Look at the body as an integrated system.
- Identify underlying causes of symptoms.
- Address multiple contributing factors simultaneously.
- Use both conventional and evidence-based natural interventions.

My Functional Medicine Journey

When I finally worked with my functional medicine doctors, they ordered tests that no previous doctor had considered: comprehensive stool analysis, SIBO breath tests, food sensitivity panels, detailed hormone assessment, and inflammatory markers that went far beyond basic bloodwork.

The results revealed what traditional medicine had missed: I had small intestinal bacterial overgrowth (SIBO), leaky gut syndrome, multiple food sensitivities, and a cascade of inflammatory responses that were affecting everything from my sleep to my mood to my energy levels.

But more importantly, they didn't just identify problems—they created a systematic approach to addressing them. Instead of prescribing medications to mask symptoms, they developed protocols to restore normal gut function, reduce inflammation, and support my body's natural healing processes.

The treatment wasn't quick or simple. It involved specific antimicrobial herbs, gut repair protocols, dietary modifications, targeted supplements, and careful monitoring of my response. But for the first time in years, I felt like someone understood what was happening in my body and had a plan to address the root causes.

When to Consider Functional Medicine

You might benefit from functional medicine if you:

- Have persistent symptoms despite "normal" lab results,
- Feel worse than your test results suggest you should,
- Have been told your symptoms are "just anxiety" or "just aging" or "just stress,"

- Have multiple seemingly unrelated symptoms,
- Have tried lifestyle changes without significant improvement, or
- Have been diagnosed with a condition, but aren't satisfied with symptom management alone.

Common Areas Where Functional Medicine Excels

- **Digestive Issues:** SIBO, IBS, leaky gut, food sensitivities,
- **Hormonal Imbalances:** Thyroid dysfunction, adrenal fatigue, sex hormone issues,
- **Autoimmune Conditions:** Hashimoto's, rheumatoid arthritis, inflammatory conditions,
- **Neurological Symptoms:** Brain fog, anxiety, depression with physical components,
- **Metabolic Dysfunction:** Insulin resistance, weight loss resistance, energy issues, and
- **Chronic Fatigue:** Persistent exhaustion despite adequate sleep and nutrition.

Finding the Right Functional Medicine Practitioner

Not all practitioners who call themselves "functional medicine" doctors have the same training or approach. Look for:

- Medical degree (MD, DO) or nurse practitioner with additional functional medicine certification,
- Training through the Institute for Functional Medicine or similar accredited programs,
- Experience with your specific health concerns,
- Approach that combines lab testing with thorough history and examination,

- Willingness to work collaboratively and explain their reasoning, and
- Integration of both conventional and natural approaches when appropriate.

The Investment in Functional Medicine

Functional medicine testing and treatment are often not covered by insurance, making them a significant financial investment. Comprehensive testing can cost $1,000 to $3,000, and treatment protocols may require ongoing monitoring and adjustments.

But for people with chronic health issues that haven't responded to conventional approaches, functional medicine can be life changing. The cost of continuing to feel terrible—lost productivity, decreased quality of life, progression to more serious conditions—often far exceeds the investment in proper evaluation and treatment.

Functional Medicine as Part of Your Team

The goal isn't to replace conventional medicine but to complement it with a more comprehensive approach to health optimization. I still have a primary care doctor for routine care and acute issues. But my functional medicine practitioner helps me understand and address the underlying factors that affect my long-term health and vitality.

This integrated approach gives you the best of both worlds: the diagnostic capabilities and acute care expertise of conventional medicine combined with the root cause analysis and optimization focus of functional medicine.

Putting It All Together: Your Personal Action Plan

Now that you understand biopsychosocial needs, habit formation, and the potential role of functional medicine, let's create your personal action plan.

Step 1: Assess Your Current Capacity

Honestly evaluate where you are right now:

- What's your stress level? (High, moderate, low)
- How much time can you realistically dedicate to health changes? (Minutes per day)
- What resources do you have available? (Financial, social support, equipment)
- What's worked for you in the past?
- What's consistently failed?

Based on this assessment, start with Ready, Willing, or Able level changes.

Step 2: Choose Your Keystone Habit

Identify one small habit that could trigger positive changes in other areas. Common keystone habits include:

- Morning routine (exercise, meditation, healthy breakfast),
- Evening routine (wind-down, preparation for next day),
- Meal preparation (planning, shopping, prepping), or
- Movement practice (daily walk, regular workouts).

Start with the smallest possible version of this habit—so small it feels almost silly not to do it.

Step 3: Design Your Environment

Make good choices easier and bad choices harder:

- Prepare your space for success (gym clothes ready, healthy food visible).
- Remove temptations and barriers.
- Create visual cues for positive behaviors.
- Arrange social support and accountability.

Step 4: Track Leading Indicators

Instead of only tracking outcomes (weight, body fat), track the behaviors that lead to outcomes:

- Number of workouts per week,
- Servings of vegetables per day,
- Hours of sleep per night, or
- Minutes of stress management practice.

Step 5: Plan for Obstacles

Identify the most likely scenarios that could derail your progress and create specific plans for handling them:

- Travel (how will you maintain habits?)
- Stress (what's your backup plan?)
- Social situations (how will you navigate challenges?)
- Low motivation (what systems will keep you going?)

Step 6: Consider Professional Support

Evaluate whether you need additional help:

- Personal trainer for exercise guidance and accountability,
- Nutritionist for meal planning and dietary support,
- Therapist for stress management and behavior change, or
- Functional medicine practitioner for underlying health issues.

Your Transformation Timeline

Remember that sustainable change happens gradually. Here's a realistic timeline for significant health transformation:

Weeks 1-4: Foundation Building

- Establish one keystone habit.
- Focus on consistency over perfection.
- Track leading indicators.
- Notice how small changes affect your energy and mood.

Weeks 5-12: Expansion

- Add complementary habits.
- Increase intensity or duration gradually.
- Address obstacles as they arise.
- Begin seeing measurable changes in strength, energy, and well-being.

Months 4-6: Integration

- Habits feel more automatic.
- Results become visible to others.
- Confidence in your ability to maintain changes increases.
- Consider more advanced interventions if needed.

Months 7-12: Optimization

- Fine-tune your approach based on results and preferences.
- Address any remaining health concerns.
- Focus on long-term sustainability.
- Help others who are beginning their own transformation.

The key is to think in seasons rather than looking for immediate results. Just as a farmer doesn't expect to harvest immediately after planting, your health transformation requires patience, consistency, and faith in the process.

Beyond Personal Transformation

As you implement these changes and experience transformation in your own life, something beautiful begins to happen: You become a guide for others who are just beginning their own health journeys.

The struggles you've overcome, the obstacles you've navigated, the habits you've built—all of this becomes valuable experience that can help others avoid the mistakes you made and find the approaches that work for them.

This is why your health journey isn't just about you. It's preparation for the calling God has placed on your life to be a source of strength, wisdom, and encouragement for others.

When you're strong, energetic, and healthy, you have the capacity to serve others from abundance rather than scarcity. When you've learned to manage stress, build sustainable habits, and address health challenges systematically, you become a resource for your family, friends, and community.

Your transformation becomes their hope. Your success becomes their possibility. Your journey becomes the bridge they need to begin their own.

This is the true purpose of getting fit for your calling—not just personal optimization, but preparation to serve others more effectively.

Recap & Actions

Scripture to Reflect On: "The mind of a person plans his way, but the Lord directs his steps" —Proverbs 16:9

Science-Backed Truth: Sustainable transformation requires matching your approach to your biopsychosocial needs rather than forcing yourself into generic programs. Small, consistent changes compound into significant results over time. When lifestyle changes aren't enough, functional medicine can address root causes that conventional medicine often misses.

Ready, Willing, Able Actions:

Ready (You can do this right now):

- Choose one tiny habit to start today (two minutes or less).
- Assess your current stress level and capacity for change.
- Identify environmental changes that would make healthy choices easier.
- Remove one barrier to healthy behavior.

Willing (You can do this within a week):

Design cues and rewards for your chosen keystone habit.

Create a weekly plan that matches your current life circumstances.

Track one leading indicator (behavior) rather than just outcomes.

Identify your most likely obstacles and create backup plans.

Able (You can do this within a month):

- Complete a biopsychosocial assessment of your health needs.
- Implement a comprehensive habit stack around your keystone behavior.
- Consider working with a functional medicine practitioner if you have persistent health concerns.
- Create accountability systems and support networks for long-term success.

Remember: You don't have to transform everything at once. Start where you are; use what you have; do what you can. Small, consistent actions aligned with your unique needs and circumstances will create the sustainable transformation that enables you to fulfill your calling.

12

WHAT ABOUT...? ADVANCED TOOLS AND HOT TOPICS

"... examine everything; hold firmly to that which is good."
— 1 Thessalonians 5:21

The Questions Everyone Asks

After speaking at conferences, leading workshops, and working with clients over the years, I've noticed a pattern in the questions people ask. They'll listen patiently through discussions about strength training, nutrition, sleep, and stress management. But inevitably, hands shoot up with the same types of questions:

"What about testosterone replacement therapy?" "Are GLP-1 medications like Ozempic® safe?" "Should I be taking peptides?" "What do you think about stem cell therapy?" "Is hormone replacement therapy dangerous?"

These are the "what about" questions—the advanced interventions that capture people's imagination and often dominate health conversations. They're also the topics surrounded by the most confusion, misinformation, and polarized opinions.

Some people treat these interventions as magic bullets that will solve all their health problems without addressing foundational issues. Others dismiss them entirely based on outdated information or unfounded fears. Neither extreme serves us well.

The truth, as usual, lies somewhere in the middle—and it requires wisdom, discernment, and a commitment to following evidence rather than emotion.

Before we dive into these topics, I need to remind you of something: I am not a physician. I have no formal medical training. Nothing in this chapter should be considered medical advice, and any decisions about these interventions should be made in consultation with qualified healthcare providers who can evaluate your individual circumstances.

What I can offer is perspective—the viewpoint of someone who has wrestled with these questions personally, studied the available research, and observed the experiences of others who have walked this path. My goal isn't to tell you what to do, but to help you think more clearly about these complex topics so you can make informed decisions with proper medical guidance.

The Biblical Filter: Testing Everything

Paul's instruction in 1 Thessalonians 5:21 to "test everything; hold fast to what is good" provides the perfect framework for evaluating advanced health interventions. This isn't a call to uncritical acceptance or reflexive rejection—it's a mandate for careful discernment.

Testing everything means:

- Examining the available evidence,
- Considering both potential benefits and risks,
- Evaluating claims against reliable sources,
- Being honest about what we know and don't know, and
- Remaining open to changing our minds when presented with better information.

Holding fast to what is good means:

- Implementing interventions that have solid evidence and favorable risk-benefit ratios,
- Being willing to abandon approaches that prove ineffective or harmful,
- Prioritizing interventions with the greatest potential impact, and
- Maintaining proper perspective on what these tools can and cannot accomplish.

This approach protects us from both the naive optimism that sees every new intervention as a miracle cure and the cynical pessimism that rejects potentially beneficial treatments based on fear or ideology.

The 80/20 Principle Applied

Remember our 80/20 principle? It's especially important when considering advanced interventions. For most people, eighty percent of their health results will come from mastering the fundamentals we've already discussed: strength training, nutrition, sleep, stress management, and community.

These advanced interventions belong in the twenty percent category. They're optimization tools that can provide meaningful benefits for some people in specific circumstances, but they're not substitutes for getting the basics right.

I've seen too many people chase the twenty percent while ignoring the eighty percent. They'll spend thousands on peptides while eating processed food and skipping workouts. They'll pursue hormone optimization while sleeping four hours a night and living in chronic stress. They'll seek out stem cell treatments while remaining sedentary and socially isolated.

This backwards approach rarely works. Advanced interventions are most effective when layered on top of a solid foundation, not used as substitutes for fundamental lifestyle changes.

This is why I didn't pursue testosterone replacement therapy until I had spent over a year optimizing everything else—sleep, nutrition, exercise, stress management, and targeted supplements. Only when I had exhausted all other options and still had suboptimal levels did it make sense to explore hormone replacement.

Hormone Replacement Therapy: Beyond the Fear and Hype

Let's start with one of the most controversial topics: hormone replacement therapy (HRT). This area is plagued by outdated fears, oversimplified messaging, and polarized positions that ignore the nuanced reality of how hormones affect health and aging.

The Fear Factor Much of the fear surrounding HRT stems from studies conducted decades ago using synthetic hormones in inappropriate dosages. The Women's Health Initiative study from 2002, which found increased risks of breast cancer and cardiovascular disease in women taking hormone replacement, fundamentally changed how people think about HRT.

But that study had significant limitations. It used synthetic hormones (Premarin and Provera) rather than bioidentical hormones, employed oral delivery methods that create different metabolic effects than topical applications, and studied older women who were years past menopause rather than those transitioning through it.

More recent research using bioidentical hormones, appropriate dosing, and better delivery methods has shown much more favorable risk-benefit profiles. But the fear from those early studies persists, often preventing people from accessing treatments that could significantly improve their quality of life.

The Male Perspective For men, the stigma around testosterone replacement therapy often centers on the misconception that it's "cheating" or equivalent to taking steroids. This misunderstanding conflates therapeutic hormone replacement with supraphysiological doses used for performance enhancement.

Testosterone replacement therapy for men with clinically low levels isn't about achieving superhuman performance—it's about restoring normal physiological function. When done properly under medical supervision, it's remarkably safe and can dramatically improve energy, mood, cognitive function, and quality of life.

My Personal Experience I mentioned earlier that I'm on testosterone replacement therapy, but let me provide more context. After a year of optimizing every lifestyle factor—eliminating alcohol, perfecting my sleep, maintaining high protein intake, consistent strength training, proper circadian rhythm management, and trying various natural supplements including tongkat ali and others—my testosterone levels remained consistently below 300 ng/dL.

At 300 ng/dL, I was technically within the "normal" range according to standard lab references (which typically span from 250-1000 ng/dL). But these ranges are based on averages that include unhealthy men and older men with declining hormones, not optimal levels for health and vitality.

Working with a knowledgeable physician, we determined that testosterone replacement therapy was appropriate for my situation. My levels now range between 750-900 ng/dL—still within normal physiological ranges, but in the optimal zone for energy, recovery, and overall well-being.

The difference has been significant. Better energy, improved recovery from workouts, enhanced mood stability, and greater overall vitality. But here's what's important: These benefits came on top of an already solid foundation of health habits, not as a replacement for them.

The Research Reality Current research on properly administered hormone replacement therapy is largely positive. Studies show that bioidentical hormone replacement, when initiated at appropriate times with proper monitoring, can:

- Improve energy levels and mood,
- Enhance cognitive function and memory,
- Increase bone density and reduce fracture risk,
- Improve cardiovascular health markers,
- Enhance sexual function and libido, and
- Reduce the risk of metabolic diseases.

The key factors for safety and effectiveness are:

- Using bioidentical rather than synthetic hormones,
- Individualizing dosing based on testing and response,
- Choosing appropriate delivery methods,
- Regular monitoring and adjustment, and
- Working with experienced practitioners.

Who Might Benefit Hormone replacement therapy may be worth considering if you:

- Have symptoms of hormone deficiency (fatigue, mood changes, decreased libido, cognitive issues),
- Have laboratory evidence of low hormone levels,
- Have optimized lifestyle factors without resolution of symptoms,
- Are working with a knowledgeable healthcare provider, and
- Understand both the potential benefits and risks.

Important Caveats HRT isn't appropriate for everyone. People with certain medical conditions, family histories, or risk factors may not be good candidates. This is why working with experienced physicians who can properly evaluate your individual situation is essential.

Pilates, Red Light Therapy, and Other "What Abouts"

The Questions That Never Stop

Every time I speak at a workshop, I can predict certain questions with near-perfect accuracy. After we've covered strength training, nutrition, sleep, and stress management, hands inevitably shoot up:

"What about Pilates? My instructor says it builds long, lean muscles."

"Have you tried red light therapy? I heard it's amazing for inflammation."

"What about yoga? Isn't flexibility just as important as strength?"

These aren't bad questions. They're asked by people who genuinely want to optimize their health. But they reveal something important about how we think about wellness: We're often drawn to the novel, the trendy, and the comfortable while neglecting the fundamental, the proven, and the challenging.

Let's address these directly—not to dismiss them, but to put them in proper perspective.

Pilates: Good, But Not the Foundation

Let me be clear: Pilates isn't bad. It can be genuinely beneficial for:

- **Core stability and body awareness:** Pilates excels at teaching you to engage muscles you didn't know you had and to move with intention and control.
- **Flexibility and mobility:** The emphasis on controlled movement through full ranges of motion can improve how your body moves in daily life.
- **Rehabilitation:** Many physical therapists incorporate Pilates principles for injury recovery.
- **Mind-body connection:** The focus on breath and precise movement can be meditative and stress-reducing.

Here's the problem: Pilates is often marketed as a complete fitness solution when it's really a complement to other training.

The claim that Pilates builds "long, lean muscles" is, frankly, marketing nonsense. Your muscle length is determined by your genetics—specifically, where your tendons attach to your bones. No exercise can make your muscles longer. And the "lean" part? That's primarily about body fat levels, not the type of exercise you do.

More importantly, Pilates doesn't provide the heavy resistance necessary to build significant muscle mass, increase bone density, or create the metabolic and hormonal benefits we discussed in Chapter Four. You cannot Pilates your way to the kind of strength that protects you from falls at eighty or maintains your independence as you age.

The bottom line: If you love Pilates, keep doing it—but don't let it replace heavy resistance training. Think of it as a valuable supporting player, not the star of your fitness program. Do your strength training twice a week and add Pilates as a complement if you enjoy it and have time.

Red Light Therapy: Optimization, Not Foundation

Red light therapy (also called photobiomodulation) has become increasingly popular, with devices ranging from small handheld units to full-body panels costing thousands of dollars. Proponents claim benefits for everything from skin health to muscle recovery to cognitive function.

Here's what the research shows:

Potential benefits with reasonable evidence:

- **Skin health:** Some studies suggest red light can improve skin texture, reduce wrinkles, and support wound healing by stimulating collagen production.
- **Inflammation reduction:** There's evidence that red light therapy can reduce inflammation in certain contexts.
- **Muscle recovery:** Some research indicates faster recovery from exercise-induced muscle damage.
- **Joint pain:** Modest benefits for certain types of arthritis and joint discomfort.

The caveats:

- Many studies are small, short-term, or industry-funded.
- Optimal dosing, wavelength, and treatment protocols aren't well established.
- Effect sizes are often modest.
- Most dramatic claims (curing depression, reversing aging, eliminating chronic disease) far outpace the evidence.

Here's my honest take: Red light therapy is probably doing *something* beneficial for some people in some contexts. But it's firmly in the "optimization" category—the twenty percent that might provide marginal benefits after you've mastered the eighty percent.

The bottom line: If you have your strength training dialed in, your nutrition optimized, your sleep on point, and your stress managed—and you have an extra $500 to $2,000 to spend—sure, experiment with red light therapy. But if you're sleeping five hours a night, skipping workouts, and eating processed food, buying a red light panel is like putting premium gas in a car that needs an engine rebuild. You're majoring in minors.

GLP-1 Receptor Agonists: The Weight Loss Revolution

Understanding the GLP Landscape: Not All "GLP-1s" Are Created Equal

If you've been paying attention to health news over the past few years, you've probably heard the term "GLP-1" used as a catch-all for medications like Ozempic®, Wegovy®, and Mounjaro®. But lumping them all together misses crucial differences that affect both effectiveness and side effects.

Let me break down what's currently happening in this rapidly evolving space.

The Three Generations of GLP Medications

Pure GLP-1 Receptor Agonists (Semaglutide) Brand names: Ozempic®, Wegovy®, Rybelsus®.

These medications mimic GLP-1, a hormone your gut produces that regulates blood sugar and signals satiety to your brain. Semaglutide was the breakthrough that launched the current weight loss medication revolution—and for good reason. The clinical results for weight loss are remarkable, averaging fifteen to twenty percent body weight reduction in trials.

But pure GLP-1 agonists (a substance—often a medication—that binds to cell receptors and activates them to produce a biological response, mimicking natural ligands) come with a notable side effect profile. Nausea, vomiting, diarrhea, and constipation are common, especially during dose escalation. Some users report more serious issues: severe gastroparesis (stomach paralysis), pancreatitis, and emerging concerns about a potential link to a rare eye condition called NAION (non-arteritic anterior ischemic optic neuropathy, often described as an eye stroke). The research on these more serious effects is still developing, but they're worth noting.

Dual GLP-1/GIP Agonists (Tirzepatide) Brand names: Mounjaro®, Zepbound®.

Here's where it gets interesting. Tirzepatide doesn't just target GLP-1 receptors—it also activates GIP (glucose-dependent insulinotropic polypeptide) receptors. You might hear people casually refer to this as "GLP-2," but that's technically incorrect. GIP is a different hormone that works synergistically with GLP-1 to regulate insulin, appetite, and metabolism.

This dual mechanism appears to be a gamechanger. In head-to-head comparisons, tirzepatide has shown greater weight loss than semaglutide—some trials showing average losses of twenty to twenty-five percent of body weight. But perhaps more importantly, many physicians and patients report significantly fewer side effects. The nausea and GI issues that plague pure GLP-1 users seem to be less common and less severe with tirzepatide.

Several functional medicine physicians I've spoken with believe tirzepatide may also have geroprotective properties—meaning it could slow aspects of biological aging beyond just weight loss. The mechanisms involve improved insulin sensitivity, reduced inflammation, and enhanced metabolic function at the cellular level. While this research is still emerging, it's one reason many integrative physicians now favor tirzepatide over pure GLP-1 agonists.

Triple Agonists (Retatrutide and Others) Coming: Expected in 2026

The next generation targets three receptors: GLP-1, GIP, and glucagon. Early trials have shown even more dramatic weight loss—some participants losing over twenty-five percent of body weight. However, there are emerging concerns about impacts on liver and kidney function that will need to be monitored closely as these medications move toward approval.

My current take: Watch this space, but don't be an early adopter. Let the data mature before jumping on the triple agonist bandwagon.

The Brain Health Connection

Here's something that doesn't get enough attention in the weight loss conversation: GLP-1 receptors aren't just in your gut—they're also in your brain.

This is why researchers are increasingly excited about these medications' potential beyond metabolic health. Studies are showing neuroprotective effects that could have profound implications:

- **Reduced neuroinflammation**: Chronic brain inflammation is linked to cognitive decline, depression, and neurodegenerative diseases. GLP-1 agonists appear to calm this inflammatory response.
- **Improved brain insulin sensitivity**: You've probably heard Alzheimer's disease called "Type 3 diabetes" by some researchers. The brain becomes insulin resistant, impairing its ability to use glucose for energy. GLP-1 medications may help restore proper insulin signaling in brain tissue.

- **Enhanced neuroplasticity**: Some research suggests these medications may support the brain's ability to form new neural connections and protect existing neurons.
- **Reduced dementia risk**: Early epidemiological data shows that diabetic patients on GLP-1 medications have lower rates of dementia than those on other diabetes treatments. This correlation is strong enough that clinical trials are now specifically studying semaglutide for Alzheimer's disease.

This isn't to say these medications are a cognitive cure-all. The research is still developing. But it does add another dimension to the risk-benefit analysis—especially for people with metabolic dysfunction, family history of cognitive decline, or early signs of insulin resistance.

The Compounding Pharmacy Question

Now let's address the elephant in the room: cost.

Mounjaro® and Zepbound® can run $1,000 to $1,500 per month without insurance coverage. For many people, that's simply not accessible, regardless of how beneficial the medication might be. This has led to a surge of interest in compounded versions of tirzepatide, which can cost $200 to $400 per month—a fraction of the brand name price.

Should you consider a compounding pharmacy? Here's my honest take:

The potential upside:

- Dramatically more affordable,
- Same active ingredient, and
- Allows more people access to potentially life-changing medication.

The real risks:

- Quality varies enormously between compounding pharmacies.
- There is no FDA oversight of the final product.
- Contamination, incorrect dosing, and stability issues are real concerns.
- Some "compounding pharmacies" are essentially operating in regulatory gray zones.

My position: Compounded tirzepatide can be a legitimate option, but only under specific conditions:

1. You must work with a qualified physician. Not an online telehealth mill that rubber-stamps prescriptions. A real doctor who understands these medications, will order appropriate labs, and will help you titrate properly. Titration matters—starting too high or increasing too fast is how people end up with severe side effects that could have been avoided.

2. Your physician should have a relationship with a reputable compounding pharmacy. Ask about their quality control processes, sterility testing, and how they source their raw materials. A good compounding pharmacy will be transparent about this. If they're evasive, that's a red flag.

3. Don't price shop to the bottom. If someone is offering compounded tirzepatide for $50 per month, something is wrong. Quality compounding requires proper facilities, testing, and expertise—that costs money.

4. Understand you're accepting some uncertainty. Even with a reputable pharmacy and qualified physician, compounded medications don't have the same quality guarantees as FDA-approved products. For many people, the cost savings justify this trade-off. But go in with eyes open.

The worst approach is ordering from random online sources without physician oversight or working with a "doctor" who will prescribe to anyone with a credit card. That's how people get hurt—and it's how this entire space risks getting shut down by regulators.

Few topics in health generate more heated debate than GLP-1 receptor agonists like semaglutide (Ozempic®, Wegovy®) and tirzepatide (Mounjaro®, Zepbound®). These medications have shown remarkable effectiveness for weight loss and metabolic health, but they've also sparked controversy about their safety, appropriateness, and long-term effects.

Understanding GLP-1 GLP-1 (glucagon-like peptide-1) is a hormone naturally produced in your intestines that regulates blood sugar and appetite. It slows gastric emptying, promotes insulin release when blood sugar is elevated, and signals satiety to the brain.

GLP-1 receptor agonists are medications that mimic this natural hormone, amplifying its effects. Originally developed for type 2 diabetes, they've shown remarkable benefits for weight loss in people with and without diabetes.

The Research Results The clinical trial results for GLP-1 medications are impressive. In the STEP trials studying semaglutide for weight loss:

- Participants lost an average of fifteen to twenty percent of their body weight.
- Many achieved weight loss comparable to bariatric surgery.
- Improvements were seen in blood pressure, cholesterol, and markers of inflammation.
- Benefits extended beyond weight loss to cardiovascular and metabolic health.

Similar results have been seen with tirzepatide, which targets both GLP-1 and GIP receptors and may be even more effective for weight loss.

Addressing the Concerns Critics of GLP-1 medications raise several concerns:

"It's just a quick fix": This criticism assumes that using medication to address obesity is somehow cheating or taking the easy way out. But obesity is a complex medical condition influenced by genetics, hormones, environment, and psychology. For many people, willpower alone isn't sufficient to overcome the biological and psychological drives that maintain excess weight.

"People will regain the weight when they stop": This is true. Weight regain often occurs when the medication is discontinued. But this doesn't negate the benefits of the treatment any more than the fact that blood pressure returns when hypertension medications are stopped negates their value.

"There could be unknown long-term risks": This is a legitimate concern with any relatively new medication. However, GLP-1 receptor agonists have been used for diabetes treatment for over a decade with a well-established safety profile. The most common side effects are gastrointestinal (nausea, vomiting, diarrhea) and typically improve over time.

My Perspective: I view GLP-1 medications as potentially valuable tools for people who have struggled with obesity despite addressing lifestyle factors. They're not magic bullets, and they work best when combined with appropriate nutrition and exercise habits. But for someone who has tried repeatedly to lose weight through lifestyle changes alone without success, they may provide the support needed to break the cycle.

The key is using them as part of a comprehensive approach rather than as standalone solutions and working with physicians who understand both the benefits and limitations of these medications.

Who Might Benefit GLP-1 medications may be appropriate for people who:

- Have struggled with obesity despite lifestyle interventions,
- Have metabolic conditions like type 2 diabetes or insulin resistance,
- Are working with physicians experienced in their use,
- Understand that lifestyle changes remain important, and
- Are prepared for the financial investment (these medications are expensive).

Peptides: The Frontier of Optimization

Peptides represent one of the most rapidly evolving areas of health optimization. These short chains of amino acids act as signaling molecules in the body, influencing everything from growth hormone release to immune function to tissue repair.

What Are Peptides? Peptides are naturally occurring compounds that serve as messengers between cells. Your body produces thousands of different peptides that regulate various physiological processes. Synthetic peptides used therapeutically are designed to mimic or enhance these natural functions.

Some of the most commonly discussed peptides include:

Growth Hormone Releasing Peptides (like Ipamorelin and CJC-1295): These stimulate natural growth hormone release, potentially improving body composition, recovery, and sleep quality.

BPC-157: Often called the "body protection compound," this peptide may accelerate healing of injuries, particularly to tendons, ligaments, and muscle tissue.

Thymosin Beta-4: Another healing peptide that may promote tissue repair and reduce inflammation.

Melanotan II: A peptide that stimulates melanin production, potentially providing protection against UV radiation while promoting tanning.

The Appeal and the Caution Peptides are appealing because they often work with the body's natural processes rather than against them. Many have favorable safety profiles compared to pharmaceutical drugs. They can be targeted to specific functions without affecting unrelated systems.

However, the peptide space is also plagued by poor regulation, questionable quality control, and overhyped marketing claims. Many peptides sold online are of unknown purity and potency. The research on many peptides is still preliminary, with most studies conducted in animals rather than humans.

My Approach to Peptides I've experimented with certain peptides under medical supervision, primarily growth hormone releasing peptides for recovery and sleep optimization. I've found some benefits, particularly for sleep quality and workout recovery. But I've also learned to be skeptical of dramatic claims and to prioritize proven interventions over experimental ones.

The peptide space changes rapidly, with new compounds emerging regularly and regulations evolving. What's available legally and safely today may be different tomorrow. This is why working with knowledgeable physicians who stay current with the research and regulations is essential.

Important Considerations If you're considering peptides:

- Work only with qualified healthcare providers.
- Be skeptical of dramatic claims or "miracle" peptides.
- Understand that research is often limited.
- Prioritize quality and legal sources.
- Start conservatively and monitor responses carefully.
- Remember that fundamentals matter more than optimization.

Stem Cell Therapy: Promise and Hype

Stem cell therapy represents one of the most promising yet controversial areas of regenerative medicine. The basic concept—using the body's natural repair cells to heal damaged tissues—is compelling. But the field is also filled with unsubstantiated claims, unregulated clinics, and treatments that may do more harm than good.

The Science Stem cells are undifferentiated cells that can develop into various specialized cell types. They play crucial roles in tissue repair and regeneration throughout life. In theory, introducing additional stem cells to damaged areas could enhance healing and restore function.

Some forms of stem cell therapy have solid research support. Bone marrow transplants for blood cancers are well-established. Certain cartilage repair procedures using stem cells show promise. But many of the stem cell treatments being marketed to consumers have limited scientific support.

The Reality Check The FDA has approved very few stem cell treatments, and most are for serious medical conditions rather than general health optimization. Many clinics offering stem cell treatments for aging, arthritis, or general wellness are operating in regulatory gray areas with treatments that haven't been proven effective.

The field is evolving rapidly, and legitimate advances are being made. But it's also an area where hope often outpaces evidence, and where people desperate for solutions may be vulnerable to exploitation.

My Perspective I remain cautiously optimistic about the potential of stem cell therapy but skeptical of current commercial offerings. The science is promising, but we're still in the early stages of understanding how to harness it safely and effectively. For most health concerns, proven interventions should be tried first.

If considering stem cell therapy, work only with legitimate medical facilities conducting approved treatments or clinical trials. Be extremely wary of clinics promising miraculous results for a wide range of conditions.

The Financial Reality of Advanced Interventions

Before pursuing any of these advanced interventions, it's important to understand the financial implications. These treatments are typically expensive and often not covered by insurance:

- Hormone replacement therapy: $100 to $500+ per month,
- GLP-1 medications: $800 to $1,500+ per month,
- Peptide therapies: $200 to $1,000+ per month, and
- Stem cell treatments: $5,000 to $50,000+ per procedure.

These costs can add up quickly, and there's no guarantee of results. This is another reason why getting the fundamentals right first is so important—you can achieve eighty percent of your health goals through lifestyle changes that cost relatively little compared to these advanced interventions.

The Framework for Decision-Making

When considering any advanced health intervention, I use this framework:

1. **Foundation First** Have I optimized the fundamentals? Sleep, nutrition, exercise, stress management, and basic health markers should be addressed before pursuing advanced interventions.
2. **Clear Rationale** Is there a specific health concern or goal that isn't being addressed by lifestyle interventions? Vague desires for "optimization" aren't sufficient rationale for expensive or potentially risky treatments.
3. **Evidence Base** What does the research say? Are there well-designed studies supporting the intervention for my specific situation, or am I relying on testimonials and marketing claims?

4. Risk-Benefit Analysis What are the potential benefits, and what are the risks? How do they compare to the status quo and to alternative approaches?
5. Qualified Guidance Am I working with healthcare providers who have legitimate expertise in this area and can provide proper monitoring and support?
6. Financial Wisdom Can I afford this intervention without creating financial stress? Am I prioritizing it appropriately relative to other health investments?
7. Realistic Expectations Do I understand what this intervention can and cannot accomplish? Am I expecting reasonable outcomes based on evidence rather than hoping for miraculous transformations?

The Integration Approach

The most successful approach to these advanced interventions is integration rather than replacement. They work best when layered on top of solid lifestyle foundations, not used as substitutes for healthy living.

My current approach includes:

- Consistent strength training and cardiovascular exercise,
- Optimized nutrition with adequate protein and whole foods,
- Prioritized sleep and stress management,
- Basic supplementation (multivitamin, omega-3, vitamin D, probiotics),
- Testosterone replacement therapy under medical supervision, and
- Occasional use of specific peptides for recovery optimization.

But the foundation remains lifestyle-based. The advanced interventions enhance what I'm already doing rather than replacing the need for healthy habits.

Beyond Individual Optimization

As we consider these advanced interventions, it's worth remembering that individual optimization isn't the ultimate goal. These tools should serve a larger purpose—enabling us to love and serve others more effectively.

When we have more energy, better mood, enhanced cognitive function, and improved physical capacity, we become more available for our families, more capable in our work, and more able to contribute to our communities.

The question isn't just "Will this intervention make me better?" but "Will being better enable me to serve my calling more effectively?"

Sometimes the answer is yes—addressing hormone deficiencies or metabolic dysfunction can dramatically improve your capacity to serve others. Sometimes the answer is no—pursuing marginal optimization gains may not be worth the cost and complexity if your basic function is already good.

Wisdom lies in discerning the difference.

The Caution Against Shortcuts

Perhaps the biggest risk with advanced interventions is the temptation to use them as shortcuts around the hard work of lifestyle change. It's human nature to want the quick fix, the magic bullet, the easy solution to complex problems.

But there are no shortcuts to sustainable health. Even the most effective interventions work best when combined with proper nutrition, regular exercise, adequate sleep, stress management, and social connection.

I've seen people spend thousands on peptides while eating fast food and skipping workouts. I've watched others pursue stem cell treatments while remaining sedentary and socially isolated. The results are predictably disappointing.

The fundamentals matter. They always have, and they always will. Advanced interventions can enhance what you're already doing well, but they can't replace the need to do it well in the first place.

Looking Forward

The field of health optimization is evolving rapidly. New interventions are being developed, existing treatments are being refined, and our understanding of how to use these tools effectively continues to grow.

This means maintaining an attitude of informed curiosity rather than closed-minded skepticism or naive optimism. We should be open to new possibilities while maintaining appropriate caution. We should test everything while being discerning about what we hold fast to.

Most importantly, we should remember that these tools are means to an end, not ends in themselves. The goal isn't to become perfectly optimized human machines—it's to become people who can love God and serve others with all our strength, energy, and capability.

When we keep that perspective, these advanced interventions take their proper place—as potentially valuable tools in service of a greater purpose, not as the purpose itself.

The 80/20 Filter

When evaluating any health intervention—whether it's Pilates, red light therapy, the latest supplement, or the newest biohacking gadget—run it through the 80/20 filter.

Ask yourself:

1. Have I mastered the fundamentals that drive eighty percent of results? (Strength training, adequate protein, quality sleep, stress management, basic nutrition.)
2. Is this intervention addressing a real limitation in my health, or am I just attracted to novelty?
3. What's the opportunity cost? (Time and money spent here is time and money not spent elsewhere.)
4. What does the quality evidence factually show—not testimonials, not influencer claims, but actual research?

If you've genuinely optimized the eighty percent and have resources to spare, then by all means explore the twenty percent. Experiment. See what works for you. Some of it might provide real benefits.

But never mistake the twenty percent for the eighty percent. Never let the sexy, novel intervention distract you from the boring, proven fundamentals.

Red light therapy cannot replace heavy resistance training. Pilates cannot replace progressive overload. No gadget, supplement, or trend can substitute for the foundational work.

Do the hard things first. Then optimize around the edges.

Recap & Actions

Scripture to Reflect On: "Test everything; hold fast to what is good." —1 Thessalonians 5:21

Science-Backed Truth: Advanced health interventions like hormone replacement therapy, GLP-1 medications, and peptides can provide significant benefits for appropriate candidates when used properly under medical supervision. However, they work best when layered on top of solid lifestyle foundations, not as replacements for fundamental health practices. The 80/20 principle applies—get the basics right first, then consider optimization tools.

Ready, Willing, Able Actions:

Ready (You can do this right now):

- Assess whether you've optimized the fundamentals before considering advanced interventions.
- Research qualified healthcare providers in your area who specialize in hormone optimization or functional medicine.
- Calculate the true cost (including time and money) of any intervention you're considering.
- Examine your motivations—are you seeking genuine health improvement or looking for shortcuts?

Willing (You can do this within a week):

- Get comprehensive lab work to establish baseline hormone and metabolic markers.
- Schedule consultation with a qualified functional medicine practitioner if you have persistent health concerns despite lifestyle optimization.

- Create clear criteria for what would constitute success with any intervention you're considering.
- Research the evidence base for any specific intervention that interests you.

Able (You can do this within a month):

- Work with qualified medical professionals to evaluate whether advanced interventions are appropriate for your situation.
- Implement a systematic approach to testing interventions—one at a time with proper monitoring.
- Develop a long-term plan that integrates any beneficial interventions with continued lifestyle optimization.
- Set realistic expectations and timelines for seeing results from any new intervention.

Remember: Advanced interventions are tools, not solutions. They work best when used to enhance an already solid foundation of health practices, guided by qualified professionals, and motivated by a desire to serve your calling more effectively rather than to achieve perfect optimization.

13

THE CALL—WHAT GOD HAS REDEEMED, HE WILL USE

"For we are His workmanship, created in Christ Jesus for good works, which God prepared beforehand so that we would walk in them."
— Ephesians 2:10

The Pursuit of Purpose

In the spring of 1945, Viktor Frankl walked out of a Nazi concentration camp weighing less than ninety pounds. He had lost his wife, his parents, and nearly his life. Everything had been stripped away—his possessions, his freedom, his health, his family, his future as he had imagined it.

But in that hell on earth, Frankl discovered something that would revolutionize psychology and challenge everything our culture believes about happiness. In the most horrific circumstances imaginable, he watched people respond in radically different ways. Some collapsed into despair and died quickly. Others found ways to maintain hope and even help others survive.

The difference wasn't physical strength, intelligence, or even faith in the traditional sense. The difference was meaning. Purpose.

Frankl observed that people could endure almost unimaginable suffering if they believed it served a purpose larger than themselves. But those who lived only for personal pleasure, comfort, or survival often couldn't withstand even minor setbacks.[38]

Years later, he would write: "Striving to find meaning in one's life is the primary motivational force in man." But here's what Frankl discovered that our culture desperately needs to understand: The pursuit of happiness is what makes you miserable. **The pursuit of meaning is what makes you happy.**

This brings us to the question that changes everything—not just about your health, but about your entire life: What if your greatest struggles aren't roadblocks to your calling, but preparation for it?

What if the emptiness you feel despite having everything you thought you wanted is instead your soul crying out for the purpose it was created to fulfill?

The Happiness Trap That's Destroying a Generation

I have a friend—let's call him Marcus—who, by every cultural metric, should be living his best life. He's in his early forties, makes seven figures, lives in a beautiful neighborhood, drives a car that turns heads, and has the freedom to travel anywhere he wants. His Instagram looks like a lifestyle magazine.

But when we grab coffee, really talk, the conversation always drifts to the same place: "I just feel ... empty, man. Like, what's the point of any of this?"

Marcus represents millions of people in our generation who have been sold a lie so seductive that entire industries exist to perpetuate it: that life is about maximizing pleasure, minimizing pain, and collecting things and experiences that make you happy.

But here's what no one tells you about that happiness-first life choice: It leads to misery. Not sometimes. Always.

Dr. Andrew Huberman, a neuroscientist and tenured professor in neurobiology at Stanford University School of Medicine, and creator of the top-ranking podcast Huberman Lab, recently had a fascinating conversation with Dr. Robert Sapolsky, one of the leading neuroscientists in the world, about this exact phenomenon.[39] The research is overwhelming: People who organize their lives around personal happiness report higher rates of depression, anxiety, and life dissatisfaction than those who organize their lives around meaning and purpose.

Why? Because happiness is an emotion—a fleeting chemical reaction in your brain. When you chase emotions, you become enslaved to circumstances. Good day? You're up. Bad day? You're down. New thing? Temporary high. Same thing? Crushing boredom. Happy? For now.

You become what psychologists call a "hedonic treadmill runner"; constantly needing more, bigger, better, newer just to feel normal.[40] The salary that thrilled you at twenty-five feels insufficient at thirty. The house that seemed amazing becomes ordinary within months. The vacation that was supposed to change your life becomes just another set of photos on your phone.

This is why so many people in our hyper-affluent, hyper-connected, hyper-entertained society are taking antidepressants, seeing therapists, and still feeling fundamentally unsatisfied with life. They're pursuing a dead-end strategy that can never deliver what it promises.

But there's another way—an ancient way that modern science is now proving works.

The Ancient Secret to Modern Fulfillment

Viktor Frankl's breakthrough wasn't just observational—it was deeply practical. He developed what became known as "logotherapy," a form of psychology based on the idea that human beings are primarily motivated by the search for meaning rather than pleasure.[41]

And his findings align perfectly with what Scripture has been saying for thousands of years.

Jesus himself said it most clearly: "For whoever wants to save his life will lose it; but whoever loses his life for My sake will find it." (Matthew 16:25). This isn't religious rhetoric—it's psychological truth. The paradox of human flourishing is that you find your life by giving it away.

Paul echoed this when he wrote that we are "...created in Christ Jesus for good works, which God prepared beforehand so that we would walk in them." (Ephesians 2:10). Notice the sequence: We were created for works that were prepared for us. Our lives have purpose baked into them from before we even existed.

Modern research confirms what ancient wisdom always knew: People who live purpose-driven lives live longer, have better physical health, stronger immune systems, lower rates of depression, and report higher life satisfaction. They don't just live better—they die better, with fewer regrets and greater peace.

But here's where it gets interesting: Your purpose isn't separate from your struggles. Your purpose is forged through your struggles.

What if the health crisis that brought you to your knees was designed to give you compassion for others who are struggling? What if the anxiety you've battled taught you tools that could help someone else find peace? What if the addiction you overcame equipped you to guide others to freedom? What if the depression that nearly destroyed you became the foundation for helping others find hope?

What if nothing—absolutely nothing—in your story has been wasted?

This is the heart of the Gospel: What God has redeemed in you He wants to use through you. Your pain becomes your platform. Your struggle becomes your strength. Your healing becomes your ministry.

You didn't get healthy just for you. You got healthy for them—for the people whose lives will be changed because you chose to become who God called you to be.

Throughout Scripture, God has a pattern of using broken people to do beautiful things. He doesn't choose the qualified—He qualifies the chosen. And often, the very thing that seems to disqualify us is exactly what He uses to reach others.

Moses had a speech impediment and a criminal record. David was an adulterer and murderer. Paul was a terrorist who persecuted Christians. Peter was impulsive and denied Jesus when it mattered most. Yet these flawed, broken people became instruments of world-changing impact.

Consider the story of Mephibosheth that we looked at in Chapter One. There's a deeper meaning within that story that reveals God's redemptive heart. Remember: Mephibosheth was the grandson of King Saul, crippled in both feet from a childhood accident. He lived in exile, convinced the new king would want him dead. But King David sought him out, not to destroy him but to restore him.

When David brought Mephibosheth to the palace and seated him at the royal table, he didn't hide his disability. Everyone could see that this man was lame in both feet. Yet there he sat, not despite his brokenness, but as a living testimony to the king's grace. Every meal was a reminder to everyone present: "This is what redemption looks like. This is how the king treats those who would be outcasts. This is the kind of kingdom we live in."

Your story—including the broken parts, especially the broken parts—isn't an obstacle to your calling. It is your calling.

The executive who battles depression becomes a safe harbor for others drowning in despair. The mother who struggled with addiction becomes a beacon of hope for families in crisis. The person who nearly lost everything to poor health becomes a guide for others seeking transformation.

God doesn't waste our wilderness seasons. He uses them to prepare us for the Promised Land—not so we can retire in comfort, but so we can help others make the same journey.

The False Gospel of Self-Improvement

We live in a culture obsessed with self-improvement, life hacking, and personal optimization. (I know this all too well.) The message is everywhere: You can become the best version of yourself, achieve your dreams, live your best life now.

There's nothing wrong with growth, discipline, or reaching your potential. But when self-improvement becomes the end goal rather than the means to serve others, it becomes a sophisticated form of selfishness.

The health and fitness industry is particularly guilty of this. We're told to get fit to look good, feel confident, and optimize our performance. These aren't bad motivations, but they're not deep enough to sustain long-term transformation or create lasting fulfillment.

The truth that transforms everything is this: You were created not primarily for your own happiness, but for God's glory and others' good. Your health, your strength, your energy, your mental clarity—these are gifts to be stewarded in service of something bigger than your own comfort.

This isn't a burden—it's liberation. When you understand that your life has a purpose beyond your own pleasure, suddenly the daily discipline of health makes sense. The hard workouts, the careful nutrition, the prioritized sleep, the stress management—it's all training for your calling.

You're not just building a better you. You're building a vessel capable of carrying the weight of purpose.

The Ripple Effect of Radical Health

Let me paint you a picture of what happens when someone gets truly healthy—not just physically, but holistically.

They wake up with energy and clarity. Instead of hitting the snooze button and starting the day in survival mode, they rise with purpose. Their morning routine isn't a chore—it's preparation for battle in the best possible way.

They move through their day with presence and patience. Instead of being irritable from poor sleep or scattered from bad nutrition, they're available for their family, focused at work, and resilient under pressure.

They show up differently in every room they enter. There's something in their posture, their voice, their eyes that communicates strength and peace. People are drawn to them because they embody what everyone is searching for—authentic vitality.

But here's what's most powerful: They become living proof that transformation is possible.

When your coworkers see you handling stress with grace, they start asking questions. When your friends notice your energy and joy, they want to know what's different. When your children watch you prioritize your health without making it an obsession, they learn what balanced living looks like.

You don't have to preach about health—you become a sermon that everyone can read.

This is the ripple effect of radical health. One person's transformation becomes permission for others to believe change is possible. Your healing becomes a catalyst for their healing. Your strength becomes an invitation for them to get strong.

But it starts with you being willing to do the hard work of becoming who God created you to be.

Why Your Children Are Watching (And What They Really Need to See)

If you're a parent, this next part might change everything about how you think about your health journey.

Your children are not primarily learning from your words—they're learning from your life. They're watching how you treat your body, how you handle stress, how you prioritize your well-being, how you respond to challenges. And they're making decisions about their own future based on what they observe.

But here's what they really need to see: not perfection, but purpose.

If you're constantly exhausted, they learn that being tired is normal. If you're always stressed, they learn that anxiety is inevitable. If you neglect your health, they learn that taking care of your body isn't important.

But if you prioritize sleep, they learn that rest has value. If you exercise consistently, they learn that movement is medicine. If you eat with intention, they learn that food is fuel, not just entertainment. If you manage stress well, they learn that peace is possible even in difficult circumstances.

Most importantly, if you live with purpose—if they see you stewarding your health not for vanity but for service, not for yourself but for others—they learn what it looks like to live a life that matters.

I think about my own four boys and the father I want to be for them. I don't want them to see a man who's obsessed with his appearance or addicted to optimization. I want them to see a man who takes care of his body so he can serve his family with energy and presence. I want them to watch me work through challenges with resilience rather than giving up when things get hard. I want them to observe what it looks like to live with intention rather than just drifting through life.

Your children need you to be healthy. Your spouse needs you to be healthy. Your community needs you to be healthy. The world needs you to be healthy.

Not because you're indispensable, but because God wants to use your unique gifts, experiences, and calling to touch lives that no one else can reach.

And they're watching to see if you believe that strongly enough to do something about it.

The Church That Could Change the World

Imagine what would happen if Christians took seriously the command to honor God with their bodies.

Picture churches filled with people who radiate energy, joy, and peace because they've learned to steward their physical and mental health well. Envision believers who can love tirelessly because they have the capacity that comes from proper rest, nutrition, and exercise.

Think about Christians who don't need to rely on caffeine and sugar to get through the day, who don't collapse into exhaustion every evening, who don't battle depression and anxiety because they've addressed the physical factors that contribute to mental health.

Consider the impact of a church where people live ten, fifteen, or twenty years longer in good health because they understood that their bodies are temples of the Holy Spirit. Imagine the cumulative wisdom and influence of believers who remain vital and engaged well into their eighties and nineties.

This isn't a fantasy—it's entirely possible. The research is clear, the methods are proven, and the results are reproducible. The only question is whether we'll have the courage to live differently than the culture around us.

The early church turned the world upside down not because they had perfect theology or flawless execution, but because they lived with *radical love and sacrificial service*. People were drawn to them because they embodied something the world desperately needed.

What if health—holistic health—became our witness in the same way? What if our energy, joy, and vitality became so compelling that people couldn't help but ask about the hope we carry?

What if we became living demonstrations of what human beings look like when they're fully alive?

The Deathbed Test

When you're lying on your deathbed, what will you wish you had done with the health, strength, and time you were given?

Oliver Burkeman, in his brilliant book *Four Thousand Weeks,* reminds us of a sobering reality: if you live to be eighty, you get roughly 4,000 weeks on this planet. That's it. Not 4,000 years, not even 4,000 months—4,000 weeks.[42]

When you frame life in those terms, every week becomes precious. Every month becomes significant. Every year becomes irreplaceable.

But here's what's tragic: Most people spend their 4,000 weeks in what Burkeman calls "the efficiency trap"—constantly trying to optimize their time to fit more stuff in, rather than being intentional about what deserves their finite attention in the first place.

They'll spend weeks scrolling social media. Months binge-watching shows they'll forget. Years chasing pleasure and comfort that leave them feeling empty. They'll burn through their precious, limited weeks in pursuit of a happiness that always seems just out of reach.

Will you wish you had spent more time scrolling social media? More hours binge-watching Netflix? More energy chasing pleasure and comfort?

Or will you wish you had used your vitality to love people better? To serve causes that mattered? To leave a legacy that outlasted your lifetime?

Every day you choose to prioritize your health is a vote for the second option. Every workout is preparation for service. Every healthy meal is fuel for purpose. Every night of good sleep is recovery for the calling God has placed on your life.

But here's what breaks my heart: Millions of people will reach that deathbed with deep regret, not because they didn't have opportunities to make a difference, but because they didn't have the health and energy to seize them when they came.

They'll have spent their 4,000 weeks surviving instead of thriving, consuming instead of creating, being entertained instead of making a difference. And in their final moments, they'll realize what Burkeman calls "the fundamental problem of finitude"—that we get exactly one life, and most of us waste it waiting for the right moment to really start living.

From Surviving to Thriving to Serving

Most people spend their lives in survival mode—exhausted, overwhelmed, just trying to make it through each day. They dream of someday reaching a place where they can finally breathe, finally relax, finally enjoy life.

But thriving isn't the end goal either. It's the launching pad.

When you're truly healthy—when you have abundant energy, mental clarity, emotional stability, and physical vitality—you realize that this isn't the destination. It's the equipment you need for the journey.

This is what Frankl discovered in the concentration camps. The people who survived weren't necessarily the strongest physically—they were the ones who found meaning in their suffering and purpose beyond their circumstances. They had a reason to live that was bigger than their own survival.

This is why self-improvement alone will never satisfy you. You can optimize your nutrition, perfect your workout routine, hack your sleep, and manage your stress beautifully—but if it's all in service of your own comfort, you'll eventually feel empty.

The moment you shift from "How can I feel better?" to "How can I live life with purpose?"—everything changes.

Suddenly, the discipline of health isn't a burden—it's training. The hard workouts aren't punishment—they're preparation. The careful nutrition isn't restriction—it's fuel for mission.

You stop asking "What's in it for me?" and start asking "What can I contribute?"

And paradoxically, this is when you finally find the fulfillment that all the self-improvement was supposed to deliver.

The Calling That Chose You

You don't have to go looking for your calling. It's already looking for you.

Right now, somewhere, there's a person who needs exactly what you have to offer. A teenager who needs to see that transformation is possible. A parent drowning in shame who needs to witness grace in action. A coworker losing hope who needs to watch someone fight through difficulty with resilience.

God didn't make a mistake when He allowed you to go through whatever you've been through. He didn't waste your struggles, your pain, your failures, or your victories. Every experience—especially the difficult ones—has been preparing you for something specific.

The question isn't "What is my calling?" The question is "Am I prepared for the calling that's already been prepared for me?"

And preparation isn't just spiritual—it's physical, mental, and emotional. It's developing the capacity to carry the weight of purpose without breaking under the pressure.

Think about the people in your life who inspire you most. They're probably not the ones who had it easy. They're the ones who went through fire and came out refined. They're the ones who turned their pain into purpose, their struggle into strength, their healing into hope for others.

They didn't become influential despite their struggles—they became influential because of how they chose to respond to their struggles.

This is your invitation to the same transformation. Not to avoid difficulty, but to allow difficulty to forge you into someone who can bear the weight of significance.

Your health journey isn't separate from your spiritual journey—it's part of it. Every choice to prioritize your physical well-being is a declaration that you believe God has something important for you to do. Every workout is an act of faith. Every healthy meal is a vote of confidence in your future calling.

You're not just getting fit for yourself. You're getting fit for the calling that has been waiting for you to be ready.

The Gift Only She Could Give

What It Really Means to Be Fit for Your Calling

I want to tell you a story that still moves me to tears when I think about it—not because it's sad, but because it captures something I've been trying to say throughout this entire book.

It's about my wife, Tiffani. And it's about what can happen when someone is healthy and whole enough to say yes to something impossibly beautiful.

Tiff grew up with a couple from her church—let's call them David and Sarah. They were the kind of friends who felt like family, the ones you assumed would always be around, weaving in and out of your life's major moments. After they got married, David and Sarah started trying to have children.

And then the miscarriages began.

One after another. Hope rising, then crashing. Pregnancy announcements followed by devastating phone calls. Baby showers they attended for others while their own nursery sat empty. The kind of grief that doesn't have a clear end point—just wave after wave of loss.

For years, this was their story. And Tiff watched it unfold, heartbroken for her friends but unsure what she could possibly do to help.

A Word in the Darkness

One evening, we attended a worship night at our church. I was playing drums—losing myself in the music, eyes closed, focused on keeping rhythm. Tiff was somewhere in the congregation, hands raised, heart open.

And in that space, she felt something she couldn't explain. An overwhelming sense of peace. The kind that doesn't make logical sense given your circumstances. The kind that feels like it's coming from outside yourself.

Then a word. Not audible, but unmistakable. Repeating over and over in her spirit:

Surrogate. Surrogate. Surrogate.

Tiff's eyes flew open. Her heart started racing. Surely she'd heard wrong. This couldn't be what God was asking. We had two young boys already, and we wanted more children of our own. This wasn't in our plan. This wasn't even on our radar.

She tried to shake it off, to convince herself it was just her own emotions responding to her friends' pain. But the word wouldn't leave.

After the service, she approached me with a look I'll never forget—equal parts terror and wonder. She told me what she'd experienced. What she thought she'd heard.

I didn't know what to say. My first instinct was to problem-solve, to list all the reasons this was complicated and risky and not what we'd signed up for. But something in her eyes stopped me.

"Let's not decide anything right now," I said. "Let's pray about it separately for thirty days. No discussing it, no trying to convince each other. Just listening. Then we'll talk."

She agreed.

Wrestling on the Floor

For the next month, I wrestled. I prayed, but mostly I worried. I thought about the medical risks. The emotional toll. The financial implications. The logistics of Tiff carrying a baby while raising our own young children. Every time I tried to hear from God, my own fears drowned out the signal.

Then one night, everything changed.

I was on the bedroom floor with Liam, who was maybe four years old at the time. We were wrestling—that chaotic, joyful, breathless kind of play where you're both laughing so hard you can barely move. He'd climb on my back, I'd flip him onto the carpet, he'd squeal and come back for more.

And in that moment—with my son's laughter filling the room and his small arms wrapped around my neck—a thought cut through all my careful analysis:

Who am I to keep this same treasure from these people?

David and Sarah weren't asking for a vacation or a nice gift. They were longing for what I was experiencing right now, on this carpet, with this boy. The weight of a child in your arms. The sound of your own kid's laughter. The irreplaceable, world-altering gift of being someone's parent.

And my wife might be able to give them that.

I found Tiff that night and told her I was in. I didn't have all my fears resolved. I didn't have a detailed plan. I just knew that saying no to protect our comfort would mean saying no to something sacred.

Fit for This Calling

What happened next was exactly as hard and as beautiful as you might imagine. Tiffani carried their baby—a healthy little girl—and handed her to David and Sarah in a hospital room filled with tears that had nothing to do with sadness.

I watched my wife do one of the most physically demanding, emotionally complex, and spiritually profound things a person can do. She gave her body—literally—so that another family could experience the joy we knew so well.

And here's why I'm telling you this story in a book about health and fitness:

Tiff could only say yes because she was able to.

She was physically healthy enough to carry a pregnancy safely. She was emotionally whole enough to navigate the complexity without being destroyed by it. She was spiritually grounded enough to hear God's voice and trust it even when it terrified her.

What if she'd been too exhausted, too depleted, too overwhelmed by her own health struggles to even consider it? What if her body couldn't have handled the pregnancy? What if she'd been so disconnected from God that she never heard the word *surrogate* in the first place?

That little girl might not exist.

This Is Why

This is why we steward our bodies. Not to look good in pictures. Not to hit arbitrary fitness goals. Not to optimize our personal performance for our own benefit.

We steward our bodies so that when the sacred moment comes—when God asks us to do something beautiful and hard—we can say yes.

Your calling might not be surrogacy. But it might be:

- Having the energy to be truly present with your kids after a long workday;
- The strength to care for an aging parent who needs physical help;
- The mental clarity to make a crucial decision that affects your family's future;
- The emotional resilience to walk with a friend through their darkest valley; or
- The physical capacity to serve on a mission trip, build a house, or simply show up when someone needs you.

Every workout is preparation for a moment you can't yet see. Every healthy meal is an investment in a future yes. Every hour of sleep is building the reserves you'll need when the call comes.

You don't know what God is preparing you for. But you can make sure you're ready when it arrives.

The Gift of Being Ready

Sometimes I think about all the things that had to be true for that little girl to exist. David and Sarah's persistent hope through years of loss. The worship night where Tiff heard that word. Thirty days of prayer. One wrestling match on the living room floor. Tiff's willing heart. Her capable body. Our combined faith that this inexplicable thing might was what we were supposed to do.

So many points where the chain could have broken.

But it didn't. Because when the moment came, Tiffani was fit for her calling.

That's what I want for you. Not just health for health's sake. Not just strength to admire in the mirror. Not just energy to enjoy your own life.

I want you to be ready. For the moment. For the call. For the impossible, beautiful thing that only a healthy, whole, available version of you can accomplish.

Because what God has redeemed in you, He wants to use through you.

And someone out there is waiting for you to be ready.

Starting Where You Are

Maybe you're reading this and thinking, "This sounds inspiring, but I'm not there yet. I'm still struggling with the basics. I'm still tired, still addicted, still fighting the same battles I've been fighting for years."

That's okay. That's exactly where you should start.

You don't have to wait until you're perfectly healthy to begin serving others. In fact, the most powerful ministry often happens in the middle of the mess.

Maybe your calling right now is to be honest about your struggles. Maybe it's to show others that it's okay to not be okay while still fighting for something better. Maybe it's to demonstrate that transformation is a process, not an event.

Maybe someone needs to see you choosing the salad instead of the fries not because you're perfect, but because you're working toward something greater. Maybe someone needs to watch you go to the gym even when you don't feel like it because they need to see what discipline looks like when it's not easy.

Maybe someone needs to hear your story of struggle and slow progress because they've been waiting for permission to believe that change is possible for ordinary people, not just the success stories.

Your calling doesn't begin when you achieve some perfect state of health. It begins the moment you decide to stop making excuses and start making progress.

And here's the beautiful truth: As you take steps toward your own healing, you automatically become a guide for others who are a few steps behind you on the same path.

You don't have to be a perfect example—you just have to be a moving example.

The Leadership That's Waiting

As you become healthy—truly, holistically healthy—something inevitable begins to happen: People start looking to you for guidance.

It might be subtle at first. A coworker asking what you're doing differently. A friend wanting to know about your workout routine. A family member commenting on your energy and asking for advice.

But leadership isn't just about answering questions—it's about taking responsibility for outcomes beyond your own life.

True leaders don't wait for permission to lead. They don't wait for titles or positions or official authority. They lead by example, and people follow because they want what the leader has.

When you embody health, you become a leader whether you intended to or not. The question is: What kind of leader will you be?

Will you be the kind who hoards their success, keeping the secrets of transformation to yourself? Or will you be the kind who generously shares what you've learned, helping others find their own path to wholeness?

Will you be satisfied with personal optimization, or will you use your vitality to lift others up?

The world is desperate for leaders who can show the way to abundant life—not just success or achievement, but genuine flourishing. People who are strong enough to carry others' burdens, wise enough to offer real solutions, and generous enough to invest in others' growth.

This kind of leadership isn't optional for followers of Christ—it's inevitable. When you've been transformed by grace, you can't help but want to see others experience the same transformation.

And leadership—real, transformational leadership—requires everything we've talked about in this book. It requires physical strength to endure the demands. It requires mental clarity to make good decisions under pressure. It requires emotional stability to remain calm in chaos. It requires spiritual depth to maintain perspective in difficulty.

In short, leadership requires you to be fit for your calling.

But here's what's coming next in this journey: Once you're fit for your calling, the real questions begin. How do you lead well? How do you influence others positively? How do you build teams, create culture, and make an impact that lasts beyond your lifetime?

Coming Full Circle: The Beloved Who Serves

Do you remember where we started this journey? Identify: You are beloved.

Not because of what you do, but because of who you are in Christ. Not because you've earned it, but because you've inherited it. Not after you get healthy, but right now, in this moment, exactly as you are.

That truth hasn't changed. It never will.

But now I want you to see the fuller picture. You are beloved—and the beloved lead.

Not out of obligation, but out of overflow. Not to earn love, but to share it. Not because you have to, but because you're compelled to.

When you truly understand that you are God's beloved, something profound happens: You start looking for ways to help others discover the same truth. Your healing becomes an invitation for their healing. Your strength becomes a shelter for their weakness. Your peace becomes a pathway for their freedom.

This is why getting fit for your calling matters so deeply. It's not about personal optimization—it's about becoming a vessel capable of carrying hope to a hopeless world.

The teenager cutting herself in her bedroom needs to see that healing is possible. The middle-aged man drowning his sorrows in alcohol needs to witness freedom in action. The mother overwhelmed by anxiety needs to observe peace in the midst of chaos.

They need you—not the perfect version of you that might exist someday, but the real version of you that exists right now, willing to grow, willing to serve, willing to become who God created you to be.

The Time Is Now

Let me close with something that might make you uncomfortable: You already know enough to get started.

You don't need more information. You don't need a perfect plan. You don't need ideal circumstances or unlimited resources or complete motivation.

You need to decide.

Decide that your life matters enough to fight for it. Decide that your calling is worth the discipline required to prepare for it. Decide that the people who need what you have to offer deserve the best version of you.

Decide that you're going to stop waiting for someday and start building today.

Because here's the truth: There will never be a perfect time to start. There will always be obstacles, challenges, and reasons to wait. The people who transform their lives aren't the ones who wait for ideal conditions—they're the ones who start where they are with what they have.

Your body is the only one you'll ever get. Your life is the only one you'll ever live. Your calling is the only one that's uniquely yours.

The world needs you—healthy, strong, and fully alive. Your family needs you present and engaged. Your community needs your unique contribution. The kingdom of God needs your hands, your feet, your mind, your heart—all of it working at full capacity in service of others.

But first, you have to become fit for your calling.

The journey starts now. The invitation has been extended. The path has been laid out.

What remains is your response.

Will you answer the call? Will you do the hard work of transformation? Will you become the person you were created to be?

Your story isn't over—it's just beginning. And the best chapters are still to be written.

But those chapters won't write themselves. They require a protagonist who is strong enough to carry the weight of purpose, healthy enough to sustain the journey, and courageous enough to step into the fullness of their calling.

The world is waiting for that person.

The world is waiting for you.

But first—you have to learn how to lead.

And that's exactly the topic of my next book.

Recap & Actions

Scripture to Reflect On: "For we are His workmanship, created in Christ Jesus for good works, which God prepared beforehand so that we would walk in them." —Ephesians 2:10

Life-Changing Truth: What God has redeemed in you, He wants to use through you. Your struggles weren't roadblocks to your calling—they were preparation for it. Getting healthy isn't the end goal—it's the equipment you need for the journey of serving others. You don't have to wait for perfect health to begin serving, but the world needs you to be as strong, clear, and vital as possible for the work ahead.

Ready, Willing, Able Actions:

Ready (You can do this right now):

- Write down three ways your health struggles have given you compassion for others.
- Identify one person in your life who needs to see an example of transformation.
- Choose one healthy habit you can model today, regardless of how imperfect your overall health is.
- Make a declaration: "I will get healthy not just for me, but for the people God wants me to serve."

Willing (You can do this within a week):

- Share your health journey (including struggles) with someone who might be encouraged by your story.
- Begin viewing your health habits as training for service rather than just personal improvement.
- Identify the specific calling or purpose that your health journey is preparing you for.
- Start seeing yourself as a leader-in-training, not just someone getting personally healthy.

Able (You can do this within a month):

- Develop a clear vision of the impact you want to make once you're operating at full capacity.
- Create accountability with others who share your commitment to health as a platform for service.
- Begin looking for opportunities to guide others who are earlier in their health journey.
- Start preparing for the next level of leadership by developing the skills you'll need to serve others more effectively.

Remember: Your calling isn't waiting for you to be perfect—it's waiting for you to be willing. Start where you are, use what you have, do what you can. The world needs the healthy, vibrant, fully alive version of you, and it needs that person now. Your story of transformation will become someone else's hope. Your journey to health will light the path for others. What God has redeemed in you, He will use through you—but first, you must become fit for your calling.

14

FLYING BACK TO THE SUN

You already know about the Superman movies.

I told you earlier about those visits my dad made to our small apartment in Webster, Texas—how we'd curl up together on the La-Z-Boy, my small body pressed against his large belly, watching Christopher Reeve fly across the screen. I told you about the one-armed action figure he brought me. How I loved it fiercely. How my dad was Superman to me. Distant, yes. Missing pieces, sure. But special. Powerful. *Mine.*

What I didn't tell you was how he smelled.

Cigarettes and cheap Aspen cologne. That's what I remember when I close my eyes and go back to being three years old, wedged into that recliner with him. My sister, brother, and mom were somewhere in the apartment, but this memory is just the two of us. His belly rising and falling beneath his stretched t-shirt, somehow as comfortable as the chair itself. The flicker of the TV in a dim room. The faint rocket-ship playground visible through the window—one of those old metal deathtraps they don't make anymore.

And Superman, flying.

That's the image that stayed with me. Not the cape or the bullets bouncing off his chest or even the way he caught Lois Lane mid-fall. What I remember is *how he recharged.*

There's a scene in those old movies that I must have watched a dozen times without understanding it.

Superman gets beaten down. Kryptonite—his one weakness—strips away everything that makes him who he is. His strength drains. His powers fail. He's gasping, barely able to stand, while the villains circle.

And then he does the only thing that can save him.

He flies toward the sun.

You watch him struggle upward through the atmosphere, fighting against the very weakness trying to destroy him. Higher and higher. Closer and closer to that blazing yellow star.

And as the sun's rays wash over him—strength returns. Wounds heal. Power floods back.

Then he streaks back to earth to finish the fight.

I didn't understand it then. I was three, maybe four, snuggled against my dad's belly, breathing in cigarettes and Aspen, just happy he was there.

But now I understand.

The sun wasn't just a power source. It was a part of Superman's *origin*. Where he came from. What made him who he was. Yellow sun radiation is literally what transforms an ordinary Kryptonian into the Man of Steel.

When the kryptonite poisoned him—when he forgot his own strength and lay gasping on the ground—the only remedy was to return to his source.

To fly back to where he came from.

To remember who he was made to be.

This is the gospel.

And it's the thing I almost missed while writing this entire book.

I could give you all the health practices in the world—the strength training, the nutrition, the sleep protocols, the stress management, the supplements and the labs and the tracking. And they would help. They really would.

But none of it is the sun.

The sun is your identity in Christ.

It's the truth that you are *beloved*—not because of what you've accomplished or how well you've optimized your health, but because of who made you and who He says you are.

The kryptonite is real. I've felt it. Chronic illness that stripped my strength. Anxiety that made me forget who I was. A body that felt like a prison instead of a gift. You've felt it too—whatever form it's taken in your life.

But when I finally got better, it wasn't because I perfected my protocols.

It was because I flew back to the sun first.

I remembered I was beloved *before* I started healing. I received my identity as a gift *before* I tried to earn it through discipline. I let God's love restore what the kryptonite had stolen—and *then* I had the strength to do the hard work of getting well.

The practices in this book? They're what you do *after* you've been to the sun. They're how you steward the strength that flows from knowing who you are.

But if you try to white-knuckle your way through health optimization without first being rooted in your belovedness, you'll burn out. You'll turn wellness into another way to earn love. Another form of kryptonite disguised as strength.

My dad never flew back to the sun.

He stayed on the ground, gasping. Cigarettes and fast food and a body he never learned to steward. He died at fifty-five, one month after I started working at The Perfect Workout.

When I got that phone call, my mind went straight back to that La-Z-Boy. His belly. The smell of Aspen. Superman flying across a screen in a small apartment in Webster, Texas.

I think about what might have been different if someone had told him he was beloved first. If he'd known his worth wasn't tied to his failures. If he'd understood that God wasn't waiting for him to clean up his act—God was waiting to give him the power to do it.

I can't go back and save him.

But maybe I can help save you.

So, before you close this book—before you start implementing anything—I need you to do something.

Fly back to the sun.

Let God remind you who you are. Not who you're trying to become. Not the optimized version you hope these practices will create.

Who you *already are*.

Beloved.

That's the foundation everything else is built on.

And when the kryptonite comes—when the exhaustion and the setbacks and the shame try to strip your power—you'll know what to do.

You'll fly back to the sun. You'll remember whose you are. And you'll return to the fight with strength that doesn't come from you.

That one-armed Superman action figure is long gone. The La-Z-Boy is gone. The rocket-ship playground in Webster has probably been torn down and replaced with something safer and less magical.

My dad is gone.

But the story remains. And it's yours now too.

The sun is always there, beloved.

Fly toward it.

Then fly back down and save your world.

BONUS CHAPTER

FINANCIAL FITNESS MATTERS

"The one who is faithful in a very little thing is also faithful in much; and the one who is unrighteous in a very little thing is also unrighteous in much." — Luke 16:10

The Christmas Hustle

I need to tell you about the Christmas I realized money wasn't just about numbers.

I was twelve years old, walking door-to-door through our neighborhood with a wrinkled order form, selling cookie dough and pies to anyone who'd listen. Mrs. Henderson from three houses down ordered two apple pies. The Johnsons wanted chocolate chip cookie dough. Mr. Martinez, who always seemed grumpy but had a soft spot for entrepreneurial kids, ordered one of everything.

By the time I'd knocked on every door within bike-riding distance, I had enough orders to make Christmas happen for our family. But here's the thing—I then had to go home and tell my mom she needed to make all of it. Every pie. Every batch of cookies. Because that was the only way we'd have money for Christmas presents.

I share this story not to paint a picture of hardship, but to illustrate something important about how scarcity shapes you. We didn't have much, so we had to get creative with what we had. That reality—the necessity of making something from nothing—became part of my operating system.

And here's what I remember most: my mom enjoyed those baking marathons. Yes, I'm sure she was exhausted by the time the last pie came out of the oven. But she had always encouraged us to be entrepreneurial, to find creative solutions to problems rather than waiting for someone else to fix things. Watching her twelve-year-old hustle door-to-door with an order form? That was exactly the kind of initiative she'd been nurturing in us.

There was also something about the festivity of it all—the kitchen warm with the smell of cinnamon and chocolate, Christmas music playing, flour dusted across the counter. Even if it got old toward the end of those orders, I think she genuinely loved the ritual of it. But most importantly, those sales meant we'd have a real Christmas that year. The look on her face when we counted the orders—that mixture of relief and pride—told me everything. It wasn't just about the pies. It was about being able to provide for her kids in a way that felt abundant, even when our circumstances weren't.

That memory is seared into me, not because it was traumatic, but because it was formative.

Growing up without much money creates patterns in your brain—some helpful, some destructive. The helpful ones: work ethic, resourcefulness, the ability to make something from nothing. The destructive ones: scarcity thinking, the belief that money equals security, and the overwhelming urge to spend whenever you finally have it.

I carried both sets of patterns into adulthood. And while the work ethic served me well, the spending patterns nearly destroyed my financial future before it even began.

The Lifestyle Inflation Trap

Fast forward to my twenties. I'm making decent money for the first time in my life, and I'm doing what millions of Americans do: spending more as I make more.

Better apartment. Nicer car. Eating out instead of cooking. Clothes that fit properly. It felt like I was finally living the life I was "supposed" to have. The life I'd watched other families live while we were selling cookie dough to afford Christmas.

But here's what nobody tells you about lifestyle inflation: It's a trap disguised as progress.

Every raise I got was immediately absorbed by upgraded expenses. Every bonus went toward something I'd been "needing" for months. I looked successful from the outside—and honestly, it felt good after years of scarcity—but I was essentially living paycheck to paycheck, just at a higher level.

I was like the guy Jesus described who started building a tower without counting the cost. I had plans and dreams and ambitions, but no financial foundation to support them. And eventually, that foundation would be tested.

The wake-up call came when I realized I couldn't say yes to opportunities that excited me because they didn't pay enough. I couldn't take risks that might lead to greater impact because I needed every dollar of my current income just to maintain my lifestyle. I couldn't be generous with others because I was barely covering my own expenses.

I had traded financial freedom for the appearance of success. And that trade was slowly suffocating my ability to pursue the calling God had placed on my life.

The Truth About Money and Calling

You can't be fit for your calling if you're financially handcuffed.

I don't care how spiritually mature you are, how physically strong you've become, or how mentally sharp you are. If you're trapped by debt, living paycheck to paycheck, and constantly stressed about money, your capacity to serve is severely limited.

This isn't about prosperity gospel nonsense or the idea that God wants everyone to be rich. It's about the simple mathematical reality that financial stress creates barriers to purpose.

When you're financially stressed, you can't:

- Say yes to opportunities that align with your purpose, but don't pay the most;
- Take calculated risks that could lead to breakthroughs;
- Be genuinely generous with others in need;
- Invest in your own development and the relationships that matter; or
- Have the peace of mind that allows you to focus on what really matters.

We all know that money problems are one of the leading causes of divorce, one of the major sources of anxiety in modern life, and a distraction that keeps millions of people from pursuing their deepest dreams.

But here's what's deeper: When you get your finances right, money becomes a tool that serves your calling instead of a master that constrains it.

The Ancient Secrets That Still Work

Over the years, I've devoured every book I could find about money management, trying to understand what actually works versus what just sounds good. What I discovered (shocker) is that the most powerful financial wisdom is often the oldest and simplest.

Let me tell you about the books that fundamentally changed how I think about money—and how they can help you build the financial foundation your calling requires.

The Richest Man in Babylon: Timeless Truth

George S. Clason's *The Richest Man in Babylon* reads like ancient parables, but it contains financial principles that have worked for thousands of years. The core wisdom is beautifully simple:

> **Pay yourself first.** Before you pay anyone else—your landlord, your credit card company, the government—pay yourself by saving at least ten percent of everything you earn.
>
> This isn't just about accumulating money. It's about rewiring your brain to see yourself as someone whose future matters more than immediate gratification. It's about developing the discipline that wealthy people have and poor people lack: the ability to delay pleasure for greater gain.

Live on less than you earn. This seems so obvious it's almost insulting to mention. But most Americans violate this principle constantly. They finance their lifestyle with credit cards, stretch their housing payments to the limit, and then wonder why they feel trapped and stressed.

Make your money work for you. Once you've saved money, invest it wisely so it grows while you sleep. The goal isn't to get rich quick—it's to harness the most powerful force in the universe: compound interest.

These principles worked in ancient Babylon, and they work in modern America because they address fundamental human nature and mathematical reality.

The Millionaire Next Door: The Shocking Truth

Dr. Thomas Stanley and Dr. William Danko, authors of *The Millionaire Next Door: The Surprising Secrets of America's Rich*, spent decades researching actual millionaires—not the ones you see on TV, but the ones living quietly in middle-class neighborhoods across America. What they found completely shattered my assumptions about wealthy people.

Most millionaires don't look like what you'd expect. They don't drive luxury cars, wear designer clothes, or live in mansions. They're often teachers, plumbers, and small business owners who have consistently saved and invested over decades.

They live in modest homes, drive used cars, and spend money carefully. Meanwhile, many people who *look* wealthy—with expensive cars, designer clothes, and impressive homes—actually have negative net worth. They're spending everything they make (and often more) to maintain an image.

The book taught me the crucial difference between looking rich and being rich. Looking rich is about spending money on things that lose value. Being rich is about accumulating things that gain value over time.

This was a paradigm shift for me. I realized I'd been trying to look successful instead of trying to become financially secure. And those are often opposite strategies.

The Psychology of Money: Why Smart People Do Dumb Things

Morgan Housel's *The Psychology of Money* helped me understand something that changed everything: personal finance is more personal than it is finance.

Your relationship with money isn't primarily about math or intelligence. It's about psychology, emotions, and experiences—especially the experiences you had with money as a child.

Housel shows that financial success isn't about being the smartest person in the room or having the highest income. It's about controlling your behavior over long periods of time. And behavior is driven by psychology, not intelligence.

For someone who grew up with financial scarcity, this was revelatory. Some of my spending patterns weren't rational economic decisions—they were emotional responses to childhood experiences of not having enough.

Understanding the psychology behind my financial decisions helped me make better choices based on logic rather than emotion.

The Algebra of Wealth: A Simple Formula for Complex Results

Scott Galloway breaks down wealth building into an equation so simple it fits on a napkin:

Focus + Stoicism + Time + Diversification = Wealth

Focus: Get really, really good at something valuable. Don't chase every opportunity—develop rare skills that command high compensation.

Stoicism: Live below your means, delay gratification, and don't let lifestyle inflation destroy your progress. Be content with less than you can afford.

Time: Start as early as possible and let compound interest work for decades. Time is your most powerful ally in building wealth.

Diversification: Don't put all your eggs in one basket. Spread risk across different investments and asset classes.

This formula is simple but not easy. It requires the discipline to think in decades when our culture rewards thinking in minutes.

Happy Money: The Science of Spending Well

Elizabeth Dunn and Michael Norton's *Happy Money* revealed something that completely challenged how I thought about the relationship between money and happiness.

The research shows that how you spend money matters more for your happiness than how much money you have. Most people think that having more money will automatically make them happier, but the data tells a different story.

The book identifies five principles for spending money in ways that increase well-being:

Buy experiences, not things. A vacation creates lasting memories and stories; a new gadget becomes normal within weeks.

Help others instead of yourself. Spending money on others—whether gifts or charitable giving—creates more happiness than spending on yourself.

Buy time. Paying to eliminate time stress (like hiring a house cleaner or living closer to work) increases happiness more than most material purchases.

Pay now, consume later. The anticipation of a future purchase often brings more joy than the purchase itself.

Think about what else that money could buy. Every financial choice is a trade-off; conscious trade-offs create more satisfaction.

This book helped me realize that financial health isn't just about accumulating wealth—it's about spending money in ways that align with what makes human beings flourish.

The Grace-Filled Approach to Giving

Now let's talk about the elephant in the Christian financial room: tithing and giving.

I believe deeply in the transformative power of generosity. When you give, you break the hold that money can have on your heart. You declare that your security comes from God, not your bank account. You participate in God's work of caring for others.

But I'm not dogmatic about the ten percent tithe rule, and here's why.

The New Testament Reality

While the Old Testament law required a tithe plus additional offerings, the New Testament doesn't prescribe a specific percentage. Instead, it emphasizes the heart behind the giving:

"Each one must do just as he has decided in his heart, not reluctantly or under compulsion, for God loves a cheerful giver." (2 Corinthians 9:7).

The focus shifts from law to love, from obligation to opportunity, from percentage to heart.

The Danger of Magical Thinking

I've watched too many people give money they couldn't afford while expecting God to miraculously solve their financial problems despite poor choices. They treat tithing like a spiritual lottery ticket—give ten percent and God will make you rich.

But that's not how God works, and it's not what Scripture teaches.

Your financial choices create consequences in the real world. You can't give your way out of financial irresponsibility any more than you can pray your way out of the consequences of poor health choices while continuing to eat garbage and avoid exercise.

God expects us to be wise stewards, not careless givers hoping for bailouts.

A Biblical Alternative

Here's what I've learned works better than rigid tithing rules:

Start where you can. If ten percent would create financial hardship, start with what you can sustainably give. Even one percent or two percent develops the muscle of generosity.

Increase gradually. As your financial foundation strengthens, increase your giving. Many truly wealthy people give far more than ten percent because they can afford to be more generous.

Give wisely. Don't just write checks to feel good. Invest time in understanding where your money is going and whether it's creating real impact.

Include everything. Giving isn't just money. Your time, skills, and energy are often more valuable than your dollars.

Focus on the heart. The purpose of giving is to remind you that everything belongs to God and that your joy comes from serving others, not accumulating wealth.

The Unjust Steward: Jesus's Most Controversial Money Story

Jesus told what might be his most puzzling parable about money—and it's the one that completely changed how I think about financial wisdom and kingdom impact.

A rich man discovers that his manager has been wasting his possessions and is about to fire him. The manager, panicking about his future, comes up with a brilliant scheme: He goes to all his master's debtors and reduces their bills. One guy owes one hundred measures of oil? Make it fifty. Another owes one hundred measures of wheat? Make it eighty.

The manager is essentially buying friendships and securing his future by being generous with someone else's money. And here's the shocking part—when the rich man finds out, he commends the dishonest manager for his shrewdness.

Then Jesus drops this bombshell: "And his master complimented the unrighteous manager because he had acted shrewdly; for the sons of this age are more shrewd in relation to their own kind than the sons of light. And I say to you, make friends for yourselves by means of the wealth of unrighteousness, so that when it is all gone, they will receive you into the eternal dwellings." (Luke 16:8-9).

Wait, what? Jesus is praising financial shrewdness? He's telling us to use money strategically to build relationships and secure our eternal future?

This parable isn't about being dishonest—it's about being intentional. The unjust steward understood something that many Christians miss: Money is a tool, and how you use that tool determines your outcomes, both in this life and the next.

The manager didn't hoard resources for himself. He didn't waste them on luxury. He used them strategically to build relationships and create a future where people would welcome him.

Most Christians approach money reactively—they earn it, spend it, maybe give a little, and hope for the best. But Jesus is calling us to be shrewd with our resources. To think strategically about how our financial choices can advance the kingdom and build relationships that matter for eternity.

Your money will be gone someday. The question is: What will you have built with it while you had it?

The Compound Miracle

Compound interest is the closest thing to magic that exists in the financial world.

Albert Einstein allegedly called it "the eighth wonder of the world," and when you see the math, you'll understand why.

If you invest $300 per month starting at age twenty-five and earn an average of seven percent annual returns, you'll have over $650,000 by age sixty-five. That's $144,000 of your money that became over half a million dollars through the magic of compound growth.

But here's the kicker: If you wait until age thirty-five to start, you'd need to invest $600 per month to reach the same amount. Wait until forty-five, and you'd need to invest $1,200 per month.

Time isn't just money—time IS money. The earlier you start, the less you need to contribute to achieve financial freedom.

This is why getting your finances right in your twenties and thirties is so crucial. Not because money is the most important thing, but because financial freedom gives you choices that financial bondage never can.

The Freedom Fund Philosophy

Instead of just saving for retirement, I want you to think about building what I call a "Freedom Fund."

A Freedom Fund is money that gives you options. It's the difference between having to take any job and being able to choose work that aligns with your calling. It's what allows you to say yes to opportunities that excite your soul even if they don't maximize your salary.

Your Freedom Fund might allow you to:

- Start a business that serves others;
- Take a lower-paying job at a nonprofit that aligns with your values;
- Support family members going through difficult times;
- Give generously to causes that matter to you; or
- Take calculated risks that could lead to greater kingdom impact.

The goal isn't to retire and play golf for thirty years. The goal is to have enough financial security that you can pursue your calling without being constrained by immediate financial pressures.

The Practical Path Forward

Alright, enough theory. Let's talk about what you need to do to build financial fitness that serves your calling.

Step 1: Stop the Bleeding

Before you can build wealth, you need to stop destroying it. That means eliminating high-interest debt, especially credit cards.

If you're paying eighteen to twenty-four percent interest on credit cards while hoping to earn seven to ten percent in investments, you're guaranteed to lose money. Pay off credit card debt as aggressively as possible using either the debt snowball method (smallest balances first) or debt avalanche method (highest interest rates first).

Step 2: Build Your Foundation

Create an emergency fund of three to six months of expenses. Keep this money in a boring savings account where you can access it quickly if needed.

This isn't an investment—it's insurance against life's inevitable surprises. The point isn't to make money on this fund—it's to avoid going into debt when unexpected expenses arise.

Step 3: Automate Your Success

Set up automatic systems so that building wealth happens without requiring willpower or memory:

- Automatic transfer to savings on payday,
- Automatic investment in retirement accounts,
- Automatic bill pay to avoid late fees, and
- Automatic transfer to a giving fund.

When good financial behaviors happen automatically, you don't have to rely on motivation or discipline to maintain them.

Step 4: Invest Simply and Consistently

For most people, the best investment strategy is also the simplest: Buy low-cost index funds that track the overall stock market and hold them for decades.

Don't try to pick individual stocks, time the market, or chase the latest investment trend. Just consistently invest in diversified index funds and let compound growth do the heavy lifting.

The math is remarkable: $500 invested monthly for thirty years at seven percent annual returns grows to over $600,000. Consistency and time matter more than clever strategies.

Step 5: Live Below Your Means

The most important financial habit is spending less than you earn. This requires fighting against cultural pressure to upgrade your lifestyle every time your income increases.

Instead of lifestyle inflation, practice lifestyle deflation—find ways to reduce expenses and increase the gap between what you earn and what you spend.

This doesn't mean living miserably. It means being intentional about purchases and making sure your spending aligns with your values rather than your impulses or insecurities.

Money as Ministry

When you get your finances right, something beautiful happens: Money becomes a ministry tool rather than a source of stress.

You can model financial wisdom for your children. You can be generous when you encounter people in need. You can support causes that align with your values. You can take risks in service of your calling. You can remove financial anxiety that interferes with your relationships and spiritual life.

I think about the people in my life who have had the greatest kingdom impact, and many of them were able to serve so effectively because they weren't worried about money. They had enough financial margin to focus on what really mattered.

This doesn't mean you need to be wealthy to serve God effectively. Some of the most impactful people I know have modest incomes. But they manage what they have wisely, live within their means, and don't let financial stress dominate their emotional and spiritual lives.

The Integration Point

Everything we've discussed in this book—physical health, mental clarity, spiritual vitality, and financial fitness—works together to prepare you for whatever God is calling you to do.

When you're physically strong, mentally sharp, emotionally stable, and financially free, you become a skilled weapon in God's hands. You can say yes to opportunities others can't pursue. You can serve from abundance rather than scarcity. You can take risks that could lead to breakthrough impact.

But when any of these areas is broken—when you're physically exhausted, mentally foggy, emotionally unstable, or financially trapped—your capacity to serve is severely limited.

This is why financial fitness matters for your calling. It's not about getting rich for the sake of being rich. It's about removing barriers that prevent you from pursuing your God-given purpose with full intensity.

The Long View

Building wealth is like building physical strength—it happens slowly through consistent daily choices, not through dramatic short-term efforts.

Just as you can't get physically fit with one great workout, you can't get financially fit with one great month of saving. But you can achieve both through small, consistent actions over time.

The key is thinking in decades, not quarters. Making choices today that your future self will thank you for. Living in a way that creates more options rather than fewer.

Your financial situation today doesn't determine your future. Your financial choices starting today do.

And remember: The goal isn't just personal financial success. It's positioning yourself to be maximally useful in whatever calling God has for your life.

When you're fit for your calling—physically, mentally, spiritually, and financially—you become someone who can change the world.

That's worth working toward, one choice at a time.

Recap & Actions

Scripture to Reflect On: "For which one of you, when he wants to build a tower, does not first sit down and calculate the cost, to see if he has enough to complete it?" —Luke 14:28

Life-Changing Truth: Financial fitness isn't about getting rich—it's about removing barriers that prevent you from pursuing your calling. When you manage money wisely, you gain the freedom to say yes to opportunities that align with your purpose rather than being trapped by financial constraints. Your financial choices today create the foundation for your future freedom to serve.

Ready, Willing, Able Actions:

Ready (You can do this right now):

- Calculate your actual net worth by listing all assets and subtracting all debts.
- Set up one automatic transfer to savings, even if it's just $25 per paycheck.
- Track where your money goes for one week without judgment—just awareness.
- Write down three ways financial stress has limited your ability to pursue your calling.

Willing (You can do this within a week):

- Create a simple budget based on your actual spending patterns, not your ideal ones.
- Set up automatic bill pay for all fixed expenses to avoid late fees.
- Research low-cost index funds at Vanguard, Fidelity, or Schwab for future investing.
- Decide on a giving percentage that challenges you but doesn't create financial stress.

Able (You can do this within a month):

- Build a starter emergency fund of $1,000 in a separate savings account.
- Create and begin executing a debt elimination plan for any high-interest debt.
- Start investing in a retirement account or taxable investment account with index funds.
- Develop a five-year plan for increasing your financial margin and freedom to serve.

Remember: Small, consistent financial choices compound over time into life-changing freedom. You don't have to be perfect—you just have to start where you are and keep making progress toward the financial fitness that will serve your calling and enable you to impact others for the kingdom.

REFERENCES

Theological/Spiritual Authors

- Pastor Joseph Prince, *Destined to Reign*
- Rob Bell, *Love Wins*
- Richard Rohr, *Falling Up*
- John Crowder, *Cosmos Reborn*

Health & Fitness Experts

- Dr. Gabrielle Lyon, *Forever Strong*
- Dr. Layne Norton Podcast
- Dr. Michael Ruscio, *Healthy Gut Healthy You*
- Dr. Doug McGuff, *Body by Science*
- Dr. Matthew Walker, *Why We Sleep*
- Dr. John Ratey, *Spark*

Psychology/Neuroscience Authors

- Dr. Caroline Leaf, *Switch On Your Brain*
- Dr. Anna Lembke, *Dopamine Nation*
- Daniel Kahneman, *Thinking, Fast and Slow*

- Dr. Brené Brown, *Atlas of the Heart*
- Dr. Maxwell Maltz, *Psycho-Cybernetics*
- Dr. BJ Fogg, *Tiny Habits*
- Charles Duhigg, *The Power of Habit*
- Viktor Frankl, *Man's Search for Meaning*

Financial Authors

- George S. Clason, *The Richest Man in Babylon*
- Thomas Stanley & William Danko, *The Millionaire Next Door*
- Morgan Housel, *The Psychology of Money*
- Scott Galloway, *The Algebra of Wealth*
- Elizabeth Dunn & Michael Norton, *Happy Money*

ENDNOTES

1. https://www.bible.com New American Standard Bible 2020

2. https://thedecisionlab.com/biases/dunning-kruger-effect

3. https://drleaf.com

4. https://med.stanford.edu/profiles/anna-lembke

5. https://www.instagram.com/biolayne/?hl=en

6. https://brenebrown.com

7. https://pmc.ncbi.nlm.nih.gov/articles/PMC5125296/

8. https://www.mayoclinic.org/healthy-lifestyle/stress-management/in-depth/stress/art-20046037

9. https://news.harvard.edu/gazette/story/newsplus/global-burden-of-mental-illness-underestimated/

10. https://www.proactivepsychiatry.com/post/dopamine-burnout-how-overstimulation-is-draining-your-motivation-and-happiness

11. https://medicine.yale.edu/news-article/new-evidence-supports-autoimmunity-as-one-of-long-covids-underlying-drivers/

12. https://www.sciencehistory.org/education/scientific-biographies/ignaz-semmelweis/

13. https://www.frontiersin.org/journals/pharmacology/articles/10.3389/fphar.2024.1431204/full

14. https://pubmed.ncbi.nlm.nih.gov/17062768/

15. https://drmichaelholick.org

16. https://www.ifm.org/functional-medicine

17. https://my.clevelandclinic.org/health/treatments/22466-low-fodmap-diet

18. https://bjsm.bmj.com/content/56/13/755

19. https://link.springer.com/article/10.2165/00007256-199826020-00002;https://dariusjwright.com/wp-content/uploads/2022/11/hypertrophy-2.pdf

20. https://www.webmd.com/fitness-exercise/what-to-know-about-vo2-max

21. https://corpwarrior.libsyn.com/435-a-masterclass-with-dr-jurgen-giessing-exploring-the-science-of-hit-vs-high-volume-training-debunking-muscle-building-myths-cardios-role-in-hit-and-agings-impact-on-muscle-recovery

22. https://www.jeantwenge.com; https://courses.grainger.illinois.edu/cs565/sp2018/Live1_Depression&ScreenTime.pdf

23. https://rickhanson.com

24. https://centerforbrainhealth.org/article/walker-joins-brainhealth-and-utd

25. https://www.urmc.rochester.edu/people/112359252-maiken-nedergaard#research;https://www.science.org/content/article/scientists-uncover-how-brain-washes-itself-during-sleep

26. https://www.acu.edu.au/research-and-enterprise/our-research-institutes/sprint-research-centre/our-people/dr-shona-halson; https://www.youtube.com/watch?v=_cz0x-LdffU

27. https://www.kevinhallphd.com

28. https://drgabriellelyon.com

29. https://www.cc.nih.gov/news/2019/summer/story-01

30. https://danmillerwellness.com

31. https://en.wikipedia.org/wiki/Nassim_Nicholas_Taleb

32. https://saunasupplyco.com/dr-jari-laukkanen-finnish-traditional-sauna-study-explained/

33. https://www.wimhofmethod.com

34. https://www.precisionnutrition.com

35. https://www.bjfogg.com

36. https://charlesduhigg.com

37. https://jamesclear.com/habit-stacking

38. https://pmc.ncbi.nlm.nih.gov/articles/PMC8763215/

39. https://www.hubermanlab.com;https://www.hubermanlab.com/episode/essentials-science-of-stress-testosterone-aggression-motivation-robert-sapolsky

40. https://www.healthline.com/health/hedonic-treadmill

41. https://viktorfranklamerica.com/what-is-logotherapy/

42. https://www.oliverburkeman.com

ACKNOWLEDGMENTS

This book exists because of the countless people who invested in my life, especially during seasons when I couldn't see the way forward.

To my mom, who planted the first seeds of health consciousness in our small family health store and taught me that what goes into your body matters as much as what comes out of your mouth. To my dad, whose early passing reminded me that good intentions without action aren't enough, but whose love remains a driving force in my life.

To my grandparents, who modeled that readers are leaders and that success comes through clarity, grit, and faith. Your example taught me to think big while staying grounded in something larger than myself.

To my siblings, who walked through every season with me and helped shape the man I've become.

To my in-laws, who welcomed me into their family and supported us in countless ways during our early years together. Your generosity and belief in our future helped us get on our feet when we needed it most. Thank you for raising the woman who would become my anchor and for treating me like a son.

To the spiritual voices who dared to challenge religious dogma and reveal the scandalous beauty of grace—Pastor Joseph Prince, Rob Bell, Richard Rohr, and others whose writings cracked open my understanding of what it means to be beloved. Your willingness to ask hard questions and offer fresh perspectives on ancient truths helped me discover that God's love isn't something to be earned, but something to be awakened to. You taught me that sometimes the most radical thing you can do is simply believe you are loved.

To my closest friends who never wavered during the darkest chapters of my health crisis. You know who you are, and you know what your presence meant when everything felt uncertain.

To James Pitkin, whose pastoral bedside manner consists mainly of calling people out on their excuses—which was exactly what I needed. Your invitation to "lift weights during lunch breaks because you've got tube arms" launched my strength training journey and taught me that sometimes the most loving thing a friend can do is tell you the truth you don't want to hear. And to Stephanie, our lead pastor at Living Stones, who somehow manages to balance James's bluntness with actual pastoral care. You both have been mentors and friends who model what it looks like to lead with both strength and grace.

To Matt Hedman, founder of The Perfect Workout, for creating a company culture where transformation isn't just what we do—it's who we are. Your vision gave me a platform to discover my calling. You're not only my personal and professional mentor, you're a best friend.

To Nancy and Cassie, my business coaches, who challenged me to think differently about leadership and life. Iron sharpens iron, and you've been iron for me.

To Dan Miller, my health coach and mentor, whose conversation about Finnish sauna studies planted the seed that would revolutionize how I think about stress, resilience, and human potential. Your ability to connect seemingly random dots continues to amaze me.

To Dr. Michael Ruscio, who listened when others dismissed my symptoms and provided the roadmap that led to healing. Your humility, curiosity, and willingness to adapt protocols saved not just my health, but my hope.

To Christopher Short and the team at Mark Graham Communications—and especially to Peg Brantley, whose editorial eye and ghostwriting craft helped shape the words on these pages. You took my stories, my research, and my heart for this message and helped me say what I've been trying to say for years. This book is immeasurably better because of your partnership.

To my executive team and coworkers at FastFit & The Perfect Workout, who carried the mission forward during my wilderness season and continue to serve our members with excellence. You make it possible for thousands of people to reclaim their strength and vitality.

To the researchers, physicians, and thought leaders whose work forms the foundation of this book—Dr. Gabrielle Lyon, Dr. Layne Norton, and countless others who dedicate their lives to understanding human flourishing. Your courage to challenge conventional wisdom creates space for breakthrough.

To every client who trusted me with their transformation story, every person who shared their struggles and victories—you taught me that health isn't just about the body, but about becoming who God created us to be.

And finally, to the One who never wasted any of it. Every struggle, every setback, every moment of despair was preparation for something I couldn't have imagined when the journey began. What You have redeemed, You will use.

ABOUT THE AUTHOR

KYLE RECCHIA is CEO of FastFit & The Perfect Workout, leading the largest privately owned one-on-one strength training company in the United States with over 80 studios nationwide. With certifications from NASM and Precision Nutrition and additional training from Harvard Business School, Kyle has spent over a decade at the intersection of exercise science, business leadership, and whole-person health.

After years of battling chronic illness—including a misdiagnosed parasitic infection that doctors repeatedly dismissed—Kyle's journey through functional medicine, faith, and evidence-based health practices became the foundation for this book. His story of healing transformed not only his body but his understanding of what it means to be available for God's calling.

Kyle is a long-time Vistage member, worship drummer, and outdoor enthusiast. He lives in Alvin, Texas, with his wife, Tiff, and their four sons.

For more information please visit: kylerecchia.com/book

www.ingramcontent.com/pod-product-compliance
Lightning Source LLC
LaVergne TN
LVHW020658110826
845149LV00012B/2032

* 9 7 9 8 9 9 4 2 7 3 9 3 7 *